THE
PACKAGE DESIGN
BOOK

Jean Jacques & Brigitte Evrard

pentawards

THE
PACKAGE DESIGN
BOOK

TASCHEN

diamond

Interview with Lars Wallentin
Worldwide packaging expert and consultant

beverages

Interview with Jennifer Tsai
Proad Identity Taipei, Taiwan

food

Interview with Stan Church
Wallace Church Inc., New York

body

Interview with Adrian Pierini

Pierini Partners, Buenos Aires

222

luxury

Interview with Mark Cowan

Cowan Group of companies, Australia

264

other markets

Interview with Bruce Duckworth

Turner Duckworth, London & San Francisco

358

FOREWORD

Jean Jacques & Brigitte Evrard
Founders of Pentawards

After 35 years devoted to the creation of packaging within major design groups, such as Carré Noir and Desgrippes Gobé, and after years of travelling and visiting supermarkets all over the world, we decided to turn our attention to promoting a medium we love and consider to be the most important of all communication tools – packaging!

In 2007 we created Pentawards, a worldwide competition devoted exclusively to packaging design in all its forms and open to everyone, everywhere, who is involved in creating and marketing packaging.

Our aim is to highlight creativity, innovation, quality of finish, willingness to push the boundaries, visual impact, and communication. We also invite you to take a closer look at the packaging of mass-market goods, which are not always aesthetically pleasing but whose designers nevertheless produce remarkable results.

The packaging is judged by an international panel of judges from 12 countries and different cultures. They select the winners according to the creative and innovative qualities of the entries. The winners receive bronze, silver, gold, platinum, and diamond Pentawards.

For the last editions of Pentawards, the award-winning designs in the five major categories are examples of creativity, simplicity, naturalness, and authenticity. These trends reveal what people expect today when the consumer is bombarded with information, images, and a whole array of different messages.

Six well-known personalities, all of them members of the jury, were asked five basically identical questions. Here you will discover their thoughts, their favourite entries, their passions, and the things that have fascinated them throughout their careers.

We hope you will enjoy reading this beautiful book. We hope, too, that it will be a source of inspiration to you, inspiring you to create your own packaging which – who knows? – could be a future Pentaward winner.

Happy reading!

VORWORT

Jean Jacques & Brigitte Evrard
Gründer von Pentawards

35 Jahre lang widmeten wir uns in führenden Designagenturen wie Carré Noir und Desgrippes Gobé der Entwicklung von Verpackungen. Nachdem wir jahrelang die Welt bereist und Supermärkte besucht haben, beschlossen wir, unsere gesamte Energie in das Medium zu stecken, das wir lieben und für das Wichtigste aller Kommunikationsinstrumente halten: die Verpackung! Dafür wollen wir ab sofort die Werbetrommel rühren.

2007 schufen wir Pentawards, einen weltweiten Wettbewerb, der sich ausschließlich der Verpackungsgestaltung in all ihren Formen widmet. Er steht allen offen, die sich für das Schaffen und Vermarkten von Verpackungen engagieren.

Uns ist daran gelegen, Kreativität, Innovation, qualitative Vollendung, die Bereitschaft zum Ausloten von Grenzen, visuelle Wirkung und Kommunikation zu fördern. Wir laden Sie außerdem ein, sich die Verpackung von Massenartikeln genauer anzuschauen, die ästhetisch nicht immer ansprechend sind, aber deren Designer nichtsdestotrotz bemerkenswerte Ergebnisse schaffen.

Die Arbeiten werden von einer international besetzten Jury mit Fachleuten aus zwölf Ländern und verschiedenen Kulturkreisen beurteilt. Die Preisträger werden aufgrund der kreativen und innovativen Qualität der eingereichten Arbeiten ermittelt. Es werden Pentawards in Bronze, Silber, Gold, Platin und Diamant verliehen.

Bei den letzten Pentawards-Verleihungen stehen die preisgekrönten Designs in den fünf Hauptkategorien beispielhaft für Kreativität, Einfachheit, Natürlichkeit und Authentizität. Diese Trends enthüllen, was heute erwartet wird, wenn die Konsumenten mit Informationen, Bildern und einem ganzen Arsenal verschiedener Botschaften bombardiert werden.

Sechs bekannten Persönlichkeiten, allesamt Mitglieder der Jury, wurden fünf ähnliche Fragen gestellt. Hier erhalten Sie Einblicke in deren Gedanken, ihre Lieblingsbeiträge, ihre Leidenschaften und die Dinge, die sie im Laufe ihrer Karriere fasziniert haben.

Wir hoffen, dass Sie viel Freude mit diesem Buch haben. Und wir wünschen uns, dass Sie sich davon inspirieren und anregen lassen, eigene Verpackungen zu gestalten, die möglicherweise ja selbst zukünftige Gewinner eines Pentawards werden.

Viel Spaß beim Lesen!

PRÉFACE

Jean Jacques & Brigitte Evrard
Fondateurs des Pentawards

Après 35 années consacrées à la création d'emballages au sein de grands groupes de design (Carré Noir, Desgrippes Gobé), après des années de voyage et de visites dans tous les supermarchés du monde, nous avons décidé de nous consacrer à la promotion d'un média que nous adorons et que nous considérons comme le premier outil de communication : le packaging !

En 2007, nous avons créé les Pentawards, une compétition mondiale exclusivement dédiée au packaging design sous toutes ses formes, ouverte à tous ceux et celles qui dans tous les pays du monde sont associés à la création ou la mise sur le marché d'un emballage.

Notre ambition est de mettre en valeur la créativité, l'innovation, la qualité de finition, la rupture avec les codes existants, l'impact visuel, la communication. Nous voulons aussi vous faire découvrir les emballages issus de la grande consommation, qui ne présentent pas toujours des aspects purement esthétiques, mais pour lesquels les designers font un travail remarquable.

Les emballages sont jugés par un jury lui aussi international, issu de 12 pays et cultures différents, qui sélectionne les gagnants en fonction de la qualité créative et innovante des œuvres présentées. Les lauréats reçoivent des Bronze, Silver, Gold, Platinum et Diamond Pentawards.

Pour les dernières éditions des Pentawards, créativité, simplicité, naturalité et authenticité se retrouvent dans les meilleurs designs couronnés, voyez les grands prix des 5 grandes catégories. Ces tendances sont révélatrices de ce que le monde attend aujourd'hui, alors que le consommateur est submergé d'informations, d'images et de communications de toutes origines.

Cinq questions similaires ont été posées à six personnalités du monde du design, toutes font partie du jury, vous découvrirez leurs réflexions, leurs coups de cœur, leurs passions et ce qui les a fasciné tout au long de leur carrière.

Nous vous souhaitons beaucoup de plaisir à parcourir ce beau livre, et espérons qu'il sera une source d'inspiration et vous donnera envie de créer vous aussi les emballages qui seront couronnés de succès et, qui sait, d'un Pentaward dans le futur.

Bonne lecture !

INTRODUCTION

Gérard Caron
Founder of Carré Noir
Designer of the website www.admirabledesign.com, Paris
Chair of the Pentawards jury since 2007

Packaging design. Reflecting the realities of the modern world.

Just think ... experts claim that every day our senses are subjected on average to 20,000 visual stimuli, that we will probably hear more than 800 different words, and be exposed to 150 different commercial brands. Of course, the average varies from one continent to another, but even so ...

The question for a designer is how to promote my brand amid this patchwork of assorted sounds, images, and emotions of all kinds. We know the answers to this question. It's a simple matter of capturing and holding consumers' attention and urging them to buy this brand, finding a way to touch them in some way, and finally of keeping the promises advertised by the makers of the product.

That's all very well but as far as packaging is concerned, can we express ourselves as clearly as a poster, a TV commercial or a website? In short, are there not actually more limits with packaging to the ways in which we can communicate with consumers and appeal to them?

The answer to both these questions can be found in this book devoted to the packaging designs chosen each year for the prestigious Pentawards. It comes as no surprise that the designers Brigitte and Jean Jacques Evrard were the ones who set up this worldwide competition. They recognised the huge potential of packaging and the public wasn't disappointed. The event was an immediate success.

The consumer? What else?

The jury, which I chair, is made up of marketing and design specialists based in around 12 countries on four continents. For a brand, winning a Pentaward means that its design will be universally recognised, and that it has a special quality to it that transcends the notions of frontiers and markets.

The jury's main task is to respond to the following question: Does this packaging have sufficient factors to appeal, even if only partially, to the part of the consumer's imagination that tells them they must have this product? A question like that might leave us open to charges of working with the irrational. Of course we do. We can't deny it.

The language that designers use is drawn from the sphere of emotions, instincts, archetypes, and received ideas with which we are all bombarded, especially when we are in a buying situation. The rational aspect of buying is most commonly supplied by the product itself – it is the product's quality, usefulness, reliability, etc. which encourages us to buy it again or not. Even so, we know that the consumer, when faced with a product, does not behave in one simple, easily identifiable way. Irrational responses are mixed with rational considerations in proportions that vary according to the nature of the product and the circumstances under which the purchase may take place.

Do people buy a Vuitton handbag for its hardwearing qualities? Do they smoke Marlboros because they have a better taste than other brands? And what about Barilla pasta, marketed as a premium product and therefore more expensive than other pastas? Or again the famous little catchphrase "what else?" from Nespresso?

Of course, packaging designers worthy of the name and steeped in the culture of their profession will rely on marketing approaches and surveys to create packaging that will meet consumer expectations. But they will also draw on their personal experience and feelings to find the "right signals" that will key in to the consumer's conscious and unconscious desires.

The attempt to strike a balance between reason and emotion must be repeated time and time again and, although there are no fixed rules, the process must be precise and methodical. Just as the consumer bases a specific choice on a blend of the rational and the irrational, designers, too, behave in the same way when they practise their profession.

Does packaging indicate know-how?

Yes, but there's more to it than that.

The main purpose of a brand will always be to present to the public an industrial practice within the framework of a particular culture, and therefore it must also demonstrate the relevant and corresponding know-how. But these days it is not enough just to stick to that.

In recent years, consumers have been asking much more. The economic crisis has highlighted expectations of a new kind of consumption, although the crisis itself is not the cause. Consumers now require – as an absolute minimum – that a brand name guarantees a product is manufactured to the highest quality. For them, low prices are – quite rightly – the least consideration. "The best quality at the fairest price" is a received idea which is here to stay and marks the emergence of a new breed of consumer who might be termed a "professional buyer".

This means that packaging must offer something more than the minimum. Let's not forget that "commerce" comes from the Latin *commercium* meaning "mutual trade". I think that says it all.

Packaging should be a pleasure!

There is no other explanation than this for the universal success of open-air and covered markets. Does today's consumer simply want shopping to be fun?

Consider the number of products in this book that speak to the consumer in a friendly, relaxed, almost intimate manner. In other words, they are fun. What they are really communicating is the pleasure of buying – despite the fact that the consumer may be only too aware that some huge manufacturing conglomerate could be lurking behind the traditional, home-spun style of the packaging.

This is the price we have to pay for the pleasure of buying a brand. It is one of the irrational aspects of a packaging's consumer appeal. Packaging does indeed have its part to play as a means of carrying a message and a promise of an easier life.

Can packaging create a better world?

There are several possibilities, sometimes simultaneously, which can be explored when creating packaging that conveys the idea of pleasures to come. Let's not forget that consumers tend to pinpoint images on the supermarket shelf that reflect their own lives. Nostalgia is an example – the same nostalgia expressed in music, television, cinema, and commercial architecture can find its way into packaging design. Just turn the pages and you will see. Once again it is a kind of search for authenticity. The product proclaims its origins and its history and how well it fits into a present-day environment.

Today, well-being can be achieved by taking part in local life or through trying to live more healthily by consuming an authentic product. And if it is organic and fairtrade, what more could one ask?

Behind this attempt to express ideas there lies a genuine but confused awareness which reminds us of the need to protect ourselves in a cruel world, to take care of our health, and to play our part in local affairs while continuing to be responsible citizens of the world.

Is that too great a mission for packaging? Far from it! We will have realised that these partly conscious, partly unconscious demands fall over one another to get noticed at the moment of buying when time is short and there are so many products on offer. When it comes to the moment of decision, I shall choose the packaging that best promises to make the act of buying pleasant, reassuring, life-enhancing, and personally satisfying.

Can packaging bring about a better world? It can contribute by seeking to be an ideal means of communication and even education. And what about packaging designers? Now more than ever they have a duty to reflect the reality of the modern world.

EINLEITUNG

Gérard Caron
Gründer von Carré Noir
Designer der Website www.admirabledesign.com, Paris
Seit 2007 Vorsitzender der Pentawards-Jury

Verpackungsdesign – Spiegel der Realität der modernen Welt

Stellen Sie sich das mal vor: Experten gehen davon aus, dass wir über unsere Sinne täglich durchschnittlich 20.000 optische Reize aufnehmen, dass wir wahrscheinlich mehr als 800 unterschiedliche Wörter hören und über 150 verschiedenen kommerziellen Marken begegnen. Natürlich fällt dieser Mittelwert je nach Kontinent anders aus, aber selbst dann ist er beeindruckend.

Die Frage, die sich für einen Designer daraus ergibt, lautet: Wie kann sich meine Marke angesichts dieses Flickenteppichs mannigfaltiger Klänge, Bilder und Gefühle durchsetzen? Wir kennen die Antworten auf diese Frage. Es geht um nichts anderes, als darum, die Aufmerksamkeit der Verbraucher auf die Marke zu lenken und aufrecht zu erhalten, die Konsumenten dazu zu bewegen, diese Marke zu kaufen, sie irgendwie zu berühren und schließlich darum, die Versprechen einzuhalten, mit denen die Hersteller der Produkte werben.

Das ist alles schön und gut, aber können wir uns hinsichtlich der Verpackung ebenso eindeutig ausdrücken wie mittels eines Plakats, eines Werbespots oder einer Website? Anders gefragt: Sind der Verpackung nicht viel mehr Grenzen gesetzt, was die Art und Weise betrifft, wie wir mit Konsumenten kommunizieren und sie ansprechen können?

Die Antworten auf diese beiden Fragen finden sich in diesem Buch. Hier werden die jährlich für die renommierten Pentawards ausgewählten Verpackungsdesigns vorgestellt. Es wundert nicht, dass es die Designer Brigitte und Jean Jacques Evrard waren, die diesen weltweiten Wettbewerb ins Leben gerufen haben. Sie erkannten das immense Potenzial von Verpackungen, und das Publikum war nicht enttäuscht – die Veranstaltung war sofort ein voller Erfolg.

Der Verbraucher? What else?

In der Jury, die ich leite, kommen Spezialisten aus den Bereichen Marketing und Design zusammen, die aus zwölf Ländern und vier Kontinenten stammen.

Wenn eine Marke einen Pentaward gewinnt, heißt das, dass ihr Design einen universellen Wiedererkennungswert hat und dass ihr eine besondere Qualität eigen ist, die die Vorstellungen von Grenzen und Märkten überschreitet.

Die Hauptaufgabe der Jury ist es, die folgende Frage zu beantworten: Verfügt eine Verpackung über ausreichend Faktoren, um jenen Bereich der Fantasie des Konsumenten (eventuell auch nur teilweise) anzusprechen, der ihm sagt, dass er dieses Produkt unbedingt braucht? Für die Antwort müssten wir möglicherweise mit dem Irrationalen arbeiten. Natürlich machen wir das, es ist nicht zu leugnen.

Die von Designern eingesetzte Sprache bezieht sich auf die Sphäre der Gefühle, Instinkte, Archetypen und des allgemeinen Gedankenguts, mit dem wir alle bombardiert werden – vor allem dann, wenn wir uns in einer Kaufsituation befinden. Der rationale Aspekt des Kaufens wird hauptsächlich von der Ware selbst bestimmt. Dabei geht es um die Qualität und die Nützlichkeit eines Produkts, seine Zuverlässigkeit etc. Diese Faktoren beeinflussen unsere Entscheidung, einen Artikel zu kaufen oder ihn liegen zu lassen. Wir wissen aber auch, dass sich der Konsument nicht so einfach und berechenbar verhält, wenn er sich mit einem Produkt beschäftigt. Irrationale Reaktionen mischen sich mit rationalen Erwägungen, und das Mischungsverhältnis verändert sich jeweils abhängig von der Natur des Produkts und den Umständen, unter denen es erworben werden soll.

Kaufen die Leute eine Vuitton-Handtasche, weil sie so robust ist? Raucht man Marlboro, weil die Zigaretten besser schmecken als die anderer Marken? Und was ist mit Barilla-Pasta, die als Premium-Produkt vermarktet wird und somit teurer ist als andere Pasta-Sorten? Oder mit dem berühmten kurzen Slogan „What else?" von Nespresso.

Natürlich werden sich Verpackungsdesigner, die diese Bezeichnung verdienen und von der Kultur ihrer Profession tief durchdrungen sind, auf Marketing-Ideen und Umfragen verlassen, um Verpackungen so zu gestalten, dass sie den Erwartungen der Kunden entsprechen. Doch sie werden auch ihre persönlichen Erfahrungen und Gefühle zu Rate ziehen, um die „richtigen Signale" zu finden, mit denen die bewussten und unbewussten Wünsche und Begehrlichkeiten des Kunden angesprochen werden.

Der Versuch, einen Ausgleich zwischen Vernunft und Gefühl zu schaffen, muss ständig wiederholt werden, und obwohl es keine festen Regeln gibt, muss dieser Prozess präzise und methodisch vonstattengehen. So wie der Konsument bei seiner Wahl durch eine Mischung aus Rationalem und Irrationalem beeinflusst wird, muss sich auch der Designer verhalten, wenn er seine Profession ausübt.

Weist Verpackung auf ein Know-how hin?

Ja, aber es steckt noch mehr dahinter.

Der Hauptzweck einer Marke wird es immer sein, der Öffentlichkeit die Praxis einer Branche innerhalb eines bestimmten kulturellen Rahmens zu präsentieren, und somit muss er auch das relevante und dazugehörige Know-how demonstrieren. Doch heutzutage reicht es nicht aus, sich nur daran zu halten.

In den letzten Jahren haben die Verbraucher deutlich mehr als das verlangt. Bei der aktuellen ökonomischen Krise werden die Erwartungen an eine neue Art des Konsums deutlich, obwohl die Krise selbst nicht der Grund dafür ist. Das Mindeste, das die Konsumenten heute erwarten, ist, dass ein Markenname garantiert, ein Produkt sei unter den höchsten Qualitätsansprüchen hergestellt worden. Für sie sind niedrige Preise – und zwar zu Recht – eine nachrangige Überlegung. „Die beste Qualität zum fairsten Preis" ist ein allgemein anerkanntes Konzept, das uns erhalten bleiben wird und das Erscheinen eines neuen Konsumententypus kennzeichnet, den man als „professionellen Käufer" bezeichnen kann.

Das bedeutet, eine Verpackung muss mehr anbieten als das Minimum. Wir dürfen nicht vergessen, dass „Kommerz" vom lateinischen „commercium" abstammt, was „miteinander handeln" bedeutet. Ich finde, das sagt schon alles.

Verpackung sollte Spaß machen!

Das ist die einzig mögliche Erklärung für den universellen Erfolg von Märkten – egal ob überdacht oder unter freiem Himmel. Will der heutige Verbraucher nichts weiter, als dass der Einkauf Spaß machen soll?

Schauen Sie sich einmal die verschiedenen Produkte in diesem Buch an, die den Konsumenten auf eine freundliche, entspannte, beinahe intime Weise ansprechen. Anders ausgedrückt: Sie machen Spaß. Was sie wirklich vermitteln, ist die Freude beim Kaufen – selbst dann, wenn sich der Verbraucher vielleicht nur allzu bewusst ist, dass sich hinter einem traditionellen, eher hausbackenen Verpackungsstil ein gigantisches Unternehmen verbergen kann.

Das ist der Preis, den wir für das Vergnügen zahlen müssen, eine Marke zu kaufen. Es ist einer der irrationalen Aspekte, den eine Verpackung als Reiz auf den Konsumenten ausüben kann. Die Verpackung hat wirklich den Zweck, eine Botschaft und das Versprechen eines einfacheren Lebens zu transportieren.

Können Verpackungen für eine bessere Welt sorgen?

Man kann verschiedene Möglichkeiten (manchmal auch gleichzeitig) hinzuziehen, wenn man eine Verpackung kreiert, die beim Konsumenten die Vorstellung von zu erwartenden Vergnügungen hervorruft. Wir sollten nicht vergessen, dass Verbraucher im Supermarktregal jene Bilder ganz genau erkennen, die ihr eigenes Leben reflektieren. Nostalgie ist dafür ein gutes Beispiel: Die gleiche Nostalgie, die in Musik, Fernsehen, Kino und kommerzieller Architektur ihren Ausdruck findet, kann auch im Verpackungsdesign umgesetzt werden. Blättern Sie einfach durch dieses Buch, und Sie werden auf Beispiele dafür stoßen. Auch das ist eine Art Suche nach Authentizität: Das

Produkt verweist auf seine Ursprünge und seine Geschichte und zeigt gleichzeitig, wie gut es in das heutige Umfeld passt.

Heutzutage fördert man das eigene Wohlbefinden, indem man sich lokal engagiert oder versucht, durch das Konsumieren zuverlässiger Produkte gesünder zu leben. Und wenn die dann auch noch biodynamisch sind und fair gehandelt werden, was will man mehr?

Hinter diesem Versuch, Ideen auszudrücken, verbirgt sich ein aufrichtiges, aber verstörtes Bewusstsein. Es erinnert uns daran, dass wir uns in einer grausamen Welt selbst schützen müssen, dass wir uns um unsere Gesundheit kümmern und uns vor Ort einbringen müssen, während wir gleichzeitig als Bürger auch für die Welt verantwortlich sind.

Ist dieser Auftrag für Verpackungen ein paar Nummern zu groß? Ganz im Gegenteil! Wir werden genau im Moment des Kaufens erkennen, dass diese teils bewussten, teils unbewussten Anforderungen zusammenfallen, wenn die Zeit knapp ist und viele Produkte angeboten werden. Im Moment der Entscheidung werde ich die Verpackung wählen, die das Versprechen, den Kaufakt angenehm zu gestalten, mich zu beruhigen, mein Leben zu verbessern und mich persönlich zu befriedigen am ehesten einzulösen verspricht.

Können Verpackungen eine bessere Welt bewirken? Sie können dazu beitragen, indem sie versuchen, sich als ideales Kommunikationsmittel und vielleicht sogar als Bildungsinstrument zu verstehen. Und was ist mit den Verpackungsdesignern? Sie stehen jetzt mehr denn je in der Pflicht, die Realität der modernen Welt zu reflektieren.

INTRODUCTION

Gérard Caron
Fondateur de Carré Noir
Editeur de www.admirabledesign.com, Paris
President du jury Pentawards depuis 2007

Le design packaging ? Si proche de la réalité du monde ...

Rendez-vous compte : chaque jour, en moyenne, les sens de l'homme moderne seraient soumis à percevoir 20 000 stimuli visuels, à entendre plus de 800 mots différents et à être exposés à ... 150 marques commerciales ! Certes, il s'agit de moyennes variables d'un continent à un autre, mais tout de même ...

La question se pose : comment valoriser mes marques dans tout ce patchwork de sons, d'images, de sensations diverses ? Nous connaissons les réponses à cette question : il suffit d'intriguer, d'attirer l'attention, de valoriser l'acte d'achat, d'émouvoir et au final de respecter les promesses du produit.

Bien, mais en ce qui concerne le packaging, avons-nous les mêmes possibilités d'expression qu'une affiche, un spot TV ou un site internet ? Bref, ne sommes-nous pas plus limités pour dialoguer, émouvoir le consommateur ?

La réponse est dans ce livre consacré aux meilleurs designs de packagings distingués chaque année par les prestigieux prix Pentawards. Il n'est pas étonnant que ce soient des designers, Brigitte et Jean Jacques Evrard, qui ont mis sur pied ce formidable concours mondial. Ils connaissent le potentiel énorme de ce média qu'est le packaging. Le public ne s'y est pas trompé, le succès a été immédiat

Le consommateur ? What else ?

Le jury que je préside est composé de spécialistes du marketing et du design établis dans une dizaine de pays, sur quatre continents. Pour une marque, être lauréate Pentawards signifie donc que son design est universellement reconnu, qu'il possède une dimension dépassant les notions de frontières et de marchés.

L'essentiel pour les membres du jury étant de répondre à cette question : Ce packaging possède-t-il les éléments suffisants pour ouvrir, voire entrouvrir, un territoire de désirs dans l'imaginaire du consommateur ? On me rétorquera qu'il s'agit là de données irrationnelles. Oui, ne nous en cachons pas.

Les langages utilisés par les designers relèvent du domaine des sensations, de l'instinct, des archétypes ou des idées reçues qui assaillent tout individu, en particulier quand il est en situation d'achat ! La dimension rationnelle de l'achat étant en majorité apportée par le produit lui-même : qualité, service, sérieux, etc. qui incitera ou non au réachat. Nous savons que le consommateur n'a pas un comportement unique devant les produits. L'irrationnel se mêle au rationnel avec des dosages qui varient selon la nature du produit et les circonstances de l'achat ...

Achète-t-on un sac Vuitton pour sa solidité ? Fume-t-on des Marlboro pour leur goût qui serait supérieur aux autres ? Que dire des pâtes Barilla, dites haut de gamme et à ce titre vendues plus cher que les autres ? Et la fameuse petite phrase « what else ? » de Nespresso ?

Certes, un designer de packagings digne de ce nom, possédant la culture de son métier, s'appuiera sur les études et démarches marketing pour créer des packagings en lien avec les attentes du consommateur. Mais il puisera en lui-même pour trouver les « signes justes » qui correspondent aux désirs conscients et inconscients.

Cette recherche de l'équilibre entre le rationnel et l'émotionnel est un exercice sans cesse renouvelé, sans règles figées où pourtant, la rigueur et la méthode s'imposent. Tout comme le consommateur qui dans ses choix mêle le rationnel à l'irrationnel, le designer agit de même dans l'exercice de sa profession.

Le packaging signe d'un savoir-faire ?

Oui, mais pas seulement ...

Le principal rôle d'une marque sera toujours de témoigner d'une pratique industrielle dans le cadre d'une culture particulière, donc d'un savoir-faire qui lui est propre. Aujourd'hui, s'en tenir à ce seul rôle ne suffit plus !

Depuis quelques années, le consommateur réclame d'avantage que cela ; la crise financière a mis l'attente d'un nouveau mode de consommation en pleine lumière, mais elle n'en n'est pas la cause. Pour le consommateur, qu'une marque donne la garantie de sa capacité à fabriquer un produit de qualité est devenu le minimum ! Qu'elle le vende au meilleur prix est la moindre des choses (ce en quoi il a raison ...). « Le meilleur au plus juste prix » est une notion acquise et irréversible qui marque l'émergence du professionnalisme dans la consommation, pour ainsi dire.

Le packaging doit donc offrir quelque chose de plus que ce minimum. Rappelons que « commerce » vient du latin « commercium » association de négoce et relations. Tout est dit, n'est-ce pas ?

Des packagings de plaisir svp !

Le succès universel des marchés populaires, couverts ou en plein air, ne s'explique pas autrement. Le consommateur d'aujourd'hui rechercherait donc simplement du plaisir dans son shopping ?

Regardez le nombre de créations dans ce livre qui proposent un discours familier, fun, où le tutoiement n'est pas loin. Il s'agit bien de plaisir. Elles proposent en réalité le bonheur d'acheter ... bien que le consommateur ne se fasse aucune illusion sur la dimension industrielle de la multinationale qui se cache souvent derrière des designs au style traditionnel ou rustique.

La recherche du plaisir que peut apporter une marque est à ce prix, avec toute la part d'irrationnel que cela comporte. Le packaging a bien une place à tenir, en tant qu'outil véhiculant un message et une promesse de mieux-être.

Un monde meilleur ?

Il existe bien plusieurs voies à exploiter , parfois simultanément, pour créer un packaging porteur de notions de plaisirs. Ne perdons pas de vue que le consommateur tente de retrouver des images de sa propre vie dans les rayons des magasins ! La nostalgie, par exemple, qui s'exploite dans la musique, à la télévision, au cinéma ou dans l'architecture commerciale, s'invite également dans le design de packaging : tournez les pages pour vous en convaincre ! Il s'agit encore d'une forme de quête de l'authenticité. Le produit laissera apercevoir ses origines, son histoire inscrite dans un environnement contemporain.

Aujourd'hui le bien-être peut passer par le plaisir de participer à la vie locale, ou par la recherche d'une vie plus saine en consommant un produit authentique. Et s'il est biologique et issu du commerce équitable, là on touche au summum...

Il y a derrière cette quête l'expression d'un sentiment réel mais confus. Celui de se protéger d'un monde inhumain, celui de veiller à sa santé, celui de s'inscrire dans un contexte local tout en revendiquant le statut de citoyen du monde responsable.

Une mission bien trop grande pour le packaging ? Que nenni. On aura compris que ces revendications mi-conscientes, mi-inconscientes, se bousculent au moment de l'achat quand le temps est compté et que les offres sont nombreuses. Au moment du choix, le packaging qui promet un acte d'achat agréable, sécurisant, valorisant et proche de moi, emportera ma décision.

Un monde meilleur ? Le packaging peut y participer, en cherchant à être un support idéal d'information, voire d'éducation. Le designer de packagings ? Plus que jamais, il se doit de refléter la réalité du monde moderne.

diamond

Best of the show

LARS WALLENTIN

Former Packaging Design and Communication Director at Nestlé Switzerland
Currently, worldwide packaging expert and consultant
Member of the Pentawards Jury 2007/2008/2009

How do you explain why a jury spread over 12 different countries around the world finally selected the same best designs?

Most people believe that in the marketing and design worlds, advertising, packaging, copywriting is a matter only of creativity. How wrong can they be. A good design is the result of solid knowledge of human behaviour, basic communication and media rules, technology, materials as well as creativity.

The jury members clearly have solid knowledge in all of the above areas. It is therefore just normal that they more or less arrive at the same conclusions when judging a package which is as well as a piece of art, a piece of communication, of design, of persuasion, and last but not least, common sense.

When purchasing fmcg (Fast Moving Consumer Goods) products, cultural differences are small as shops display products in more or less the same way.

How would you advise young people wishing to become a packaging designer?

To be a packaging designer is to have a multi-task profession. You can't become a fully fledged designer in this field without knowledge of:
- all design rules: ergonomics, simplicity, functionality, honesty, aesthetics, efficiency...
- communication (verbal, visual, symbolic)
- human behaviour (sociology)
- materials (glass, plastic, cardboard, aluminium, steel, etc.)
- how to surprise
- how to analyse and understand briefings
- ecology, legislation, branding, positioning, typography, etc.

The schooling should therefore include periods in the main areas of production, printing, editing, sales, marketing. But most of all, you must be able to sell the designs you develop to people with or without an understanding of what design can do and cannot do!

Who impressed you the most in your professional life and why?

Three people taught me most of the knowledge I've used during my 50 professional years. Two are great designers: the Canadian Don Watt and the Swede Eric Lilius, both left-handed and with very high aesthetic taste. The third person was my boss during many years at Nestlé, the Belgian Jean Volckaert who taught me how to analyse, how to prepare a presentation, and how to sell ideas. If I could mention one more it would be the present chairman of Nestlé, the Austrian Peter Brabeck, from whom I learned basic marketing thinking.

Through your worldwide experience at Nestlé, how do you see the British as one of the leading creative countries in the world?

I find British design very creative (verbally, visually, symbolically). It's graphically and shape-wise very sophisticated and entertaining, i.e. with the typical British humour. However, I doubt its efficiency somewhat.

My favourite designs are those from the Innocent company as there is always something to read and learn on their packages.

Kleenex has won the prestigious Diamond Pentawards 2009, Best of the Show, how do you analyse this?

A professional designer appreciates what is: attractive, surprising, new, simple, and not full of useless information.

Kleenex Summer Triangles have all of the above! Of course this is great design but most of all the consumer is not "bombarded" with information they don't need or want. I just hope that marketing people and designers learn (from Kleenex) to know:
   a) what legislation says, which in most cases is less than what they think;
   b) what consumers really need and want as information;
   c) that management often pretends a lot of information in order to "cover themselves".

Thus making it impossible to amplify the product advantages that help SALES! *Chapeau* Kimberly-Clark!

Wie erklären Sie sich, dass eine Jury, deren Mitglieder kontinentübergreifend aus zwölf Ländern stammen, sich schließlich auf dieselben besten Designs einigen konnte?

Die meisten Leute glauben, dass Werbung, Verpackung und Text in der Welt von Marketing und Design nur eine Frage der Kreativität ist. Wie sehr man sich irren kann! Ein gutes Design ist das Ergebnis eines profunden Wissens über menschliches Verhalten, Grundlagen der Kommunikation, Medienregeln, Technologien, Materialien und natürlich von Kreativität.

Die Jurymitglieder haben eindeutig solide Kenntnisse in allen oben angegebenen Bereichen. Es ist von daher nur normal, dass sie mehr oder weniger zu den gleichen Schlussfolgerungen kommen, wenn sie eine Verpackung beurteilen, die ebenso ein Werk der Kunst, der Kommunikation, von Design und Überzeugung und *last, but not least* auch des gesunden Menschenverstandes ist.

Beim Kauf der sogenannten schnell drehenden Produkte (Fast Moving Consumer Goods) sind kulturelle Unterschiede nur gering, weil die Produkte in den Läden mehr oder weniger ähnlich präsentiert werden.

Was würden Sie jungen Menschen raten, die Verpackungsdesigner werden wollen?

Verpackungsdesigner zu sein bedeutet, in einem Beruf mit einer vielschichtigen Aufgabenverteilung zu arbeiten. Man kann in dieser Branche nicht als vollwertiger Designer bestehen, ohne sich in den folgenden Bereichen auszukennen:
- in allen Gestaltungsgrundsätzen bezüglich Ergonomie, Einfachheit, Funktionalität, Ehrlichkeit, Ästhetik, Effizienz usw.
- in der Kommunikation (verbal, visuell, symbolisch)
- in menschlichem Verhalten (Soziologie)
- in Materialkunde (Glas, Plastik, Karton, Aluminium, Stahl etc.)
- in Ökologie, gesetzlichen Vorschriften, Branding, Positionierung, Typografie etc.
- wie man überrascht
- wie man Briefings analysiert und umsetzt

Aufgabe der Ausbildung ist es also dafür zu sorgen, dass die Auszubildenden Erfahrungen in den wichtigen Bereichen Produktion, Druck, Bearbeitung, Verkauf und Marketing sammeln. Doch vor allem muss man selbst in der Lage sein, die eigenen Gestaltungsentwürfe an den Mann zu bringen – egal ob die Leute verstehen, wozu Design in der Lage ist, oder nicht.

Wer hat Sie als Profi am meisten beeindruckt und warum?

Es gibt drei Menschen, denen ich einen Großteil der Kenntnisse verdanke, die ich in meinen 50 Jahren als Profi eingesetzt habe. Zwei sind großartige Designer, und zwar der Kanadier Don Watt und der Schwede Eric Lilius – beides Linkshänder mit einem ausgezeichneten ästhetischen Geschmack. Der Dritte war während vieler Jahre bei Nestlé mein Chef, nämlich der Belgier Jean Volckaert, der mir beibrachte, wie man Analysen vornimmt, Präsentationen vorbereitet und Ideen verkauft. Wenn ich noch einen weiteren nennen dürfte, wäre das der aktuelle Vorsitzende von Nestlé, der Österreicher Peter Brabeck. Von ihm habe ich die Grundlagen im marketingbezogenen Denken gelernt.

Was können Sie aufgrund Ihrer weltweiten Erfahrung bei Nestlé darüber sagen, welche Rolle die Briten als eine der führenden kreativen Nationen weltweit einnehmen?

Ich finde britisches Design sehr kreativ – sowohl verbal und visuell als auch symbolisch. In Bezug auf Grafik und Formensprache ist es sehr anspruchsvoll und unterhaltsam, das heißt mit jenem typischen britischen Humor. Allerdings bezweifele ich in gewisser Hinsicht dessen Effizienz.

Meine Lieblingsdesigns stammen von der Firma Innocent, weil es auf deren Verpackungen immer etwas zu lesen und zu lernen gibt.

Kleenex hat als „Best of the Show" den angesehenen Diamant Pentaward 2009 gewonnen. Wie analysieren Sie das?

Ein professioneller Designer würdigt das, was attraktiv, überraschend, neu, einfach und nicht voller nutzloser Informationen ist.

Bei „Kleenex Summer Triangles" finden wir all das! Natürlich ist es ein ausgezeichnetes Design, aber vor allem wird der Konsument nicht mit Informationen „bombardiert", die er nicht benötigt oder nicht will. Ich hoffe nur, dass Marketing-Leute und Designer von Kleenex lernen und begreifen, worum es geht:
a) darum, was die Gesetzgebung verlangt, nämlich in den meisten Fällen weniger ist, als sie glauben;
b) darum, was die Konsumenten als Informationen wirklich brauchen und wollen;
c) darum, dass das Management oft eine Vielzahl von Informationen vorgaukelt, um sich dahinter zu verstecken.

Ansonsten wird es unmöglich sein, ein Produkt um weitere Vorteile zu verstärken, die den Verkauf vorantreiben! Meine Hochachtung also für Kimberly-Clark!

LARS WALLENTIN

Comment expliquez-vous qu'un jury issu de 12 pays différents des quatre coins du globe ait finalement sélectionné les mêmes meilleurs designs ?

La plupart des gens pensent que, dans les mondes du marketing et du design, la publicité, le packaging et la rédaction publicitaire ne sont qu'une affaire de créativité. Comme ils se trompent. Un bon design est le résultat d'une connaissance profonde du comportement humain, des règles de base de la communication et des médias, de la technologie et des matériaux, ainsi que de la créativité.

Les membres du jury ont clairement de solides connaissances dans chacun de ces domaines. Il est donc tout à fait normal qu'ils arrivent plus ou moins aux mêmes conclusions lorsqu'ils jugent un emballage, qui est une œuvre d'art, un vecteur de communication, de design, de persuasion, mais aussi de bon sens.

Dans l'achat de PGC (produits de grande consommation), les différences culturelles sont réduites, car les magasins présentent les produits plus ou moins de la même façon.

Quels conseils donneriez-vous aux jeunes qui veulent devenir designer de packaging ?

Être designer de packaging, c'est exercer un métier aux multiples facettes. Dans ce domaine, on ne peut pas devenir un designer à part entière sans connaître :

- toutes les règles du design : ergonomie, simplicité, fonctionnalité, honnêteté, esthétique, efficacité…
- la communication (verbale, visuelle, symbolique)
- le comportement humain (sociologie)
- les matériaux (verre, plastique, carton, aluminium, acier, etc.)
- les techniques pour surprendre
- l'art d'analyser et de comprendre les briefings
- l'écologie, la législation, la stratégie de marque, le positionnement, la typographie, etc.

La formation doit donc comprendre des périodes d'études dans les domaines de la production, de l'impression, de l'édition, des ventes et du marketing. Mais il faut surtout être capable de vendre les designs que vous créez aux gens, qu'ils comprennent ou non ce que le design peut et ne peut pas faire !

Dans votre parcours professionnel, qui vous a le plus marqué et pourquoi ?

Trois personnes m'ont appris l'essentiel ce que j'ai utilisé pendant mes 50 ans de carrière. Deux d'entre elles sont de grands designers : le Canadien Don Watt et le Suédois Eric Lilius. Ils sont tous les deux gauchers et ont un grand sens de l'esthétique. La troisième personne a été mon supérieur chez Nestlé pendant de nombreuses années, le Belge Jean Vockaert. Il m'a appris à analyser, à préparer une présentation et à vendre des idées. Si je pouvais mentionner quelqu'un d'autre, ce serait le président actuel de Nestlé, l'Autrichien Peter Brabeck, qui m'a enseigné à réfléchir en termes de marketing.

À partir de l'expérience que vous avez acquise chez Nestlé sur le marché mondial, que pensez-vous du Royaume-Uni, en tant que l'un des plus grands pays créatifs du monde ?

Je trouve le design anglais très créatif (verbalement, visuellement et symboliquement). Les graphismes et les formes sont très sophistiqués et ludiques, et illustrent l'humour typiquement « british ». Pourtant, je doute un peu de son efficacité.

Mes designs préférés sont ceux de la société Innocent, parce qu'il y a toujours quelque chose à lire et à apprendre sur leurs emballages.

Kleenex a remporté le prestigieux Diamond Pentaward 2009, Best of the Show, qu'en pensez-vous ?

Un designer professionnel apprécie ce qui est : séduisant, surprenant, nouveau, simple, et débarrassé des informations inutiles.

Les Summer Triangles de Kleenex sont tout cela ! Bien sûr c'est un excellent design mais, surtout, le consommateur n'est pas « bombardé » d'informations dont il n'a pas besoin ou dont il ne veut pas. J'espère simplement que les spécialistes du marketing et du design apprennent (grâce à Kleenex) :

a) à se renseigner sur la législation, qui en général est moins stricte qu'ils ne le pensent ;
b) à analyser les véritables attentes et besoins des consommateurs en termes d'informations ;
c) à réaliser que les dirigeants des entreprises veulent souvent afficher beaucoup d'informations pour « se couvrir ».

Ce qui rend impossible de mettre en valeur les avantages du produit qui font augmenter les VENTES ! Chapeau Kimberly-Clark !

Some of the greatest creative ideas are also the simplest. There are few things more banal (hygienic and practical) nowadays than paper tissues. **Kleenex** has emerged as the uncontested leader in this field, and up to now their boxes too were at most decorative. In this case, the designers working for Kleenex were asked to create a limited-edition carton that would celebrate the summer season and drive consumer delight. And Kleenex (Kimberly-Clark Corporation) has broken the rules to offer a fresh combination of structure and graphics in perfect harmony, christened a **"slice of summer"**. A triangular box illustrated to appear like a section of different juicy fruits, watermelon, orange or lemon, that look enticing enough to eat.

Einige der besten kreativen Ideen sind gleichzeitig auch die einfachsten. Heutzutage ist in hygienischer und praktischer Hinsicht kaum etwas banaler als Papiertücher. **Kleenex** hat sich in diesem Bereich zum unangefochtenen Marktführer entwickelt, aber bisher waren die dazugehörigen Kartons bestenfalls dekorativ. In diesem Fall bekamen die für Kleenex tätigen Designer den Auftrag, einen Karton als „Limited Edition" zu gestalten, mit dem der Sommer gefeiert werden und der die Verbraucher begeistern sollte. Kleenex (Kimberly-Clark Corporation) hat die Regeln gesprengt, um in perfekter Harmonie eine ganz neue Kombination aus Struktur und Grafiken anzubieten, und taufte das Ganze „A Slice of Summer" (Eine Scheibe Sommer). Eine dreieckige Schachtel wurde so gestaltet, dass sie wie das saftige Stück einer Wassermelone, einer Orange oder einer Zitrone erscheint – so verführerisch, dass man reinbeißen möchte.

Les grandes idées créatives sont parfois aussi les plus simples. Aujourd'hui, peu de produits sont aussi courants (hygiéniques et pratiques) que les mouchoirs en papier. **Kleenex** s'est imposé en tant que leader incontesté dans ce secteur, et jusqu'à présent leurs boîtes étaient tout au plus décoratives. Dans ce cas, les designers de Kleenex ont été chargés de créer une boîte en édition limitée pour fêter l'été et réjouir les consommateurs. Et Kleenex (Kimberly-Clark Corporation) a brisé les règles pour proposer une combinaison fraîche de structure et de graphisme en parfaite harmonie, baptisée « **une tranche d'été** ». C'est une boîte triangulaire déguisée en tranche de fruit juteux, pastèque, orange ou citron, suffisamment appétissante pour mettre l'eau à la bouche.

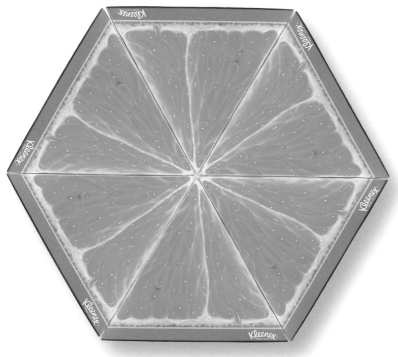

KLEENEX
SLICE OF SUMMER

Creative Director: Christine Mau
Senior Designer: Jennifer Brock
Brand Design Manager: Jane Kelly
Illustration: Hiroko Sanders
Company: Kimberly-Clark
Country: USA

DIAMOND PENTAWARD 2009

PIPER HEIDSIECK
VIKTOR & ROLF

Design: Viktor & Rolf; BETC France
Company: Sleever International
Country: France
DIAMOND PENTAWARD 2008

How to create something new with a timeless product? The answer from Dutch fashion designers **Viktor & Rolf** for **Piper Heidsieck** was to reverse the directions. Still keeping the main classic graphic features (bottle, cork, ice bucket, glass, and labels) vital to the champagne market, the idea was that, if champagne could turn one's head, it was only necessary to reverse all these visual elements to amplify this impression, and especially to differentiate the brand from its competitors by recreating the packaging. The bottles of Piper Heidsieck Rosé Sauvage signed by Viktor & Rolf were launched on the market in October 2007 in several duty-free shops and in exclusive bars and wine bars. The glass bottles are covered by a sleeve produced by Sleever International.

Wie kann man mit einem zeitlosen Produkt etwas ganz Neues schaffen? Die Antwort der niederländischen Modedesigner **Viktor & Rolf** für **Piper Heidsieck** lautete, die Richtung zu wechseln. Hier werden die für den Champagnermarkt wichtigen klassischen grafischen Merkmale (Flasche, Korken, Eiskühler, Glas und Etikett) bedient. Gleichzeitig wird aber mit der Idee gespielt, dass Champagner einem den Kopf verdreht. Alles, was man tun muss, um diesen Eindruck zu verstärken, ist, diese visuellen Elemente umzukehren. Dadurch, dass die Verpackung neu geschaffen wurde, hob sich die Marke vor allem auch von ihren Konkurrenten ab. Die von Viktor & Rolf signierten Piper-Heidsieck-Rosé-Sauvage-Flaschen wurden im Oktober 2007 auf dem Markt eingeführt und zwar in verschiedenen Duty-Free-Shops sowie in exklusiven Bars und Weinläden. Die Glasflaschen werden von einer von Sleever International produzierten Hülle bedeckt.

Comment innover avec un produit intemporel? La réponse des créateurs de mode néerlandais **Viktor & Rolf** pour **Piper Heidsieck** a été de renverser les directions. Tout en gardant les éléments graphiques classiques (bouteille, bouchon, seau à glace, verre et étiquettes) essentiels sur le marché du champagne, l'idée était que, si le champagne peut vous faire tourner la tête, il suffisait de renverser tous ces éléments visuels pour amplifier cette impression, et plus particulièrement pour différencier la marque de ses concurrents en réinventant le packaging. Les bouteilles de Piper Heidsieck Rosé Sauvage signées Viktor & Rolf ont été lancées sur le marché en octobre 2007 dans plusieurs boutiques duty-free et dans des bars et bars à vins exclusifs. Les bouteilles en verre sont recouvertes d'un manchon fabriqué par Sleever International.

Hoyu is a well-established brand in the Japanese professional hair-colour products market, but a newcomer in professional hair-styling products. The brief was to introduce **Hoyu** professional styling products into the very competitive, top-class hair salons, and establish a presence, using a very bold and memorable approach. The concept for this brand is "countdown". As the hairdresser is about to finish the customer's hair, the customer's anticipation reaches a high point. The product is then used to conclude this "countdown" to the finish.

Hoyu ist auf dem japanischen Markt eine gut eingeführte Marke für professionelle Haarfärbeprodukte, aber ein Newcomer bei den Profi-Hairstyling-Produkten. Das Briefing lautete, die Profi-Styling-Produkte von **Hoyu** in den heiß umkämpften Topclass-Friseursalons zu etablieren. Auf sehr mutige und prägnante Weise sollte dort die Präsenz des Produkts verankert werden. Diese Marke greift das Konzept „Countdown" auf: Wenn der Coiffeur sich daran macht, den Haaren der Kundin den letzten Schliff zu verleihen, erreichen ihre Erwartungen den Höhepunkt. Das Produkt wird nun eingesetzt, um diesen „Countdown" bis zur Vollendung abzuschließen

Hoyu est une marque reconnue sur le marché japonais des produits de coloration professionnelle, mais c'est une nouvelle venue dans le domaine des produits de coiffage. La mission était d'introduire les produits de coiffage professionnel de **Hoyu** dans les salons haut de gamme, où la concurrence fait rage, et de leur y donner une présence grâce à une démarche audacieuse et mémorable. Le concept de cette marque est le « compte à rebours ». Lorsque le coiffeur est sur le point de terminer le coiffage des cheveux, l'impatience du client atteint son paroxysme. Le produit sert alors à accompagner ce « compte à rebours » jusqu'à sa conclusion.

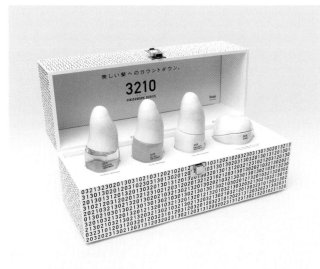

HOYU 3210

Creative Director: Tomohiro Sakurai (ADK)
Art Director: Mutsumi Ajichi (ADK), Kunikazu Hoshiba (Katachi)
Designer: Murakami Takashi, Hiro Kinoshita (Katachi), Yasuhiro Nagae (Iro)
Company: ADK
Country: Japan

DIAMOND PENTAWARD 2010

beverages

Interview with

JENNIFER TSAI

Proad Identity Taipei, Taiwan
Member of the Pentawards Jury 2009/2010

How do you explain why a jury spread over 12 different countries around the world finally selected the same best designs?

Excellent designs share something in common despite cultural, historic, and geographical differences. For example, they must be creative and meticulously executed, which is readily distinguishable to any professional jury member with well-trained eyes.

Coming from different countries, the jury members have their own particular experience and professional ability. With the perceptive insight and accurate judgement this gives, the selected design works are not only above the general level but also gain special credibility.

How would you advise young people wishing to become a packaging designer?

In the context of keen competition on the market, packaging must be more than just beautiful design. It must respond to market analysis, brand strategy, and correct positioning in relation to other designs. Choice of material for the packaging must not become a burden for our environment after use. Together, these are new challenges for young designers, because even though packaging is only one part of the product, it continues to grow in importance in every industry since a creative and integrated packaging design creates new value for the product.

Who impressed you the most in your professional life and why?

Throughout my professional career, Kazumasa Nagai and Koichi Sato have impressed me the most. These two designers have something very much in common even if they employ differing styles. Taking a cue from the culture they came from, Nagai and Sato both use innovative approaches in their designs, in which the traditional East meets the modern West, to achieve intense visual effects that are profound, thought-provoking, unique, and reflect their own personal style.

With your large expertise and knowledge of Eastern and Western design, how do you see Russian design developing today?

Given the long-term, extensive influence of Communism, I think Russian designers tend to utilise a limited number of elements, and are relatively lacking in variety, in terms of the overall design concepts and palette adopted. In my opinion, a design is created out of the mixture, or interaction, of historic, cultural, educational, and commercial elements. For sure there is potential in Russian design but, in order to improve the diversity of their works, the country's designers must engage themselves further in cultural exchanges and learn from other countries.

For three consecutive years, Coca-Cola has been highly awarded by Pentawards, how do you explain such a phenomenon?

Upholding the brand's original identity with a hint of playfulness and humour in everyday life, the design concepts of Coca-Cola are extremely ingenious and very creative. That is why I consider it only right and proper for Coca-Cola to have been honoured by Pentawards for three consecutive years.

Wie erklären Sie sich, dass eine Jury, deren Mitglieder kontinentübergreifend aus zwölf Ländern stammen, sich schließlich auf dieselben besten Designs einigen konnte?

Ausgezeichnete Designs haben trotz der kulturellen, historischen und geographischen Unterschiede etwas gemeinsam. Sie müssen beispielsweise kreativ sein und sorgfältig ausgeführt werden, was für jedes professionelle Jurymitglied mit gut geschultem Auge leicht erkennbar ist.

Was würden Sie jungen Menschen raten, die Verpackungsdesigner werden wollen?

Die Verpackung wird in jeder Branche zunehmend wichtiger, weil ein kreatives und vollendetes Package Design dem Produkt einen neuen Wert verleiht. Es ist nicht nur ein ausschlaggebender Faktor für den Verkaufserfolg, sondern spielt auch bei der Vermittlung des Produktimages eine wesentliche Rolle. Daher kann ich junge Designer nur dazu ermutigen, sich der Herausforderung zu stellen, die Verpackungen von Markenprodukten zu gestalten und sich darauf zu konzentrieren.

Wer hat Sie als Profi am meisten beeindruckt und warum?

Während meiner gesamten beruflichen Laufbahn haben Kazumasa Nagai und Koichi Sato mir am meisten imponiert. Obwohl sie stilistisch unterschiedlich arbeiten, haben diese beiden Designer doch eine ganz wesentliche Gemeinsamkeit: Nagai und Sato richten sich nach der Kultur, der sie entstammen. Sie arbeiten in ihren Designs mit innovativen Ansätzen, in denen der traditionelle Osten auf den modernen Westen trifft, um eindringliche visuelle Effekte zu erzielen, die sehr tief gehen, zum Nachdenken anregen und einzigartig sind sowie ihren ganz persönlichen Stil widerspiegeln.

Wie beurteilen Sie die Entwicklung des russischen Designs vor dem Hintergrund Ihres profunden Fachwissens und Ihrer Kenntnis des östlichen und westlichen Designs?

Wenn man den langfristigen und umfassenden Einfluss des Kommunismus berücksichtigt, bin ich der Ansicht, dass russische Designer dazu neigen, eine begrenzte Anzahl von Elementen einzusetzen. Dabei mangelt es an Abwechslung, wenn man es unter dem Aspekt der Designkonzepte insgesamt und der gewählten Palette betrachtet. Meines Erachtens entsteht ein Design aus der Mischung oder Interaktion von historischen, kulturellen, kommerziellen und Bildungselementen. Beim russischen Design gibt es gewiss einiges an Potenzial, doch damit ihre Arbeiten vielfältiger werden, müssen sich die dortigen Designer noch mehr am kulturellen Austausch beteiligen und von anderen Ländern lernen.

In drei aufeinander folgenden Jahren wurde Coca-Cola von Pentawards besonders hoch ausgezeichnet. Wie erklären Sie ein solches Phänomen?

Die Marke bewahrt ihre ursprüngliche Identität, der ein Hauch von Verspieltheit und Humor im Alltag anhaftet. Ihre Designkonzepte sind extrem genial und sehr kreativ. Darum halte ich es nur für folgerichtig und angemessen, dass Coca-Cola gleich drei Jahre nacheinander von Pentawards gewürdigt wird.

JENNIFER TSAI

Comment expliquez-vous qu'un jury issu de 12 pays différents des quatre coins du globe ait finalement sélectionné les mêmes meilleurs designs ?

Tous les designs vraiment bons ont quelque chose en commun malgré les différences culturelles, historiques et géographiques. Par exemple, ils doivent être créatifs et réalisés avec soin, ce que n'importe quel jury professionnel au regard exercé sait distinguer sans peine.

Les membres du jury viennent de différents pays, et possèdent chacun leurs propres expériences et compétences professionnelles particulières. Avec ces facultés de compréhension, de perception et d'analyse, les designs sélectionnés sont non seulement au-dessus du niveau général, mais acquièrent aussi une crédibilité unique.

Quels conseils donneriez-vous aux jeunes qui veulent devenir designer de packaging ?

Le marché est livré à une concurrence intense, et le design des emballages ne doit pas se contenter d'être esthétique. Il doit répondre à une étude de marché, à une stratégie de marque, et à un positionnement approprié par rapport aux autres designs. Le choix des matériaux ne doit pas peser sur l'environnement après l'utilisation du produit. Tout cela représente de nouveaux défis pour les jeunes designers, car même si l'emballage n'est qu'une partie du produit, son importance continue de croître dans tous les secteurs, car un emballage créatif et intégré crée de la valeur ajoutée pour le produit.

Dans votre parcours professionnel, qui vous a le plus marquée et pourquoi ?

Tout au long de ma carrière professionnelle, ce sont Kazumasa Nagai et Koichi Sato qui m'ont le plus marquée. Ces deux designers partagent une caractéristique commune, même si leurs styles sont différents. Inspirés par la culture dont ils sont issus, dans leurs designs Nagai et Sato utilisent tous deux des démarches où l'Orient traditionnel rencontre l'Occident moderne, pour obtenir des effets visuels intenses, profonds, uniques, qui poussent à la réflexion et reflètent leur style personnel.

Avec votre vaste expérience du design oriental et occidental, comment voyez-vous l'évolution du design russe aujourd'hui ?

Étant donné l'influence profonde et persistante du communisme, je pense que les designers russes ont tendance à utiliser un nombre d'éléments limité, et que leur travail souffre d'un manque relatif de variété, en termes de concepts généraux et de palette. Pour moi, le design est le résultat d'un mélange, ou d'une interaction, d'éléments historiques, culturels, éducatifs et commerciaux. Bien sûr le design russe a du potentiel mais, pour améliorer la diversité de leurs projets, les designers russes devraient s'intéresser davantage aux échanges culturels et apprendre des autres pays.

Les Pentawards ont beaucoup récompensé Coca-Cola pendant trois années consécutives, comment expliquez-vous ce phénomène ?

Les concepts de Coca-Cola reprennent l'identité originale de la marque et ajoutent une touche d'humour à la vie quotidienne. Ils sont extrêmement ingénieux et très créatifs. C'est pourquoi, à mon avis, il est tout à fait normal et approprié que les Pentawards aient rendu hommage à Coca-Cola trois années de suite.

For this **Coca-Cola** can, Turner Duckworth used a red print on metal which features cheerful and feel-good images from summertime in the USA, culminating in the national holiday of the 4th of July: a BBQ, Raybans, a beach-ball, surfboards, stars and stripes. To add personality, the Coca-Cola logo is used with more freedom and creativity each time. Everything is also easily adaptable to all promotional material such as T-shirts, caps, beach towels, and so on, to create a perfectly integrated marketing campaign.

Bei dieser **Coca-Cola**-Dose arbeiteten Turner Duckworth mit einem roten Aufdruck auf Metall, der fröhliche und gutgelaunte Symbole der sommerlichen USA zeigt. Zusammen spielen sie auf den amerikanischen National-feiertag an, den 4. Juli: ein Barbecue, Rayban-Sonnen-brillen, ein Beachball, Surfbretter und Stars and Stripes. Um allem noch mehr Persönlichkeit zu verleihen, wird das Logo von Coca-Cola stets freier und kreativer ver-wendet. Alles kann ganz einfach an verschiedene Werbe-materialien wie T-Shirts, Baseballcaps, Strandtücher usw. angepasst werden, um eine perfekt integrierte Marketing-Kampagne zu schaffen.

Pour cette canette de **Coca-Cola**, l'agence Turner Duckworth a imprimé en rouge sur le métal des images joyeuses et réconfortantes de l'été américain, dont le point fort est la fête nationale du 4 juillet : un barbecue, des Ray-Ban, un ballon de plage, des planches de surf, les rayures et étoiles du drapeau. Pour ajouter de la person-nalité, le logo Coca-Cola est utilisé avec plus de liberté et de créativité dans chaque déclinaison. Le tout s'adapte aussi facilement à tous les supports promotionnels comme les t-shirts, les casquettes, les serviettes de plage, etc. pour créer une campagne marketing parfaitement intégrée.

COCA-COLA
SUMMER 2009 PACKAGING

Creative Directors: David Turner, Bruce Duckworth
Design Director: Sarah Moffat; *Design:* Rebecca Williams, Josh Michels
Company: Turner Duckworth, London & San Francisco
Country: UK/USA
Category: Best of the category Beverages

PLATINUM PENTAWARD 2009

The Anglo-American Turner Duckworth agency designed the **Coca-Cola aluminium bottle**. As a successful brand like Coca-Cola becomes ever more familiar, adding new graphics is an answer for keeping it fresh. But over time the effect can be diluted, and the answer can be a return to the basics. This is what Turner Duckworth has done with its bottle, keeping the same shape, but in a very contemporary new material. The result is packaging that feels familiar and new at the same time. It's also a good way of putting into practice a "Less is More" kind of design.

Die angloamerikanische Agentur Turner Duckworth hat die **Coca-Cola-Flasche aus Aluminium** entworfen. Da eine so erfolgreiche Marke wie Coca-Cola im Laufe der Zeit immer vertrauter wird, ergänzt man sie am besten mit neuen grafischen Inhalten, um sie frisch zu halten. Doch im Laufe der Zeit verwässert sich womöglich auch dieser Effekt, und die Antwort könnte lauten, wieder zu den Grundlagen zurückzukehren. Genau das hat Turner Duckworth mit seiner Flasche gemacht: Man bewahrte die Form, jedoch in einem sehr modernen, aktuellen Material. Das Ergebnis ist eine Verpackung, die einem gleichzeitig vertraut und neu vorkommt. Es ist außerdem eine gute Möglichkeit, ein Design im Stil von „Weniger ist mehr" umzusetzen.

L'agence anglo-américaine Turner Duckworth a conçu la **bouteille en aluminium de Coca-Cola**. Une marque aussi connue que Coca-Cola finit par devenir trop familière, et lui donner un nouveau graphisme est une solution pour conserver sa fraîcheur. Mais l'effet peut se diluer avec le temps, et la réponse peut se trouver dans un retour à l'essentiel. C'est ce que Turner Duckworth a fait avec cette bouteille, en gardant la même forme, mais avec un nouveau matériau très contemporain. Le résultat est un packaging qui semble familier et nouveau à la fois. C'est aussi une bonne façon de mettre en pratique un design épuré à l'extrême.

COCA-COLA
ALUMINIUM BOTTLE

Creative Directors: David Turner, Bruce Duckworth
Designer: Chris Garvey
Company: Turner Duckworth, London & San Francisco
Country: UK/USA
Category: Best of the category Beverages

PLATINUM PENTAWARD 2008

A long-standing Spanish winemaker wanted to enter the Chinese market. This process had to be as smooth as possible. French wines, which are the most popular in China, usually choose to keep their identity 100%, showing their authenticity. **Lascala** decided to merge Western and Eastern cultures; it is also the word the Chinese use for the theatre. A face all painted to imitate a theatre mask and with Eastern features to represent China, with the merger represented by La Peineta (the ornamental comb) Rosé Wine, El Abanico (the hand fan) White Wine, and La Bailaora de Flamenco (the Flamenco dancer) Red Wine. Products that are not originally manufactured in China cannot bear Chinese writing on the front packaging, so for the main label, the brand's text is displayed on a vertical axis, like traditional Chinese script.

Ein seit langem am Markt vertretener spanischer Produzent wollte seine Weine auch in China anbieten. In China sind französische Weine besonders begehrt. Ihre Produzenten entscheiden sich normalerweise dafür, die Identität der Weine 100%ig zu behalten und damit Authentizität zu verdeutlichen. Doch **Lascala** (diesen Begriff verwenden die Chinesen auch fürs Theater) beschloss, westliche und östliche Kultur zu verschmelzen. China wird durch eine Theatermaske mit fernöstlichen Gesichtszügen repräsentiert. Für Roséwein wird auf dem Etikett der Schmuckkamm *La Peineta* ergänzt, für den Weißwein der Fächer *El Abanico* und für den Rotwein *La Bailaora de Flamenco* (die Flamenco-Tänzerin). Produkte, die nicht ursprünglich in China hergestellt worden sind, dürfen auf der Vorderseite der Packung keine chinesischen Schriftzeichen tragen. Also werden die Buchstaben für das Hauptetikett in traditioneller chinesischer Schreibweise von oben nach unten aufgedruckt.

Un producteur de vin espagnol de longue tradition voulait pénétrer le marché chinois. Il fallait que l'opération se fasse en douceur. Les vins français, qui sont les plus populaires en Chine, préfèrent habituellement garder leur identité sans rien y changer, pour montrer leur authenticité. **Lascala** a décidé de fusionner les cultures occidentale et orientale. Par ailleurs, c'est par ce mot que les Chinois désignent le théâtre. L'identité visuelle se compose d'un visage maquillé pour imiter un masque de théâtre, avec des traits orientaux pour représenter la Chine, et la fusion des cultures est symbolisée par La Peineta (peigne ornemental) pour le vin rosé, El Abanico (éventail) pour le vin blanc, et La Bailaora de Flamenco (danseuse de flamenco) pour le vin rouge. Les produits qui ne sont pas fabriqués en Chine ne peuvent pas arborer de lettres chinoises sur le devant de l'emballage. Pour l'étiquette principale, la marque est écrite verticalement, comme les lettres chinoises traditionnelles.

LASCALA

Art Direction: Eduardo del Fraile
Design: Eduardo del Fraile, Manel Quilez
Company: Eduardo del Fraile
Country: Spain
Category: Best of the category Beverages
PLATINUM PENTAWARD 2010

Isklar, "ice clear" in Norwegian, is Norway's first ever water brand to be exported to the UK, and is positioned as an "everyday premium" glacial mineral water. The task for the designers was to create an award-winning brand, including pack structure and graphics, for this everyday product, that would outshine other players in the market. Inspiration was taken from the folklore of the water's source region and its Norwegian provenance to devise the core brand ideas. The unique bottle structure dispenses with the need for structural ribbing, thus reducing the volume of raw materials used in production.

Isklar (Norwegisch für „eisklar") ist die erste norwegische Mineralwassermarke, die nach Großbritannien exportiert wurde. Sie wird als Premium-Eisbergmineralwasser für den Alltag vermarktet. Die Aufgabe für die Designer bestand darin, für dieses alltägliche Produkt inklusive Verpackungsstruktur und Grafiken eine preisverdächtige Marke zu schaffen, die die anderen Konkurrenten auf diesem Markt ausstechen sollte. Man ließ sich von volkstümlichen Elementen aus der Quellregion dieses Wassers und seiner norwegischen Herkunft inspirieren, um die zentralen Ideen für diese Marke zu entwickeln. Durch die neuartige Flaschenstruktur ersparte man sich die geriffelte Struktur und reduzierte somit die Menge der für die Produktion erforderlichen Rohmaterialien.

Isklar, « clair comme de la glace » en norvégien, est la toute première marque d'eau norvégienne exportée au Royaume-Uni, et est positionnée comme eau minérale de glacier « quotidienne haut de gamme ». La mission des designers était de créer une marque primée, notamment pour la structure et le graphisme du packaging, pour ce produit de consommation courante qui devait éclipser les autres acteurs du marché. Ils se sont inspirés du folklore de la région de la source et de sa provenance norvégienne pour concevoir le cœur de la marque. La forme originale de la bouteille la dispense de nervures structurelles, ce qui réduit le volume de matières premières utilisées pour la production.

ISKLAR

Executive Creative Director: Martin Grimer
Design Director: Reseigh Fooks
Design Director Structure: Guy Williams
Realisation Director: Shaun Jones
Account Director: Roger Hart
Company: Blue Marlin Brand Design
Country: UK
Category: Water

GOLD PENTAWARD 2009

ISKLAR SPARKLING

Design: Guy Williams, Martin Grimer
Company: Blue Marlin Brand Design
Country: UK
Category: Water

BRONZE PENTAWARD 2010

EVIAN PURE

Design: Grand Angle design team
Company: Grand Angle Design
Country: France
Category: Water

GOLD PENTAWARD 2008

DEEP ORIGIN

Design: Stephan Jelicich
Company: Grenache Bottle Design
Country: New Zealand
Category: Water

GOLD PENTAWARD 2010

Deep Origin is a tear-drop-shaped, crystal-clear glass bottle, with dimple recesses positioned in parallel. These two 9 mm-deep indentations on opposite sides of the bottle, resembling the bowl of a spoon in shape, not only function as an inviting grip for the hand, but also feature Deep Origin's company logo. To create a unique and functional package with low environmental impact Grenache Bottle Design chose packaging elements that used fewer resources and lent themselves to multiple re-use, or composting. The bottle's main label is in raised letters on the glass itself, reducing waste. The small biodegradable cellulose neck-label has water-soluble adhesive and is printed using vegetable-based inks.

Deep Origin ist eine kristallklare Glasflasche in Tropfenform mit parallelen Einkerbungen. Sie ist an zwei gegenüberliegenden Stellen 9 mm tief eingebuchtet. Diese Vertiefungen ähneln in der Form einem Löffel und dienen nicht nur als einladender Griff für die Hand, sondern tragen auch das Firmenlogo von Deep Origin. Um eine unverwechselbare und funktionale Verpackung möglichst ohne Umweltbelastungen zu schaffen, entschied sich Grenache Bottle bei der Verpackung für Elemente, die weniger Ressourcen verbrauchen und sich für Mehrfachverwendung oder Kompostierung eignen. Der Namenszug wird mit erhabenen Buchstaben auf das Glas selbst aufgebracht, was Abfall vermeidet. Das kleine Etikett, dessen Aufdruck aus pflanzlicher Druckfarbe besteht, ist biologisch abbaubar und wird mit wasserlöslichem Klebstoff befestigt.

Deep Origin est une bouteille en verre transparent comme le cristal, en forme de goutte, avec des creux en forme de fossettes placés face à face. Ces deux renfoncements profonds de 9 mm de chaque côté de la bouteille prennent la forme de la partie concave d'une petite cuiller, et invitent à y placer les doigts pour saisir la bouteille, mais servent aussi à mettre en valeur le logo de Deep Origin. Pour créer un emballage original et fonctionnel tout en minimisant l'impact sur l'environnement, Grenache Bottle Design a choisi des matériaux qui consomment moins de ressources et qui se prêtent à être réutilisés plusieurs fois, ou à être compostés. Le texte principal de la bouteille est inscrit en relief directement sur le verre, pour réduire les déchets. La petite étiquette biodégradable en cellulose placée sur le col est collée avec de l'adhésif soluble dans l'eau, et est imprimée avec des encres végétales.

LANJARÓN

Design: Oscar Fort
Company: Coleman CBX
Country: Spain
Category: Water

SILVER PENTAWARD 2010

SPADEL
SPA "ON THE GO"

Design: Ruta Figarol, Marc Sicard
Company: Design Board
Country: Belgium
Category: Water

SILVER PENTAWARD 2009

**PARIS BAGUETTE
EAU**

Design: Karim Rashid
Company: Karim Rashid Inc.
Country: USA
Category: Water
SILVER PENTAWARD 2010

CALDES DE BOÍ

Design: Emma Olive
Company: emmaolivéstudio
Country: Spain
Category: Water

BRONZE PENTAWARD 2009

PEDRAS

Design: Esme Fisher, Robyn Stevenson, Jackie Hall,
Ninja Scheel Aas, Candy Schneider, Jeremy Chestnutt,
David Muzeen, Kevin Greene, Ian Burren, Steve Elliott
Company: You
Country: UK
Category: Water

BRONZE PENTAWARD 2010

VITALIS

Creative Director: Antonia Hayward
Client Manager: Sally Westlake
Company: Design Bridge Ltd.
Country: UK
Category: Water

BRONZE PENTAWARD 2010

VERI

Creative Director: Anna Andersson
Company: Pulp
Country: France
Category: Water

BRONZE PENTAWARD 2009

Apart from the light-bulb-shaped bottle, which represents energy, the idea for the **Gloji** packaging design was based on three related elements. First, the brand name "Gloji", second, the main ingredient "goji-berry juice", and third, the slogan "The juice that makes you glow". It visually tries to communicate the ideas of "Glowing and Healthy", and fits ergonomically in the consumer's hand.

Abgesehen von der Flasche in Glühbirnenform, die für Energie steht, basiert die Idee für das Verpackungsdesign von **Gloji** auf drei zusammengehörigen Elementen: erstens dem Markennamen „Gloji", zweitens der Hauptzutat „Gojibeerensaft" und drittens dem Slogan „Der Saft, der Sie zum Leuchten bringt". So wird versucht, den Gedanken von „leuchtend und gesund" visuell zu vermitteln, und das Produkt ist sehr ergonomisch auf die Hand des Verbrauchers abgestimmt.

Outre la bouteille en forme d'ampoule électrique, qui représente l'énergie, l'idée qui se trouve derrière le packaging de **Gloji** est basée sur trois éléments voisins. Tout d'abord, le nom de la marque « Gloji » (« glow » signifie rayonner en anglais), ensuite, l'ingrédient principal « jus de baie goji », et enfin, le slogan « Le jus qui vous fait rayonner ». Le packaging essaie de communiquer visuellement la notion de rayonnement et de santé, et s'adapte ergonomiquement à la main du consommateur.

GOJI & POMEGRANATE
100% juice
8.5 fl oz (250 ml)

GOJI & PARADISE APPLE
100% juice
8.5 fl oz (250 ml)

GLOJI

Design: Peter Kao
Company: Gloji Inc.
Country: USA
Category: Soft drinks, juices

GOLD PENTAWARD 2008

GOJI JUICE
ALL NATURAL
11 fl oz (325 ml)

It is unusual to have a client who comes with a briefing for a product named after the height of the bottle it comes in. When it happens, the challenge probably requires something different. The answer for the **12 Inches** juices was a label that was exactly 12 inches long, printed on to packaging tape, that could also be used as signage and merchandising at points of sale.

Es ist schon ungewöhnlich, wenn ein Kunde mit einem Briefing für ein Getränk kommt, das seinen Namen von der Höhe der Flasche bezieht, in der es angeboten wird. Tritt dieser Fall ein, dann sollte man sich für eine solche Herausforderung wahrscheinlich etwas ganz Neues überlegen. Die Antwort für die **12**-**Inches**-Säfte lag in einem Etikett, das genau 12 Zoll lang ist und auf eine Banderole gedruckt wird, die in den Verkaufsstellen auch für die Beschilderung und die Warenwerbung eingesetzt werden kann.

Il est inhabituel d'avoir un client qui vient vous voir avec un produit baptisé d'après la hauteur de la bouteille qui le contient. Lorsque cela arrive, la mission appelle probablement une approche originale. Pour les jus **12 Inches**, la réponse a été une étiquette qui mesure exactement 12 pouces (« inches ») de long, imprimée sur de l'adhésif d'emballage, qui peut aussi servir à la signalisation et au merchandising sur le point de vente.

12 INCHES

Design: Ivana Martinovic
Company: War Design
Country: Australia
Category: Soft drinks, juices

GOLD PENTAWARD 2009

PASCUAL SELECCION

Design: Christophe Blin
Company: In Spirit Design
Country: Spain
Category: Soft drinks, juices

GOLD PENTAWARD 2010

THE FRUIT LAB

Design: Arthur van Hamersveld, Bart de Rooy
Company: PROUDdesign
Country: The Netherlands
Category: Soft drinks, juices

SILVER PENTAWARD 2009

PARIS BAGUETTE
JUS

Design: Karim Rashid
Company: Karim Rashid Inc.
Country: USA
Category: Soft drinks, juices

SILVER PENTAWARD 2010

RIJP

Design: Iwan Kempe, Bart de Rooy
Company: PROUDdesign
Country: The Netherlands
Category: Soft drinks, juices

SILVER PENTAWARD 2009

FRUITY KING
LIMONADA!

Design: Kyanne Buckmann
Company: PROUDdesign
Country: The Netherlands
Category: Soft drinks, juices

SILVER PENTAWARD 2010

ROBINSONS
FRUIT SHOOT

Design: David Beard, Pip Dale
Company: Brandhouse
Country: UK
Category: Soft drinks, juices

BRONZE PENTAWARD 2009

V8

Design: Sandrine Topart
Company: Brandimage – Desgrippes & Laga
Country: Belgium
Category: Soft drinks, juices

BRONZE PENTAWARD 2010

CUCULAND

Creative Director: Cristian "Kit" Paul
Senior Designers: Cristian Petre, Bogdan Dumitrache
Designers: Eugen Erhan, Ciprian Badalan, Iancu Barbarasa
Company: Brandient
Country: Romania
Category: Soft drinks, juices
BRONZE PENTAWARD 2010

IN FRUIT
MANDAR

Design: Fabrice Peltier
Company: P'Référence
Country: France
Category: Soft drinks, juices
BRONZE PENTAWARD 2010

Q TONIC

Design: Johan Liden
Company: Aruliden
Country: USA
Category: Soft drinks, juices

BRONZE PENTAWARD 2009

PEPSI
RAW

Design: Stuart Lelsie, Taek Kim (4sight);
Robert Lebras-Brown (Pepsi)
Company: 4sight Inc.
Country: USA
Category: Soft drinks, juices

BRONZE PENTAWARD 2009

TANGO

Design: Martin Grimer, Gavin Halford
Company: Blue Marlin Brand Design
Country: UK
Category: Soft drinks, juices

BRONZE PENTAWARD 2010

In Japanese, "Cha" means tea, and the world's finest green tea comes from Kyoto, the ancient capital of Japan. It was there in 1790 that Iyemon Fukui founded the Fukujuen tea company. This family company still produces today its **Iyemon Cha Original Green Tea**, or "Sencha". For it, a special bottle shape was designed and shrink-wrapped, using different colours to differentiate the two flavours. Fine printing allowed subtle colour gradations, and the mixture of both traditional Japanese calligraphy and Western typography gives the bottles a contemporary and yet classic feeling.

Auf Japanisch heißt Tee „Cha", und die besten grünen Tees stammen aus der vormaligen japanischen Hauptstadt Kyoto. Genau dort gründete Iyemon Fukui im Jahre 1790 die Teehandelsgesellschaft Fukujuen. Dieses Familienunternehmen produziert auch heute noch Sencha, den **Iyemon Cha Original Green Tea**. Dafür wurde eine spezielle Flaschenform gestaltet und in einer Schrumpf-folienverpackung umgesetzt, wobei zwei Geschmackssorten anhand verschiedener Farben unterschieden werden. Durch spezielle Druckvorgänge waren subtile Farbverläufe möglich, die Mischung aus traditioneller japanischer Kalligraphie und westlicher Typographie verleiht den Flaschen ein modernes und gleichzeitig klassisches Flair.

En japonais, « Cha » signifie thé, et le meilleur thé vert du monde vient de Kyoto, l'ancienne capitale du Japon. C'est là-bas que Iyemon Fukui a fondé la compagnie de thé Fukujen en 1790. Aujourd'hui, cette entreprise familiale produit toujours son **thé vert original Iyemon Cha**, ou « Sencha ». Une bouteille spéciale a été conçue pour ce thé, avec un film rétractable de deux couleurs pour différencier les deux goûts. L'impression haut de gamme autorise des dégradés de couleur subtils, et le mélange de la calligraphie japonaise et de la typographie occidentale donne aux bouteilles un style contemporain et classique à la fois.

IYEMON CHA
ORIGINAL & ROASTED GREEN TEA

Creative Director: Yoshio Kato; *Art Director:* Yoji Minakuchi
Illustration: Kozo Hayashi; *Logotype:* Noriyuki Shimada
Company: Suntory Ltd.
Country: Japan
Category: Tea (ready-to-drink)

GOLD PENTAWARD 2008

GREGORY'S
BOX'D BEVERAGES

Art director: Simon Lince
Designer: Stephanie Krompier
Photographers: Chris Vincent, Brent Taylor
Client: Gregory Packaging
Company: Sterling Brands
Country: USA
Category: Coffee & tea
(ready-to-drink)

SILVER PENTAWARD 2010

POUR TE

Design: Identity Works
Design Team
Company: Identity Works
Country: Sweden
Category: Coffee & tea
(ready-to-drink)

GOLD PENTAWARD 2010

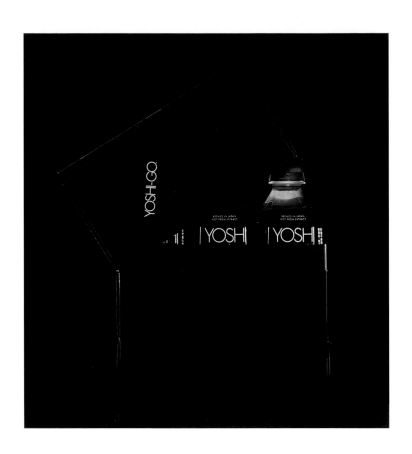

SUNTORY COFFEE BOSS SILKY BLACK

Creative Director: Yoshio Kato; Yoshiyasu Fujita
Art Director: Hiroyuki Ishiura
Designer: Satoshi Ito
Company: Suntory Ltd.
Country: Japan
Category: Coffee & tea
(ready-to-drink)

SILVER PENTAWARD 2009

YOSHI-GO HARUNA EUROPE

Art Direction: Jonas Lundin
Company: LA+B, Love for Art and Business
Country: Sweden
Category: Coffee & tea
(ready-to-drink)

SILVER PENTAWARD 2009

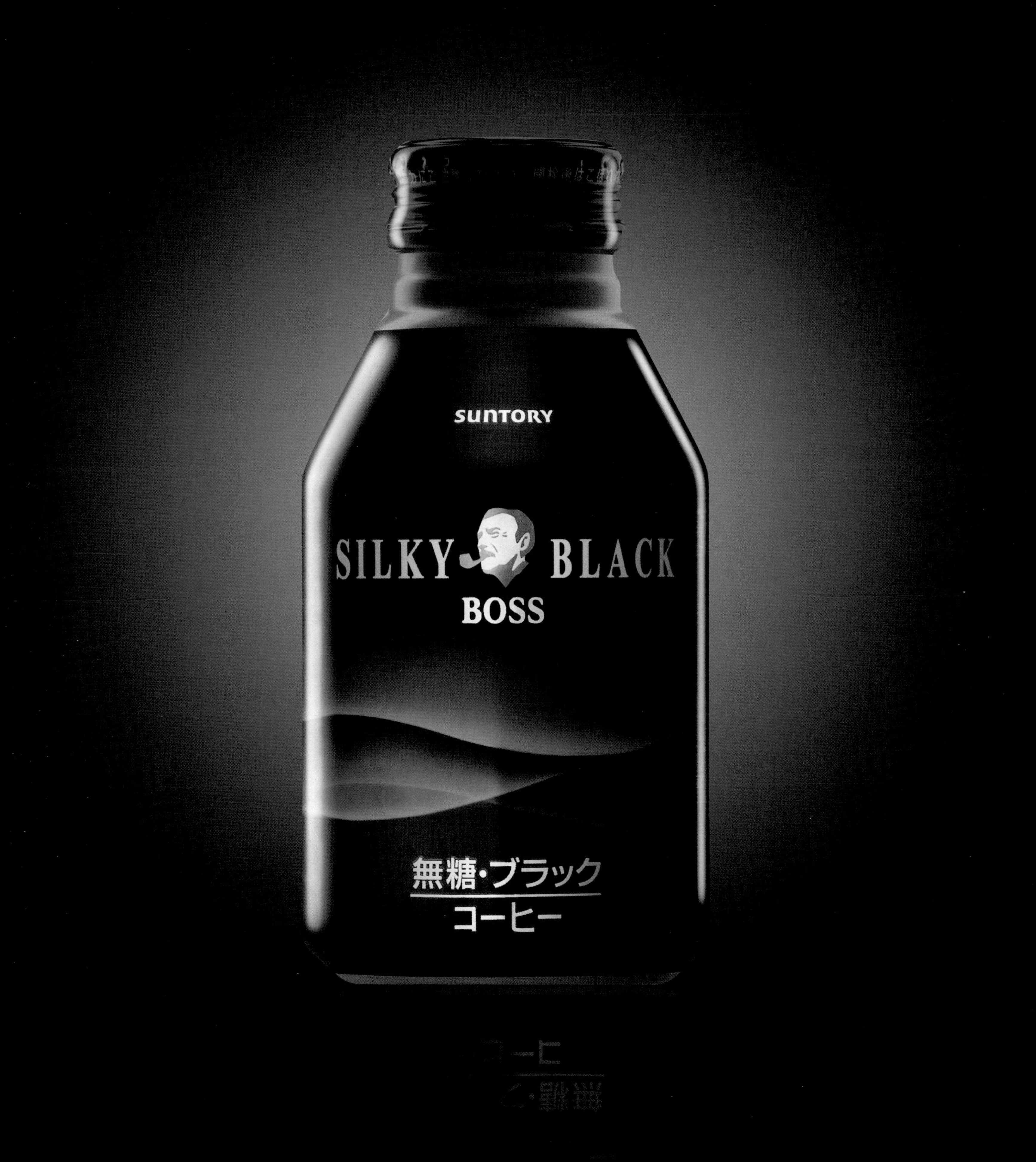
SUNTORY
SILKY BLACK
BOSS
無糖・ブラック
コーヒー

DONGWON
T2U

Art Director: Liver Ng
Senior Designer: Nayoun Kang
Creative Director: Sofan Man
Company: Brandimage – Desgrippes & Laga
Country: Hong Kong
Category: Coffee & tea (ready-to-drink)
BRONZE PENTAWARD 2009

GEORGIA EMERALD MOUNTAIN BLEND

Design: IFF Company
Company: Momentum Co., Ltd.
Country: Japan
Category: Coffee & tea
(ready-to-drink)

BRONZE PENTAWARD 2009

GEORGIA EMERALD MOUNTAIN BLEND BLACK KUROSUMI

Design: Bravis International Design Team
Company: Bravis International
Country: Japan
Category: Coffee & tea (ready-to-drink)

BRONZE PENTAWARD 2010

URURUCHA

Design: Bravis International team
Company: Bravis International
Country: Japan
Category: Coffee & tea
(ready-to-drink)

BRONZE PENTAWARD 2009

LE LAIT DE LA FORÊT

Director/Producer: Shigeki Kunimatsu
Design: Shigeki Kunimatsu, Makiko Sato
Company: Hinomoto Design
Country: Japan
Category: Milk, chocolate (ready-to-drink)

GOLD PENTAWARD 2010

ORLAIT

Design: Caracas Team
Company: Caracas
Country: France
Category: Milk, chocolate (ready-to-drink)

SILVER PENTAWARD 2009

ARLA

Design: Arthur van Hamersveld
Company: PROUDdesign
Country: The Netherlands
Category: Milk, chocolate (ready-to-drink)

BRONZE PENTAWARD 2010

YOPLAIT
YOP

Design: DIL Brands team
Company: DIL Brands
Country: Brazil
Category: Milk, chocolate
(ready-to-drink)

BRONZE PENTAWARD 2009

BYLINA

Design: Alexey Yakushik
Company: Uniqa Creative Engineering
Country: Russia
Category: Milk, chocolate (ready-to-drink)

BRONZE PENTAWARD 2010

Mood-balancing Spring Water **Sero²** is not a traditional energy drink or dietary supplement, but instead is positioned as a new health beverage. Sero² restores serotonin levels, which reinforces your sense of well-being and purpose in life. Therefore the graphic simplicity aims to express purity and general health, while the shrink-labelling enhances the appearance and guarantees a longer shelf-life.

Das stimmungsausgleichende Quellwasser **Sero²** ist weder ein traditioneller Energy-Drink noch eine Nahrungsergänzung, sondern wird vielmehr als neues Gesundheitsgetränk positioniert. Sero² baut den Serotoninspiegel auf, der das persönliche Wohlbefinden und die Lebensfreude bestärkt. Die grafische Schlichtheit zielt daher darauf ab, Reinheit und Gesundheit im Allgemeinen auszudrücken, während das Schrumpfetikett das Erscheinungsbild aufwertet und eine längere Lagerfähigkeit garantiert.

L'eau de source équilibrante **Sero²** n'est pas une boisson énergisante classique, ni un complément alimentaire, mais occupe le nouveau positionnement de boisson de santé. Sero² rétablit les niveaux de sérotonine, pour renforcer le bien-être et la motivation. La simplicité du graphisme cherche donc à exprimer les idées de pureté et de santé générale, et le film rétractable sur lequel les motifs sont imprimés améliore l'apparence et garantit une durée de vie plus longue au produit.

SERO²

Design: Nigel Kuzimski, Natalie Dawson
Company: Curious Design
Country: New Zealand
Category: Functional drinks
GOLD PENTAWARD 2008

BEAST EYE

Art Director/Illustration: Ichiji Ohishi
Company: I+Plus Design
Country: Japan
Category: Functional drinks

GOLD PENTAWARD 2009

LOL

Design: Monique Pilley, Nigel Kuzimski
Company: Curious Design
Country: New Zealand
Category: Functional drinks

SILVER PENTAWARD 2009

ÜBERSHOT

Design Director: Ian Firth
Creative Director: Natalie Chung
Creative Partner: Jonathan Ford
Company: Pearlfisher
Country: UK
Category: Functional drinks

GOLD PENTAWARD 2010

The brief was to create an identity and packaging for a new energy shot that would be launched in the UK with potential to roll out across Europe. The objective was to create a new category language. The logo is strong and striking with an arrow created out of the negative space. The aluminium packaging is a first in this category and creates stand-out next to the plastic bottles used by competitors. The formula was developed to avoid the usual crash that comes when normal energy drinks wear off.

Das Briefing lautete, für einen neuen Energy-Drink Identität und Verpackung zu schaffen. Dieser Drink soll in Großbritannien auf den Markt kommen, verfügt aber über das Potenzial, auch in Europa vertrieben zu werden. Die Herausforderung bestand darin, die Sprache für eine neue Kategorie zu finden. Das Logo ist extrem wirksam: Aus einer Negativfläche entsteht ein nach oben gerichteter Pfeil. In dieser Kategorie gab es vorher keine Aluminiumverpackungen, was dieses Produkt von den Plastikflaschen der Konkurrenz abhebt. Mit der speziell entwickelten Rezeptur soll das typische Absacken nach dem Genuss normaler Energy-Drinks vermieden werden.

La mission était de créer une identité et un emballage pour un nouvel energy shot qui allait être lancé au Royaume-Uni, et peut-être dans toute l'Europe. L'objectif était de créer un nouveau langage pour la catégorie. Le logo a une présence forte, et son espace négatif dessine une flèche. La bouteille en aluminium est une première dans cette catégorie, et se fait remarquer à côté des bouteilles en plastique des concurrents. La formule a été élaborée pour éviter la perte d'énergie que provoquent habituellement les autres boissons énergisantes lorsque leur effet s'estompe.

X GAMES ENERGY

Creative Director: Jeff Davis
Lead Designer: Jeff Boulton
Company: Davis
Country: Canada
Category: Functional drinks

SILVER PENTAWARD 2009

GORILLA

Design: Andrey Gornov, Konstantin Bubenchikov,
Elena Nekrasova, Edgar Quirey, Denis Makarov
Company: Getbrand
Country: Russia
Category: Functional drinks
SILVER PENTAWARD 2010

ATTITUDE

Design: Breathe Design, Nude Creation
Company: Energizer Brands
Country: UK
Category: Functional drinks

BRONZE PENTAWARD 2009

SOLIXIR

Design: John Norman, Traci Milner
Company: Design Resource Center
Country: USA
Category: Functional drinks

BRONZE PENTAWARD 2009

Nelson beer is a lower-carb lager developed with the help of consumers and using Nelson Sauvin hops as the key ingredient. Creatives in parts of Melbourne and Sydney received their first taste of Nelson in August 2008. Using their feedback, Nelson returned in early 2009 with a name, labelling concept, and slightly different taste. From there, Nelson has continued to change by adopting the feedback of its drinkers. Welcoming audience feedback on the brew and inviting artists to design bottle imageryhas infused it with consumer ownership. Nelson's packaging was produced with the collaboration of illustrative duo Sonny & Biddy working to an open brief in creating the first bottle artwork.

Nelson beer ist ein kohlehydratarmes Lager, das unter Mitarbeit der Verbraucher entwickelt wurde und bei dem als wesentliche Zutat die Hopfensorte Nelson Sauvin eingesetzt wird. Kreative aus Melbourne und Sydney durften im August 2008 Nelson zum ersten Mal probieren. Nach ihrem Feedback kehrte Nelson Anfang 2009 mit einem neuen Namen, einem Konzept für die Etikettierung und einem leicht veränderten Geschmack auf den Markt zurück. Nelson hat sich weiterentwickelt, indem die Zielgruppe ihre Meinung über das Getränk äußern konnte und Künstler aufgefordert wurden, sich mit der Gestaltung der Flaschen auseinanderzusetzen. Das führte dazu, dass die Verbraucher sich diese Marke regelrecht angeeignet haben. Die Verpackung von Nelson wurde in Zusammenarbeit mit dem Illustratorenduo Sonny & Biddy produziert. Nach einem offenen Briefing haben sie an den ersten Illustrationen für die Flasche gearbeitet.

La bière Nelson est une bière pauvre en hydrates de carbone. Elle est développée avec l'aide des consommateurs et son ingrédient principal est le houblon Nelson Sauvin. La marque a fait goûter Nelson en avant-première à des créatifs de Melbourne et de Sydney en août 2008. Après avoir pris note de leurs commentaires, Nelson est revenu début 2009 avec un nom, un concept d'étiquette et un goût légèrement différent. À partir de là, Nelson a continué de changer en fonction des commentaires de ses consommateurs. En prenant en compte les commentaires du public sur la bière et en invitant des artistes à créer des images pour la bouteille, la marque a donné aux consommateurs un sentiment de propriété sur le produit. Le packaging de la bière Nelson a été fabriqué avec la collaboration du duo d'illustrateurs Sonny & Biddy, qui ont eu carte blanche pour créer la première illustration de la bouteille.

NELSON BEER

Creative Director: Reece Hobbins
Company: The Taboo Group
Country: Australia
Category: Beer, cider, and low-alcohol or non-alcoholic drinks

GOLD PENTAWARD 2009

DOCTOR DIESEL SEXY LIME

Creative Director: Andrey Kugaevskikh
Company: Svoe mnenie
Country: Russia
Category: Beer

GOLD PENTAWARD 2010

ÅBRO
LEJON

Design: Identity Works team
Company: Identity Works
Country: Sweden
Category: Beer, cider, and low-alcohol
or non-alcoholic drinks

SILVER PENTAWARD 2009

CHINA TOWN

Design: Alexey Yakushik, Natalya Chigvintseva, Dmitry Valdt
Company: Uniqa Creative Engineering
Country: Russia
Category: Beer, cider, and low-alcohol or non-alcoholic drinks

GOLD PENTAWARD 2008

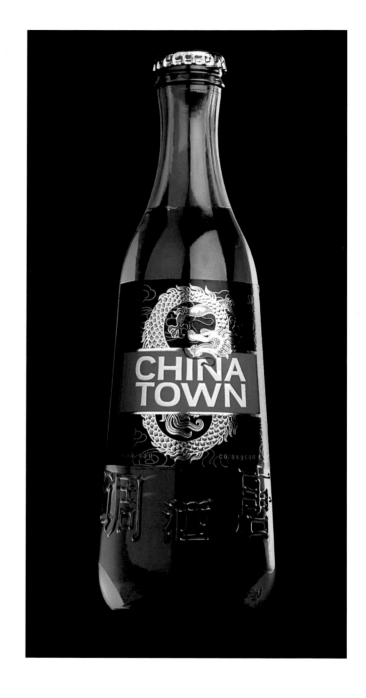

JILLZ

Design: Thea Bakker, Kyanne Buckmann
Company: VBAT
Country: The Netherlands
Category: Beer, cider, and low-alcohol or non-alcoholic drinks

SILVER PENTAWARD 2009

MACK
TASTE SERIES

Design: Bjørn Viggo Ottem, Bernt Ottem
Company: Tank Design Tromsø AS
Country: Norway
Category: Beer

SILVER PENTAWARD 2010

HANSA BORG BRYGGERIER ASA

Design: Ninja Scheel Aas, David Muzeen, Candy Schneider,
Robyn Stevenson, Jeremy Chestnutt, Esme Fisher,
Andy Seymour, Ian Burren, Steve Elliott
Company: You
Country: UK
Category: Beer

SILVER PENTAWARD 2010

TASTE OF REAL
ALFA, BUDELS, GULPENER, LINDEBOOM

Design: Anthony Siemons, Arthur de Haan, Helmich van Herpt, Martyn Graat
Company: BooM packaging
Country: The Netherlands
Category: Beer, cider, and low-alcohol or non-alcoholic drinks

BRONZE PENTAWARD 2009

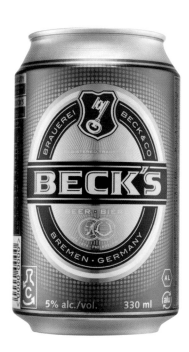

BECK'S

Design: Adrian Pierini
Company: Pierini Partners
Country: Argentina
Category: Beer

BRONZE PENTAWARD 2010

MIKE'S HARD LEMONADE

Design: Gary Oakley
Company: Anthem Worldwide
Country: Canada
Category: Beer, cider, and low-alcohol or non-alcoholic drinks

BRONZE PENTAWARD 2009

A.K. DAMM

Design: Salvatore Adduci
Company: Salvatore Adduci
Country: Spain
Category: Beer, cider, and low-alcohol
or non-alcoholic drinks

BRONZE PENTAWARD 2009

MOLSON M

Design: Ron Wong
Company: Spring Design Partners
Country: USA
Category: Beer

BRONZE PENTAWARD 2010

LT WATERS
BEACH, SPORT, NIGHT

Design: Xavier Corretje, Ana Hernando, Bruno Andrez
Company: Corretjé Comunicació Gràfica
Country: Spain
Category: Ciders and low-alcohol drinks

GOLD PENTAWARD 2010

SEAGRAM
WILD BERRY, WILD APPLE

Design: Jeff Boulton; *Account Director:* Jeff Davis
Company: Davis
Country: Canada
Category: Ciders and low-alcohol drinks

SILVER PENTAWARD 2010

MIXED APE

General Director/Photographer: Cathrin Jo Ann Wind
General Manager: Luc Bütz; *Creative Director:* Markus Lichte
Client Services: Martin Terkatz
Company: WINcommunication
Country: Germany
Category: Ciders and low-alcohol drinks

BRONZE PENTAWARD 2010

JAQK Cellars wines are the offspring of a collaboration between Hatch Design founders and a renowned Napa Valley winemaker. Named after the Jack, Ace, Queen, and King in a deck of cards, JAQK Cellars is a new company dedicated to play. The names and designs of all eight wines in the inaugural offering evoke the allure and sophistication of the world of gaming: High Roller, Soldiers of Fortune (the Jacks), Black Clover (clubs), Pearl Handle (the derringer that tamed the gambling saloons), 22 Black (roulette), Bone Dance (dice), Her Majesty (the Queen), and Charmed (the luckier the better).

Die Weine von **JAQK Cellars** sind das Resultat einer Zusammenarbeit zwischen den Gründern von Hatch Design und einer renommierten Winzerei aus Napa Valley. Die Buchstabenfolge JAQK bezieht sich auf die Bildkarten in einem Skatspiel (englisch Jack, Ace, Queen und King), und JAQK Cellars hat sich als neue Firma das Spielen zum Motto gemacht. Die Namen und Designs aller acht Weine aus dem Einführungsangebot beschwören Reiz und Raffinesse in der Welt der Glücksspiele: High Roller (Glücksspieler), Soldiers of Fortune (die Buben), Black Clover (Kreuzkarten), Pearl Handle (der Revolver, der die Spielsaloons zähmte), 22 Black (Roulette), Bone Dance (Würfelspiel), Her Majesty (die Königin) und Charmed (je mehr Glück, desto besser).

Les vins des **caves JAQK** sont le fruit d'une collaboration entre les fondateurs de Hatch Designs et un viticulteur renommé de Napa Valley. Baptisées d'après les valets, as, reines et rois (Jack, Ace, Queen et King) d'un jeu de cartes, les caves JAQK sont une nouvelle entreprise qui a pris le jeu pour thème central. Les noms et designs des huit vins de la gamme inaugurale évoquent le style et la sophistication du monde du jeu: High Roller (grand joueur), Soldiers of Fortune (les valets), Black Clover (trèfle), Pearl Handle (le nom du pistolet Derringer qui faisait la loi dans les saloons), 22 Black (roulette), Bone Dance (dés), Her Majesty (la reine), et Charmed (pour la chance).

JAQK CELLARS

Design: Eszter T. Clark, Ryan Meis
Creative Directors: Katie Jain, Joel Templin
Company: Hatch Design
Country: USA
Category: Wines

GOLD PENTAWARD 2009

FRITZ MÜLLER

Design: Schmidt/Thurner/von Keisenberg
Büro für visuelle Gestaltung; *Photographer:* Anja Prestel
Company: Fritz Müller verperlt GbR
Country: Germany
Category: Wines

GOLD PENTAWARD 2010

VIVANZA

Art Direction/Design: Eduardo del Fraile
Company: Eduardo del Fraile
Country: Spain
Category: Wines

BRONZE PENTAWARD 2010

In order to start his wine business, founder Jeff Lubin had to sell his prize possession, a 1999 C5 Corvette. In order to honour his sacrifice, the design team decided that they would tell his story. The objectives were to communicate his story in a bold, modern, and elegant manner, and the solution shows the transformation from car owner to wine-business founder in a simple and witty execution.

Um ein Weingeschäft aufmachen zu können, musste der Gründer Jeff Lubin sein Schmuckstück verkaufen: eine C5 Corvette Baujahr 1999. Um dieses Opfer gebührend zu würdigen, beschloss das Designteam, diese Geschichte zu erzählen. Ziel war es, Lubins Werdegang auf mutige, moderne und elegante Weise zu vermitteln, und die gewählte Lösung zeigt einfach und pfiffig ausgeführt die Transformation vom Sportwagenbesitzer zum Gründer eines Weinfachhandels.

Pour lancer son entreprise vinicole, Jeff Lubin a dû vendre son bien le plus précieux, une Corvette C5 de 1999. Pour rendre hommage à ce sacrifice, l'équipe de design a décidé d'en raconter l'histoire. Les objectifs étaient de l'exposer d'une façon audacieuse, moderne et élégante, et la solution montre la transformation d'un propriétaire de voiture en fondateur d'entreprise vinicole avec simplicité et intelligence.

SIDE JOB CELLARS C5

Design: Shawn Roseberger
Company: Thermostat
Country: USA
Category: Wines
GOLD PENTAWARD 2008

FIRE ROAD

Design: Tony Ibbotson, Mayra Monobe
Company: The Creative Method
Country: Australia
Category: Wines
SILVER PENTAWARD 2009

MARQUÉS DE RISCAL FINCA

Creative Director: Antonia Hayward
Design Director: Asa Cook; *Designer:* Casey Sampson
Company: Design Bridge Ltd.
Country: UK
Category: Wines

SILVER PENTAWARD 2010

EL CAMPESINO

Design: Cosi Surace, Eva Pluta
Company: Stranger & Stranger Ltd.
Country: UK
Category: Wines

SILVER PENTAWARD 2010

**BODEGAS CARCHELO
ALTICO, CARCHELO, VEDRÉ**

Design: Eduardo del Fraile
Company: Eduardo del Fraile
Country: Spain
Category: Wines

SILVER PENTAWARD 2009

LONGUE-DOG

Design: Simon Tame
Company: Dare
Country: UK
Category: Wines

BRONZE PENTAWARD 2010

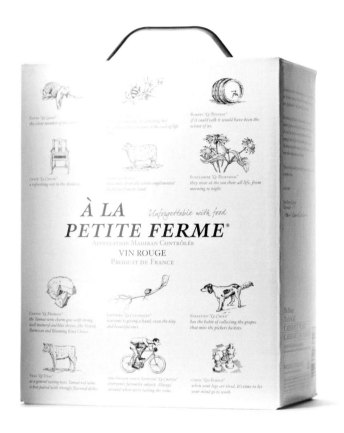

À LA PETITE FERME

Design: Erika Barbieri, Henrik Olssøn
Company: Designers.Journey
Country: Norway
Category: Wines

BRONZE PENTAWARD 2009

ASTORIA
9.5 COLD WINE

Design: Giovanni Favero
Company: Astoria Vini
Country: Italy
Category: Wines

BRONZE PENTAWARD 2010

CHANTE-CLAIR

Design: Kevin Shaw, Guy Pratt
Company: Stranger & Stranger Ltd.
Country: UK
Category: Wines

BRONZE PENTAWARD 2009

MARLBOROUGH SUN

Design: Tony Ibbotson, Andi Yanto
Company: The Creative Method
Country: Australia
Category: Wines

BRONZE PENTAWARD 2009

VERNISSAGE

Design: Sofia Blomberg, Takis Soldatos
Company: Oenoforos
Country: Sweden
Category: Wine as bag-in-box

GOLD PENTAWARD 2010

UNTOUCHED

Design: Motherland Branding & Design team
Company: Motherland Branding & Design
Country: Sweden
Category: Wine as bag-in-box

SILVER PENTAWARD 2010

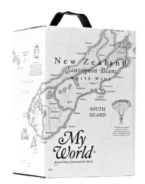

MY WORLD

Design: Erika Barbieri, Henrik Olssøn
Company: DesignersJourney
Country: Norway
Category: Wine as bag-in-box

BRONZE PENTAWARD 2010

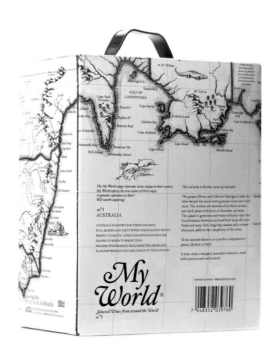

The main thrust of this project's brief was to strengthen the brand's design presence, and aim to become associated with "best in class" design. Specific aims for the **Jack Daniel's** Mayday packaging within this framework were to maintain and re-assert the brand's premium pricing and brand image, and, moreover, to reinforce the brand's iconic status and successfully cut through to consumers in a competitive and cluttered environment.

Die Haupttriebkraft für dieses Projekt-Briefing war es, die Designpräsenz der Marke zu stärken: Sie sollte mit einem „Best in class"-Design verknüpft werden. Die speziellen Ziele für die Mayday-Verpackung von **Jack Daniel's** innerhalb dieses Rahmens lauteten, die Preisgestaltung und das Markenimage dieser Premium-Marke zu bewahren und ihr erneut Geltung zu verschaffen. Obendrein sollte der Kultstatus der Marke verstärkt und die Konsumenten in einem hart umkämpften Umfeld mit Überangebot direkt erreicht werden.

L'idée maîtresse de ce projet était de renforcer la présence de la marque sur le terrain du design, et de l'associer aux meilleurs dans ce domaine.

Les objectifs spécifiques du packaging que l'agence Mayday a créé pour **Jack Daniel's** étaient en outre de renforcer le statut emblématique de la marque et d'arriver à atteindre les consommateurs dans un environnement concurrentiel et encombré.

JACK DANIEL'S

Creative Director: Roger Akroyd
Design Director: Barry Gillibrand
Account Director: Charlie Bosworth
Production Director: Andrew Smith
Production Development: Joey Schmissrauter
Production Development: Chris Hallam
Company: Mayday
Country: UK
Category: Limited editions,
limited series, event creations

GOLD PENTAWARD 2009

IYEMON CHA
TEA CEREMONY IN AUTUMN

Creative Director: Yoji Minakuchi
Art Director: Keiko Genkaku
Designer: Keiko Genkaku/Chiso Co., Ltd.
Company: Suntory Ltd.
Country: Japan
Category: Limited editions,
limited series, event creations

SILVER PENTAWARD 2010

EVIAN
PAUL SMITH

Design: Paul Smith
Company: Danone Waters
Country: France
Category: Limited editions,
limited series, event creations

GOLD PENTAWARD 2010

COCA-COLA
2008 BEIJING OLYMPIC GAMES

Executive Creative Director: Robert Swan; *Creative Director:* Scott Hardy
Production Director: Joe Durkin; *Project Strategy Director:* Michael Coleman
Company: Anthem Worldwide
Country: USA
Category: Limited editions,
limited series, event creations

SILVER PENTAWARD 2009

COCA-COLA
2010 WINTER OLYMPICS
PACKAGING AND PREMIUMS

Client: The Coca-Cola Company North America; *Client Contact:* Frederic Kahn
Designers: Tetsuya Takenomata, Josh Michels; *Design Director:* Sarah Moffat
Creative Directors: David Turner & Bruce Duckworth; *Illustration:* John Geary
Company: Turner Duckworth: London & San Francisco
Country: UK/USA
Category: Limited editions, limited series, event creations

SILVER PENTAWARD 2010

J&B

Design: Linea Global design team
Company: Linea Brand Development
Country: France
Category: Limited editions,
limited series, event creations

SILVER PENTAWARD 2009

BOMBAY SAPPHIRE

Design: Dominic Burke, Sarah Fagin, Mark Lloyd
Company: Webb Scarlett deVlam
Country: UK
Category: Limited editions,
limited series, event creations

BRONZE PENTAWARD 2009

COCA-COLA SELFRIDGES

Design: Coca-Cola UK and Selfridges
Company: Sleever International
Country: France
Category: Limited editions,
limited series, event creations

BRONZE PENTAWARD 2010

MALIBU

Design: The Brand Union Paris, MJC, Delta for Ricard
Company: The Brand Union
Country: France
Category: Limited editions, limited series, event creations

BRONZE PENTAWARD 2009

The **ICA** Grocery chain's own line of products is a key element of the brand as a whole. Each package must feel like a modern, enticing alternative on the shelves. A big part of this means having a unique, appealing design that communicates the quality of the products. The concept for ICA's fruit juices made from fresh fruit uses all four sides of the package to tell customers how a fresh orange becomes juice.

Die eigene Produktlinie der schwedischen Supermarktkette **ICA** ist ein zentrales Element der Marke insgesamt. Jede Packung soll sich im Regal als moderne und verlockende Alternative präsentieren. Dies bedeutete im wesentlichen, dass ein einzigartiges und ansprechendes Design erforderlich war, um die Qualität der Produkte zu vermitteln. Das Konzept der aus frischen Früchten hergestellten Säfte von ICA nutzt alle vier Packungsseiten, um den Verbrauchern zu erläutern, wie eine Orange zu frischem Fruchtsaft verarbeitet wird.

La gamme de produits de la chaîne de supermarchés **ICA** est un élément essentiel de la marque dans son ensemble. Chaque emballage mis en rayon doit suggérer une alternative moderne et appétissante aux autres produits concurrents. Cela signifie notamment que le design doit être original et refléter la qualité des produits. Le concept des jus de fruits frais d'ICA utilise les quatre côtés de l'emballage pour raconter aux clients comment une orange se convertit en jus.

ICA

Creative Director: Ulf Berlin
Senior Designer: Linus Ostberg
Photographer: Roland Persson
Senior Production Manager: Caiza Nyman
Company: Designkontoret Silver KB
Country: Sweden
Category: Distributors'/Retailers' own brands

GOLD PENTAWARD 2009

THE DELI GARAGE POWERFUEL

Creative Director: Kathrin Oeding
Art Director: Reginald Wagner
Copywriter: Katharina Trumbach
Graphic Design: Jan Simmerl
Illustration: Heiko Windisch
Company: Kolle Rebbe
Country: Germany
Category: Distributors'/
Retailers' own brands

SILVER PENTAWARD 2009

M&S
LAGERS, ALES, & CIDERS

Design: Bronwen Edwards, Dave Beard, Keely Jackman, Chris Nokes
Company: Brandhouse
Country: UK
Category: Distributors'/Retailers' own brands

GOLD PENTAWARD 2010

FRESH & EASY NEIGHBOURHOOD MARKET RANGE

Art Direction: Phil Curl, Simon Pemberton, Adrian Whitefoord
Company: Pemberton & Whitefoord
Country: UK
Category: Distributors'/ Retailers' own brands
SILVER PENTAWARD 2009

ALBERT HEIJN DAIRY

Design: Erik de Graaf, Danny Klein
Company: Millford Brand-id
Country: The Netherlands
Category: Distributors'/
Retailers' own brands

BRONZE PENTAWARD 2009

Lucid, an absinthe made in the traditional way, is a spectacular success in the USA. Screen-printed in eight colours, the dark-green glass is borrowed from the top-of-the-range food sector. The original and unconventional name of this product gives it an effective buzz. Lucid was created to fill a gap in the newly captivating absinthe category in the USA, which is a contemporary and trendy sector within that of "time-honoured spirits".

Lucid ist ein Absinth, der auf traditionelle Weise hergestellt wird und in den USA spektakuläre Erfolge erzielt. Das dunkelgrüne Glas ist dem gehobenen Nahrungsmittelsegment entlehnt und wird im achtfarbigen Siebdruckverfahren bedruckt. Der originelle und unkonventionelle Name dieses Produkts verleiht ihm einen wirkungsvollen Kitzel. Lucid soll in den USA eine Lücke in der ganz neuen, spannenden Kategorie Absinth füllen. Dabei handelt es sich um einen modernen und trendigen Sektor innerhalb der sogenannten „altehrwürdigen Spirituosen".

Lucid, une absinthe fabriquée à l'ancienne, remporte un succès spectaculaire aux États-Unis. Le verre vert foncé sérigraphié en huit couleurs est emprunté au secteur alimentaire haut de gamme. Le nom original et non conventionnel de ce produit fait parler de lui efficacement. Lucid a été créée pour occuper une niche vacante dans la catégorie des absinthes, qui captive les États-Unis depuis peu. C'est un secteur contemporain et tendance au sein des « alcools traditionnels ».

LUCID

Design: Linea Global design team
Company: Linea Brand Development
Country: France
Category: Spirits

GOLD PENTAWARD 2008

SOLERNO

Design: Kevin Shaw, Guy Pratt
Company: Stranger & Stranger Ltd.
Country: UK
Category: Spirits

GOLD PENTAWARD 2009

MAHIKI RUM

Art Director: Nara Watson-Ward
Company: Roger Clarke Associates
Country: Barbados
Category: Spirits

SILVER PENTAWARD 2009

For its main product range, **Tatratea** tea-based liqueurs, Karloff wished to create a new bottle combining a modern look and traditional elements. The design criteria started with a simple and original shape, a global name taken from the Tatra Mountains, and local tradition. The Tatratea bottle was thus given a thermos-flask shape together with a large initial T made out of elements inspired by Slavic symbols of the circle of life, love, and happiness, and traditional Slovak crafts. Colour-printed directly on to the bottle, in an appropriate colour scheme for all flavour variations.

Die Hauptproduktlinie von Karloff nennt sich **Tatratea**. Das sind aus Tee hergestellte Kräuterliköre, für die eine neue Flasche geschaffen werden sollte, bei der ein moderner Look mit traditionellen Elementen kombiniert wird. Beim Design ging man von einfachen und ursprünglichen Formen aus, ergänzt durch einen übergreifenden, vom slowakischen Tatra-Gebirge abgeleiteten Namen sowie lokale Traditionen. Die Tatratea-Flasche bekam eine Form wie eine Thermosflasche. Das darauf abgebildete große T wird aus Elementen geformt, die aus den slawischen Symbolen für den Zyklus des Lebens, Liebe und Glück sowie traditionellen slowakischen Künsten bestehen. Die Farben werden je nach Geschmacksvariante in einer passenden Tönung direkt auf die Flasche gedruckt.

Pour sa gamme principale, les liqueurs à base de thé **Tatratea**, Karloff souhaitait créer une nouvelle bouteille combinant un look moderne et des éléments traditionnels. Les critères de départ du design étaient une forme simple et originale, un nom collectif emprunté aux montagnes Tatra, et la tradition locale. La bouteille Tatratea a donc été dotée de la forme d'une gourde isotherme, avec un grand T composé d'éléments inspirés par les symboles slaves du cercle de la vie, de l'amour, du bonheur et de l'artisanat slave. Le texte est imprimé en couleur directement sur la bouteille, avec une palette de couleurs étudiée pour chaque parfum.

TATRATEA
HERBAL LIQUEURS

Creative Direction/Graphic Design: Juraj Demovic (Pergamen Trnava)
Concept/Graphic Design: Livia Lorinczova (Pergamen Trnava)
Creator of the Product: Jan Semanak, MD (Karloff)
Photographer: Jakub Dvorak (Pergamen Trnava)
Company: Karloff, s.r.o.
Country: Slovakia
Category: Spirits
GOLD PENTAWARD 2010

DISTILLERIE DEINLEIN
8TH TRIBE

Creative Director: Nigel Kuzimski
Designer: Monique Pilley
Company: Curious Design
Country: New Zealand
Category: Spirits
SILVER PENTAWARD 2010

THE KRAKEN

Design: Kevin Shaw
Company: Stranger & Stranger Ltd.
Country: UK
Category: Spirits
SILVER PENTAWARD 2010

BEEFEATER 24

Design: Graham Shearsby, Antonia Hayward,
Laurent Robin-Prevalle, Claire Dale, Emma Warner
Company: Design Bridge Ltd.
Country: UK
Category: Spirits

SILVER PENTAWARD 2009

BRUGEMANN PETERMAN

Design: Sylvain Vandeven
Company: Strategie Design
Country: Belgium
Category: Spirits

BRONZE PENTAWARD 2009

SVEDKA VODKA

Design: Sam O'Donahue, Stewart Devlin
Company: Spirits Marque One
Country: USA
Category: Spirits

BRONZE PENTAWARD 2009

SMIRNOFF BLUE
100 PROOF

Design Leads: JB Hartford, Tara Lubonovich
Executive Creative Director: Richard Brandt
Client Director: Patricia Verdolino
Senior Client Managers: Elizabeth Knell, Pamela Mazzocco
Company: Landor Associates
Country: USA
Category: Spirits

BRONZE PENTAWARD 2009

GIN 9 MASCARÓ

Design: Morera Design
Company: Morera Design S.L.
Country: Spain
Category: Spirits

BRONZE PENTAWARD 2010

SAMURAI DANCE
GREEN LABEL / PINK LABEL

Creative Director/Art Director: Takao Ito
Designer: Tadashi Cho, Megumi Ohtsu
Copywriter: Kazuhisa Okamoto
Company: Dentsu Kyushu Inc.
Country: Japan
Category: Spirits

BRONZE PENTAWARD 2010

MASTER'S

Design: Series Nemo team
Company: Series Nemo
Country: Spain
Category: Spirits

BRONZE PENTAWARD 2010

Every year Wallace Church designs a **Thanksgiving** wine bottle as a gift for clients and friends. For 2008's design, the solution was a simple twist on a classic fork, creating a fanciful turkey face. The message was: Thanksgiving, a turkey feast enjoyed with a good wine.

Jedes Jahr gestaltet Wallace Church zu **Thanksgiving** als Geschenk für Kunden und Freunde eine Weinflasche. Beim Design des Jahres 2008 bestand die Lösung einfach darin, die Zinke einer Gabel umzuknicken, wodurch sehr fantasievoll und einfach der Kopf eines Truthahns entstand. Die Botschaft lautete: Thanksgiving ist ein Fest, bei dem man zum Truthahn einen guten Wein genießt.

Chaque année, Wallace Church crée une bouteille de vin que l'agence offre à ses clients et amis à l'occasion de **Thanksgiving**. La solution choisie pour l'année 2008 était une réinterprétation toute simple d'une fourchette classique, qui dessinait une dinde stylisée. Le message : Thanksgiving, un festin de dinde accompagné d'un bon vin.

THANKSGIVING WINE

Creative Director: Stan Church
Design: Bird Tubkam, Chung-Tao Tu
Company: Wallace Church Inc.
Country: USA
Category: Self-promotion

GOLD PENTAWARD 2008

MOVING PICTURES VODKA

Creative Director: Stan Church
Design Director: Kevin Sams
Design: Chris Cook, Tiphaine Guillemet
Company: Wallace Church Inc.
Country: USA
Category: Self-promotion

GOLD PENTAWARD 2009

This company promotion was inspired by the Zoetrope, a Victorian novelty that produced the illusion of a moving picture through a rapid succession of spinning images. The idea is to spin this bottle of vodka while looking through the slits to see the moving images just as you would a Zoetrope. The ultimate purpose was to create a unique and creative gift for friends and clients.

Diese Firmenwerbung wurde durch das Zootrop inspiriert. Bei dieser Erfindung aus der viktorianischen Zeit wurde durch eine schnelle Abfolge sich drehender Bilder die Illusion von Bewegung geschaffen. Die zugrunde liegende Idee ist es, diese Wodkaflasche zu drehen, während man durch die Schlitze schaut, um die sich bewegenden Bilder zu sehen – genau wie bei einem Zootrop. So wurde letzten Endes für Freunde und Kunden ein kreatives und unvergleichliches Geschenk geschaffen.

Ce cadeau d'entreprise est inspiré du Zoetrope, un appareil victorien qui produisait l'illusion d'une animation en faisant tourner rapidement une séquence d'images. L'idée est de faire tourner cette bouteille de vodka tout en regardant à travers les fentes pour voir les images s'animer, comme avec un Zoetrope. L'objectif était de créer un cadeau original et créatif à offrir aux amis et aux clients.

The aim of this packaging was to create a unique gift to give our clients at Christmas and to act as a new business introduction. It needed to remind them of who we are and the long hours that we put into our work. It also needed to feature all of our staff, and reflect our creativity and sense of humour. Each label was based on one staff member and included a number of facial features and the client was encouraged to **BYO** – Build Your Own.

Mit dieser Verpackung wollten wir unseren Kunden ein einzigartiges Weihnachtsgeschenk präsentieren und gleichzeitig unser neues Angebot vorstellen. Wir erinnern unsere Kunden daran, wer wir sind und wie viele und wie lange Stunden in unserer Arbeit stecken. Außerdem soll damit unser gesamtes Personal mit seiner Kreativität und seinem Humor vorgestellt werden. Zu jedem Teammitglied gibt es ein entsprechendes Etikett. Der Kunde wird ermuntert, aus den verschiedenen Gesichtselementen ein neues Gesicht zu schaffen: **BYO** – Build Your Own!

Le but de cet emballage était de créer un cadeau de Noël original pour nos clients, qui devait également servir de cadeau de présentation pour les nouveaux clients. Il devait leur rappeler qui nous sommes, ainsi que les longues heures que nous investissons dans notre travail. Il devait aussi représenter toute notre équipe, et refléter notre créativité et notre sens de l'humour. Chaque étiquette est basée sur un membre de l'équipe, et se compose d'éléments de son visage. Le client est invité à « **BYO** » (Build Your Own – Fabriquez le vôtre).

THE CREATIVE METHOD
BYO – BUILD YOUR OWN

Creative Director: Tony Ibbotson
Designer: Andi Yanto
Company: The Creative Method
Country: Australia
Category: Self-promotion

GOLD PENTAWARD 2010

AMPRO
THE PACKAGING DESIGN BOTTLE

Concept-Creative Director: Irinel Ionescu
DTP: Danubiu Birzu; *Illustration:* Alin Patru
3D: Mario Teodoru
Company: Ampro Design
Country: Romania
Category: Self-promotion

SILVER PENTAWARD 2010

DVINE VODKA

Creative Director: Stan Church
Design Director: Kevin Sams
Design: Chris Cook, Tiphaine Guillemet
Company: Wallace Church Inc.
Country: USA
Category: Self-promotion
SILVER PENTAWARD 2009

WC HOLIDAY WINE

Creative Director: Stan Church
Designer: Lou Antonucci
Company: Wallace Church Inc.
Country: USA
Category: Self-promotion
BRONZE PENTAWARD 2010

COCA-COLA
PARIS ILLUMINE PARIS

Design: Didier Cosson
Company: P'Référence
Country: France
Category: Self-promotion

SILVER PENTAWARD 2010

CHAMPAGNE MONA LISA ART & PACKAGING

Design: Fabrice Peltier
Company: P'Référence
Country: France
Category: Self-promotion

BRONZE PENTAWARD 2009

INDEX BOOK

Design: Eduardo del Fraile
Company: Eduardo del Fraile
Country: Spain
Category: Self-promotion

BRONZE PENTAWARD 2010

MAQUINARIA CREATIVA

Design: Maquinaria Creativa
Company: Maquinaria Creativa
Country: Mexico
Category: Self-promotion

BRONZE PENTAWARD 2009

food

Interview with
STAN CHURCH

Founder, Managing Partner, and Executive Creative Director
Wallace Church Inc. New York
Member of the Pentawards Jury 2008/2009/2010

How do you explain why a jury spread over 12 different countries around the world finally selected the same best designs?

When judging design work, the judges themselves are, more often than not, award winners. They are continually involved in the process of design. In order to produce leading-edge work, you must know what has been done before and do it better. To create something that could be considered revolutionary should be the goal. The vast network of global communications today makes it possible to see the developments worldwide. Consequently jury members are well aware of what merely communicates, what is new and breakthrough, and that which is outstanding.

How would you advise young people wishing to become a packaging designer?

I inform my students and young designers that *branding* is the new opportunity. I make it clear to them that the value of package design discipline has never been greater. It is not just about the end result of a tactile package. It is how the package resonates with consumers – going beyond the surface, and grabbing their emotions. These are the items people see, purchase, and treasure. Our clients now finally understand that great packaging sells and, as a result, the consumer is demanding better and more creative solutions. After all, who buys a bottle of wine with a distasteful label?

Who impressed you the most in your professional life and why?

The most impressive designer I have ever known is Milton Glazer. I consider him my mentor, my teacher, and my friend. Milton will never stop producing outstanding work. Each project he is involved with yields another opportunity for greatness. The man is a brilliant thinker. There is no one else like him. His imagination is endless, telling entire stories with a single image. More a giver than a receiver, he continues to be generous with his time – teaching, and supporting the design community.

Having judged all over the world, and seen works from all countries, how do you see East European countries approaching the market?

I am quite impressed with what has changed so rapidly in the Eastern European countries. After years of limited access to developments worldwide in design, these designers have become current and competitive. I am quite excited to see their future contributions. After all, it takes us all to make the difference.

A Japanese noodle packaging wins the Platinum Pentaward, best of category. What would you say about it?

It is an outstanding accomplishment for Kanpyo Udon to be awarded the Platinum Pentaward in a category where brilliant design is abundant. It is refreshing to see in this category some clients acting open-minded and courageous in accepting revolutionary solutions. The characters and images in the design are visually stimulating while appealing to the consumer's humorous nature. The design concept is clever, innovative, and utilises interesting materials. Each component is well executed enabling the elements of the package to fit cohesively into a distinctive bag, with its handles falling on a maze of similar shapes. Consequently, this outstanding design is inventive and most notably original.

Wie erklären Sie sich, dass eine Jury, deren Mitglieder kontinentübergreifend aus zwölf Ländern stammen, sich schließlich auf dieselben besten Designs einigen konnte?

Wenn gestalterische Arbeiten von einer Jury begutachtet werden, sind die Juroren oft auch selbst Preisträger. Sie sind ständig mit Gestaltungsprozessen beschäftigt. Um wirklich absolut maßgebliche Arbeiten zu schaffen, muss man wissen, was bis dato gemacht wurde, und es besser machen. Ziel sollte es sein, etwas Revolutionäres zu vollbringen. Das gigantische Netzwerk der heutigen globalen Kommunikation macht es möglich, Entwicklungen weltweit zu verfolgen. Als Konsequenz sind sich die Jurymitglieder sehr wohl darüber im Klaren, was einfach nur seine Botschaft vermittelt, was neuartig und ein Durchbruch ist und was man als hervorragend und bahnbrechend werten muss.

Was würden Sie jungen Menschen raten, die Verpackungsdesigner werden wollen?

Ich informiere meine Studierenden und junge Designer und Designerinnen darüber, dass Markenbildung, also *Branding*, die neue Chance ist. Ich erkläre ihnen, dass die Disziplin des Verpackungsdesigns noch niemals so wertvoll war wie heute. Es geht nicht nur darum, im Ergebnis eine Packung zu schaffen, die man anfassen kann, sondern vielmehr darum, welchen Anklang die Verpackung bei den Konsumenten findet, ob sie ihnen also unter die Haut geht und nach ihren Emotionen greift. Solche Elemente sehen, kaufen und schätzen die Menschen. Unsere Kunden begreifen nun endlich, dass ausgezeichnete Verpackungen den Umsatz steigern, und demzufolge verlangt der Konsument bessere und kreativere Lösungen. Wer kauft schon eine Weinflasche mit einem geschmacklosen Etikett?

Wer hat Sie als Profi am meisten beeindruckt und warum?

Als Designer finde ich Milton Glazer am beeindruckendsten. Ich betrachte ihn als Mentor, Lehrer und Freund. Milton wird nie aufhören, herausragende Arbeiten zu produzieren. Aus allen Projekten, an denen er beteiligt ist, entwickeln sich neue Chancen für etwas Großartiges. Der Mann ist ein brillanter Denker. Da ist ihm niemand gleich. Seine Fantasie ist grenzenlos, und er erzählt mit nur einem einzigen Bild ganze Geschichten. Er gibt mehr, als er nimmt, und schenkt anderen sehr großzügig seine Zeit: Er vermittelt sein Wissen und unterstützt die Gemeinschaft der Designer.

Sie waren Preisrichter weltweit und haben Arbeiten aus allen Teilen der Welt begutachtet – wie beurteilen Sie vor diesem Hintergrund das Erscheinen osteuropäischer Länder auf dem Markt?

Ich bin sehr beeindruckt davon, was und wie schnell sich in den osteuropäischen Ländern alles verändert hat. Nachdem der Zugang zu den internationalen Entwicklungen im Bereich Design jahrelang nur eingeschränkt möglich war, sind die Designer dort auf der Höhe der Zeit und konkurrenzfähig. Ich bin sehr gespannt darauf, was sie uns in Zukunft noch zeigen werden. Denn im Endeffekt brauchen wir uns alle gegenseitig, um etwas zu bewirken.

Eine japanische Nudelverpackung gewinnt als Beste in ihrer Kategorie den Platin Pentaward. Was sagen Sie dazu?

Es zeugt von der herausragenden Leistung von Kanpyo Udon, dass die Verpackung mit dem Platin Pentaward ausgezeichnet wird, und zwar in einer Kategorie, in der es reichlich brillantes Design gibt. Wie erfrischend, dass sich in dieser Kategorie einige Kunden so aufgeschlossen und couragiert zeigen und revolutionäre Lösungen akzeptieren. Die Schriftzeichen und Bilder im Design sind visuell sehr spannend und sprechen auch die humorvolle Seite der Konsumenten an. Das Designkonzept ist clever, innovativ und setzt interessante Materialien ein. Jede Komponente ist so gut ausgeführt, dass die Verpackungselemente in eine auffällige Papiertüte passen. Wenn die Schlaufen der Tüte herunterhängen, liegen sie auf dem Papier auf und vermischen sich mit den darauf aufgedruckten ähnlichen Formen. Es liegt auf der Hand, dass diese hervorragende Gestaltung sehr erfinderisch und vor allem originell ist.

Interview with
STAN CHURCH

Comment expliquez-vous qu'un jury issu de 12 pays différents des quatre coins du globe ait finalement sélectionné les mêmes meilleurs designs ?

Les juges qui évaluent un projet de design sont bien souvent eux-mêmes des designers primés. Leur implication dans le processus du design est permanente. Pour produire un travail innovant, il faut savoir ce qui a déjà été fait, puis faire mieux. L'objectif devrait être de créer quelque chose qui pourrait être considéré comme révolutionnaire. Aujourd'hui, le vaste réseau mondial de communication permet de voir ce qui se passe dans le monde entier. Les membres du jury savent donc parfaitement reconnaître les projets qui se contentent de communiquer, ceux qui sont vraiment innovants, et ceux qui se démarquent de tout le reste.

Quels conseils donneriez-vous aux jeunes qui veulent devenir designer de packaging ?

Je dis à mes étudiants et aux jeunes designers que c'est dans la *stratégie de marque* que se trouvent les nouvelles opportunités. Je leur explique que le design d'emballage n'a jamais eu de plus grande valeur qu'aujourd'hui. Il ne s'agit pas seulement du résultat que l'on peut obtenir avec un emballage agréable au toucher. Il s'agit de la façon dont l'emballage entre en résonance avec les consommateurs, en passant sous la surface, et en faisant appel à leurs émotions. Ce sont ces articles-là que les gens voient, achètent et aiment vraiment. Nos clients comprennent enfin qu'un bon packaging est vendeur et que le consommateur exige donc des solutions plus créatives et de meilleure qualité. Après tout, qui achèterait une bouteille de vin affublée d'une étiquette de mauvais goût ?

Dans votre parcours professionnel, qui vous a le plus marqué et pourquoi ?

Milton Glazer est le designer le plus marquant que je connaisse. Je le considère comme mon mentor, mon professeur et mon ami. Milton n'arrêtera jamais de faire un travail remarquable. Chacun des projets auxquels il participe renferme une autre opportunité de grandeur. Cet homme est un penseur brillant. Il est unique. Son imagination est infinie, et il arrive à raconter toute une histoire en une seule image. Il donne plus qu'il ne reçoit, et il est toujours généreux de son temps : il enseigne et soutient la communauté du design.

Après avoir été juré dans le monde entier, et avoir vu ce qui se fait dans tous les pays, que pensez-vous de l'approche du marché qu'ont les pays d'Europe de l'Est ?

Je suis assez impressionné par les changements rapides qui ont pris place dans les pays d'Europe de l'Est. Après des années d'accès limité aux progrès que le design réalisait dans le monde entier, ces designers se sont mis au goût du jour et sont devenus concurrentiels. J'ai hâte de voir leurs prochaines contributions. Après tout, chacun d'entre nous compte pour changer les choses.

Un packaging de nouilles japonais a remporté le Pentaward Platinum, Best of category. Quel est votre commentaire ?

Ce n'est pas une mince affaire pour Kanpyo Udon d'avoir remporté le Pentaward Platinum dans une catégorie qui regorge d'emballages excellents. C'est agréable de voir que dans cette catégorie certains clients font preuve de courage et d'ouverture d'esprit, et acceptent des solutions révolutionnaires. Les personnages et les images de ce concept sont stimulants du point de vue visuel, tout en faisant appel à l'humour du consommateur. Le design est intelligent, innovant et emploie des matériaux intéressants. Chaque élément est bien conçu, et forme avec les autres un ensemble cohérent dans un sac plein de personnalité, avec ses anses qui retombent sur un enchevêtrement de formes similaires. Cet emballage remarquable est donc inventif, et surtout original.

The Nosigner agency in Tokyo had to design the packaging for a new type of **Udon** noodles, which are actually made from dried vegetable marrow, and not from wheat flower. The packaging design was turned into an amusing combination which mixed the shape of a pumpkin and fresh noodles that evokes a non-industrial product, quite luxurious, and yet still affordable. This design has broken the mould of what has traditionally been done in Japan for this type of product, although using traditional Japanese paper and calligraphy.

Die Agentur Nosigner aus Tokio sollte die Verpackung einer neuen Sorte **Udon**-Nudeln gestalten, die nicht aus Weizen-, sondern aus Kürbismehl hergestellt werden. Die Verpackung wurde als amüsante Kombination gestaltet, in der eine Kürbisform und frische Nudeln zusammengeführt werden. Sie weckt Assoziationen an ein nicht-industrielles Produkt, das recht luxuriös, aber doch erschwinglich ist. Diese Gestaltung sprengt die Form dessen, was traditionell in Japan für diese Art von Produkt gemacht wurde, obgleich dabei traditionelles japanisches Papier und Kalligraphie eingesetzt werden.

L'agence tokyoïte Nosigner devait créer le packaging d'un nouveau type de nouilles **Udon**, fabriquées à partir de courge déshydratée, et non de farine de blé. Le design du packaging est une combinaison amusante qui allie la forme d'une citrouille aux nouilles fraîches et suggère un produit non industriel, assez luxueux, et pourtant abordable. Le design a brisé le moule de ce qui se fait traditionnellement au Japon avec ce genre de produit, mais emploie la calligraphie et le papier japonais traditionnels.

KANPYO UDON

Design: Nosigner
Company: Nosigner
Country: Japan
Category: Best of the category Food

PLATINUM PENTAWARD 2009

TESCO TORTILLA CHIPS

Design: Simon Pemberton,
Lee Newham, Barry Crombie
Company: Pemberton & Whitefoord
Country: UK
Category: Best of the category Food

PLATINUM PENTAWARD 2008

The Pemberton & Whitefoord agency of London developed a range of tortilla chips for the British retailer Tesco by creating "the Bandito", a comical character who changes outfit and accessories according to the type of chips, bringing a touch of humour to the product. Moreover, the strong colour codes aim to increase the display impact.

Die Londoner Agentur Pemberton & Whitefoord entwickelte für den britischen Händler Tesco verschiedene Tortilla-Chips. Dazu spannte sie die spaßige Figur des „Banditos" ein, der sein Äußeres und seine Accessoires je nach Art der Chips ändert. So verleiht er dem Produkt einen humorvollen Touch. Überdies verstärken die kräftigen Farbcodes der Verpackung die Wirkung im Regal.

L'agence londonienne Pemberton & Whitefoord a conçu une gamme de tortillas pour les magasins anglais Tesco en créant le « Bandito », un personnage comique qui change de vêtements et d'accessoires en fonction du type de chips, et ajoute par la même occasion une touche d'humour au produit. Les codes couleurs très forts visent à augmenter

THE DELI GARAGE
CHOCOLATE GLUE

Executive Creative Director: Stefan Kolle
Creative Director: Katrin Oeding (Kolle Rebbe, KOREFE)
Art Director: Reginald Wagner (Kolle Rebbe, KOREFE)
Graphic Design: Jan Hartwig, Paul Svoboda (Kolle Rebbe, KOREFE)
Copywriter: Till Grabsch (Kolle Rebbe, KOREFE)
Account Manager: Kristina Wulf (Kolle Rebbe)
Producer: Frank Witte (Produktionsbüro Romey von Malottky),
Stephan Gerlach (Kolle Rebbe)
Company: Kolle Rebbe GmbH
Country: Germany
Category: Best of the category Food

PLATINUM PENTAWARD 2010

WAHAHA

Design: Yunfeng Wang
Company: Hang Zhou Wahaha Group
Country: China
Category: Cereals (cereals, bread, pasta, soya, rice, noodles, dried pulses, etc.)

SILVER PENTAWARD 2010

YARMARKA PLATINUM

Art Director: Sypko Maria; *Designer:* Morgalev Evgeny
Company: Kian brand agency
Country: Russia
Category: Cereals (cereals, bread, pasta,
soya, rice, noodles, dried pulses, etc.)

GOLD PENTAWARD 2009

SILVER HILLS

Creative Director: James Bateman; *Senior Designer:* Dan O'Leary
Designer: Jennifer Pratt; *Copywriter:* Jeff Galbraith
Senior Project Manager: Heather Tryon; *Account Director:* Megan McCord
Brand Planner: Hugh Ruthven; *Producer:* Trish Beck
Illustration: Robert Hanson
Company: DDB Canada/Karacters Vancouver
Country: Canada
Category: Cereals (cereals, bread, pasta,
soya, rice, noodles, dried pulses, etc.)

SILVER PENTAWARD 2009

KELLOGG'S SPECIAL K

Design: Sandrine Topart, Renaud Claerbout
Company: Brandimage – Desgrippes & Laga
Country: Belgium
Category: Cereals (cereals, bread, pasta,
soya, rice, noodles, dried pulses, etc.)

BRONZE PENTAWARD 2009

HEINZ BABY BREAKFASTS AND DINNERS

Design: David Pearman
Company: Cowan London
Country: UK
Category: Cereals (cereals, bread, pasta, soya, rice, noodles, dried pulses, etc.)

BRONZE PENTAWARD 2009

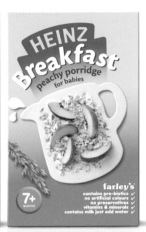

The Parisian **Chateau Rouge** brand created a line of premium teas from around the world, with Brandhouse using the name to imagine a real mansion somewhere in Paris filled with the finest art collection. Each package features the image of an antique item found and shot in the imaginary chateau's richly sumptuous interior, with each item carefully echoing a particular tea in origin, taste or name.

Die Pariser Marke **Chateau Rouge** schuf eine Produktlinie mit Premium-Tees aus aller Welt. Brandhouse nutzte den Markennamen, um sich irgendwo in Paris eine echtes Herrenhaus auszumalen, das mit einer ausgezeichneten Kunstsammlung gefüllt ist. Auf jeder Packung wird das Bild eines antiken Gegenstandes gezeigt, der in der opulenten Innenausstattung des imaginären Herrensitzes gefunden und fotografiert wurde. Jeder Gegenstand bezieht sich hinsichtlich Ursprung, Geschmack oder Name wohlüberlegt auf einen bestimmten Tee.

La marque parisienne **Château Rouge** a créé une ligne de thés haut de gamme issus des quatre coins du globe. En partant de ce nom, l'agence Brandhouse a imaginé un vrai manoir quelque part dans Paris, décoré d'une exquise collection d'art. Chaque emballage est illustré par une antiquité trouvée et photographiée dans le décor somptueux de ce château imaginaire, qui fait écho à l'origine, au goût ou au nom du thé concerné.

CHATEAU ROUGE

Design: David Beard,
Bronwen Edwards, Mel Beeson
Company: Brandhouse
Country: UK
Category: Coffee & tea (dry)
GOLD PENTAWARD 2009

CHATEAU ROUGE

FORMOSA
POUCHONG
GREEN OOLONG

CHATEAU ROUGE

JASMINE
DOWNY PEARLS
GREEN TEA

CHATEAU ROUGE

WIEDOUW
LONG CUT
ROOIBOS
TISANE

CHATEAU ROUGE

WILD HARVEST
HONEYBUSH
TISAN

CHATEAU ROUGE

ILAM
FIKKAL
ETGIOPE
BLACK TEA

CHATEAU ROUGE

IMPERIAL
EARL GREY
BLACK TEA

CHATEAU ROUGE

WHITE
MONKEY
GREEN TEA

CHATEAU ROUGE

SIKKIM
TEMI
1st FLUSH ETGIOPE
BLACK TEA

RUBRA
KOKOLICIOUS

Art Director: Geoff Bickford
Graphic Design: Esther Lee
Company: Dessein
Country: Australia
Category: Coffee & tea (dry and capsules)

SILVER PENTAWARD 2010

RUBRA

Graphic Design/Photography: Geoff Bickford
Graphic Design: Esther Lee
Company: Dessein
Country: Australia
Category: Coffee & tea (dry and capsules)

SILVER PENTAWARD 2010

NANA'S GREEN TEA MACCHA LATTE

Art Director: Akihiro Nishizawa; *Designers:* Akihiro Nishizawa,
Etsuko Sanada, Wakako Shibata
Company: Eight Co., Ltd.
Country: Japan
Category: Coffee & tea (dry and capsules)
GOLD PENTAWARD 2010

LANGUAGE OF THE LEAF

Design: Andrei Procopie, Marius Ursache
Company: Grapefruit
Country: Romania
Category: Coffee & tea (dry)
SILVER PENTAWARD 2009

CLIPPER TEAS

Design: Big Fish team
Company: Big Fish
Country: UK
Category: Coffee & tea (dry)

SILVER PENTAWARD 2009

REGENT'S PARK

Design: Hélène Sagné
Company: Bug
Country: France
Category: Coffee & tea (dry)

BRONZE PENTAWARD 2009

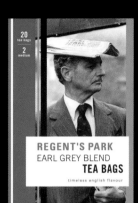

REGENT'S PARK
EARL GREY BLEND
TEA BAGS
timeless english flavour

REGENT'S PARK
BREAKFAST BLEND
TEA BAGS
classic english flavour

REGENT'S PARK
EXTRA STRONG BLEND
TEA BAGS
boosting english flavour

REGENT'S PARK
DECAFFEINATED BLEND
TEA BAGS
relaxing english flavour

REGENT'S PARK
FINE FLAVOUR BLEND
TEA BAGS
lovely english flavour

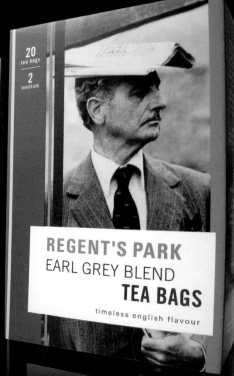

REGENT'S PARK
BREAKFAST BLEND
TEA BAGS
classic english flavour

REGENT'S PARK
EARL GREY BLEND
TEA BAGS
timeless english flavour

REGENT'S PARK
LEMON
CURD
surprising english flavour

REGENT'S PARK
PINK GRAPEFRUIT
MARMALADE
amusing english flavour

BEAR BRAND
CERIO

Design: Navaporn Phongwan,
Kittikoon Pakdeekaew, Perus Saranurak
Company: FiF House
Country: Thailand
Category: Coffee & tea (dry and capsules)

BRONZE PENTAWARD 2010

SPECIAL T BY NESTLÉ

Design: Béatrice Mariotti, Emmanuelle Binet
Company: Carré Noir
Country: France
Category: Coffee & tea (dry and capsules)

BRONZE PENTAWARD 2010

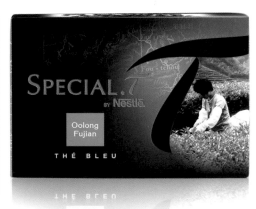

BIOGURT

Design: Gilberto Sanchez
Company: Guti Sanz Diseño
Country: Mexico
Category: Dairy products

SILVER PENTAWARD 2009

PHILADELPHIA

Creative Director: Nick Hanson; *Senior Designer:* Sarah Hilsley
Junior Designer: Tim Nelis; *Artwork:* Jon Goldingay
Company: Holmes & Marchant
Country: UK
Category: Dairy products

SILVER PENTAWARD 2009

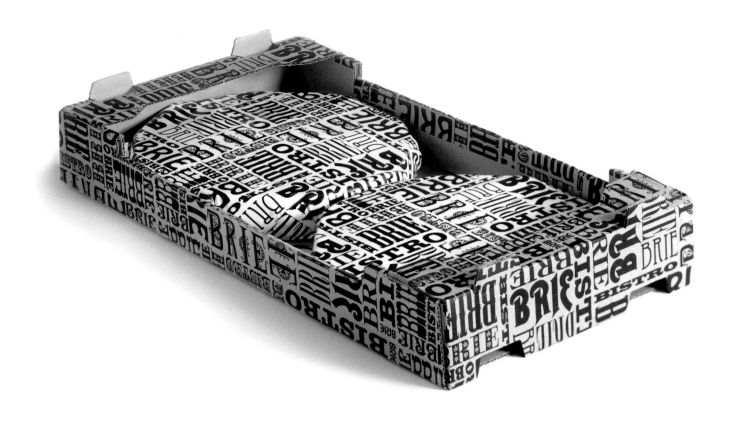

BRIE BISTRO

Design: Emma Ringsberg, Per Hallin, Mr. Golv
Company: ID kommunikation
Country: Sweden
Category: Dairy products

GOLD PENTAWARD 2010

FONTERRA BRANDS
MAINLAND SPECIAL RESERVE

Creative Director: Jure Leko
Designer: Jeremy Tombs
Photographer: Steven Popovich
Company: The Grain
Country: Australia
Category: Dairy products

BRONZE PENTAWARD 2010

ARRIGONI VALTALEGGIO

Design: Gianfranco Siano
Company: CB'a Design Solutions
Country: France
Category: Dairy products

BRONZE PENTAWARD 2010

HEINZ
DAILY SPREAD

Design: Claire Parker, Martina Rosati, Jordy Huisman,
Chantal Roberti, Stefan Hermsen, James McAllister, Nanne Gepken
Company: Design Bridge Ltd.
Country: The Netherlands
Category: Dairy products

BRONZE PENTAWARD 2009

KRAFT
AMOOZA! TWISTS

Creative Director: Don Chisholm
Creative Strategy: Patrick Ho
Design: Patrick Smith
Production Design: Rob Sunderland
Production Management: Reg Dick
Company: Dossier Creative Inc.
Country: Canada
Category: Dairy products

BRONZE PENTAWARD 2010

TINE
NORVEGIA

Design: Kristine Lillevik, Tonje Jæger,
Caroline Dahlstrøm
Company: Dinamo Design
Country: Norway
Category: Dairy products

BRONZE PENTAWARD 2009

Soso is the name of a high-quality salt brand from Spain, and means "lacking salt or short of salt" in Spanish. The client was looking for a distinguished container that could be used both to store salt and as a salt-cellar. Inspired by the egg, Eduardo del Fraile used the form of its shell for the packaging of the container, and an egg-box tray to serve as the product's base and support. Moreover, both shape and colour are very unusual in this category of products.

Soso ist der Name einer qualitativ hochwertigen spanischen Salzmarke. Auf Spanisch bedeutet Soso etwa „ungesalzen" in der Bedeutung von „fade" oder „langweilig". Der Auftraggeber suchte nach einem charakteristischen Behälter, mit dem man Salz nicht nur verpacken, sondern den man auch als Salzstreuer verwenden kann. Eduardo del Fraile ließ sich von Eiern inspirieren und nutzte die Form der Eierschale für die Verpackung des Containers und ein Tablett mit Eierkartons, das als Basis und Support für das Produkt dienen soll. Überdies sind sowohl Form als auch Farbe in dieser Produktkategorie sehr ungewöhnlich.

Soso est le nom d'une marque espagnole de sel haut de gamme, et signifie « qui manque de sel » en espagnol. Le client voulait un récipient distingué qui pourrait servir à entreposer et conserver le sel. Eduardo del Fraile s'est inspiré de l'œuf et a repris la forme de sa coquille pour le packaging, et a créé une boîte d'œufs qui fait office de base et de support du produit. Cette forme et ces couleurs sont en outre très inhabituelles dans cette catégorie de produits.

SOSOFACTORY
SOSO

Design: Eduardo del Fraile, Aurelia Gonzalez
Company: Eduardo del Fraile
Country: Spain
Category: Spices, oils & sauces
(oil, vinegar, mayonnaise,
mustard, spices, sauces, etc.)

GOLD PENTAWARD 2009

SO
SO

sal natural
natural salt

100 g

SO
SO

sal negra
black salt

100 g

SO
SO

flor de sal picante
spicy fleur de sel

100 g

SO
SO

flor de sal dulce
sweet fleur de sel

100 g

Guzman y Gomez were releasing their own range of sauces to be sold in restaurants and selected supermarkets. The design used the faces of Mexican store managers and photographed them tasting the sauces, their expressions reflecting the amount of chilli or heat in each one. This approach gave the sauces immediate personality and quick communication of the product. Along with using the images of the staff there is also a blurb on the side of each bottle that describes the person's experience with it, which gives great authenticity and adds further personality.

Guzman y Gomez brachten ihre eigene Auswahl an Saucen auf den Markt, die in Restaurants und ausgewählten Supermärkten verkauft werden sollten. Für das Design wurden Fotos von mexikanischen Geschäftsinhabern verwendet, die zeigen, wie sie die Saucen probieren. Dabei entsprechen ihre Gesichtsausdrücke der Menge an Chili in der jeweiligen Sauce beziehungsweise deren Schärfegrad. Dieser Ansatz verlieh den Saucen sofort eine Persönlichkeit, und das Produkt erschloss sich schnell.

Guzman y Gomez lançait sur le marché sa propre gamme de sauces, qui devait être vendue en restaurants et dans des supermarchés sélectionnés. Sur les bouteilles, on voit les visages de gérants mexicains de filiales de la marque, photographiés en train de goûter aux sauces. Leur expression reflète la quantité de chili ou d'épices dans chaque variété. Cette approche confère de la personnalité aux sauces et transmet instantanément des informations sur le produit. Sur le côté de la bouteille, un petit texte décrit les impressions que la personne photographiée a ressenties en goûtant la sauce, ce qui donne une grande authenticité et assoit encore davantage la personnalité du produit.

GUZMAN Y GOMEZ

Creative Director: Tony Ibbotson
Designer: Andi Yanto
Artwork: Paul Rumens
Company: The Creative Method
Country: Australia
Category: Spices, oils & sauces (oil, vinegar, mayonnaise, mustard, spices, sauces, etc.)

GOLD PENTAWARD 2008

HEINZ TWISTED KETCHUP

Design: David Pearman
Company: Cowan London
Country: UK
Category: Spices, oils & sauces
(oil, vinegar, mayonnaise, mustard, spices, sauces, etc.)
SILVER PENTAWARD 2009

HAECHANDEUL RED PEPPER

Design: Jisun Kim, Kangkook Lee, Byungyong Moon,
Sangsik Yoon, Seungpyo Lee, Moonchan Bae, Wonseok Lee
Company: CJ Cheiljedang Design Center
Country: South Korea
Category: Spices, oils & sauces
(oil, vinegar, mayonnaise, mustard, spices, sauces, etc.)
BRONZE PENTAWARD 2009

To revitalise **Bull's-Eye** and re-ignite consumer interest, the re-design needed to be contemporary, masculine, unpretentious, and genuinely convey the BBQ expertise that is inherent in the Bull's-Eye brand. This was achieved through bold typography, distressed textures, and a re-invention of the brand's icon of the Bull.

Die Neugestaltung des Designs für **Bull's-Eye** sollte aktuell, maskulin und einfach sein, um die Marke mit neuem Leben zu erfüllen und das Kundeninteresse neu zu entfachen. Dazu sollte authentisch all das Grillfachwissen vermittelt werden, das der Marke Bull's-Eye eigen ist. Erzielt wurde dies durch eine kraftvolle Typografie, eine veränderte Oberflächenbeschaffenheit und die Neugestaltung des Stiers als Markensymbol.

Pour revitaliser **Bull's-Eye** et relancer l'intérêt des consommateurs, la refonte du design se devait d'être contemporaine, masculine, sans prétention, et d'exprimer avec authenticité l'expertise du barbecue qui est au cœur de la marque. C'est réussi avec une typographie originale, des textures vieillies, et une réinvention du taureau emblème de la marque.

KRAFT
BULL'S-EYE

Design: Kai Muller; *Account Director:* Ben Blaber
Company: Davis; *Country:* Canada
Category: Spices, oils & sauces
(oil, vinegar, mayonnaise, mustard, spices, sauces, etc.)

GOLD PENTAWARD 2010

TORO
MATKUNST

Design: Jeremy Chestnutt, Candy Schneider, David Muzeen, Ninja Scheel Aas, Jackie Hall, Robyn Stevenson, Esme Fisher, Andy Seymour, Ian Burren, Steve Elliott
Company: You
Country: UK
Category: Spices, oils & sauces
(oil, vinegar, mayonnaise, mustard, spices, sauces, etc.)

SILVER PENTAWARD 2010

VERSTEGEN
SPICES & SAUCES
HERB AND SPICE SHAKERS

Design: Erik de Graaf, Robert Stakenburg
Company: Millford Brand-id
Country: The Netherlands
Category: Spices, oils & sauces
(oil, vinegar, mayonnaise, mustard,
spices, sauces, etc.)

SILVER PENTAWARD 2009

DOMAINE FENDRI

Design: Souheil Nachi, Sonia Benzid
Company: Snash Design
Country: Tunisia
Category: Spices, oils & sauces
(oil, vinegar, mayonnaise, mustard,
spices, sauces, etc.)

BRONZE PENTAWARD 2010

VERSTEGEN SPICES & SAUCES
VERSTEGEN GRINDERS

Design 2D: Millford Brand-id
Design 3D: Flex/theINNOVATIONLAB
Designers: Robert Stakenburg, Erik de Graaf (Millford
Brand-id), Sven van Westreenen (Flex/theINNOVATIONLAB)
Photography: Marc Wauters
Company: Millford Brand-id
Country: The Netherlands
Category: Spices, oils & sauces (oil, vinegar,
mayonnaise, mustard, spices, sauces, etc.)

BRONZE PENTAWARD 2010

CASTILLO DE CANENA

Design: Gloria de Castro, Belen de Pedro
Company: Castillo de Canena
Country: Spain
Category: Spices, oils & sauces
(oil, vinegar, mayonnaise, mustard, spices, sauces, etc.)

SILVER PENTAWARD 2010

CLEARSPRING

Creative Director: Roger Akroyd
Design Director: Barry Gillibrand
Account Director: Charlie Bosworth
Company: Mayday
Country: UK
Category: Spices, oils & sauces
(oil, vinegar, mayonnaise, mustard,
spices, sauces, etc.)

BRONZE PENTAWARD 2009

AKZO NOBEL SALT
JOZO SALT

Design: Erik de Graaf, Edwin Everling
Company: Millford Brand-id
Country: The Netherlands
Category: Spices, oils & sauces
(oil, vinegar, mayonnaise, mustard,
spices, sauces, etc.)

BRONZE PENTAWARD 2009

Norgården is a new range of high-quality ecological meat and poultry products from Nortura, certified to ensure that each one follows the rules and regulations for organic production in Norway. Norgården's main goal is to be the consumer's number one choice for ecological meat and a challenger to well-established competitors.

Norgården ist ein neues Angebot mit biodynamisch produzierten Fleisch- und Hühnerprodukten von Nortura, deren Zertifizierung sicherstellt, dass alle Produkte die Auflagen und Regularien der biologischen Produktion in Norwegen einhalten. Norgårdens Hauptziel besteht darin, beim Bio-Fleisch zur ersten Wahl für die Konsumenten zu werden und die etablierten Konkurrenten herauszufordern.

Norgården est une nouvelle ligne de produits écologiques haut de gamme à base de viande et de volaille de Nortura. Elle est certifiée pour garantir que chaque produit est conforme à la réglementation norvégienne sur la production organique. L'objectif principal de Norgården est d'être le premier choix des consommateurs dans le secteur de la viande écologique, et de faire de la concurrence aux autres marques bien établies sur le marché.

ØKOLOGISKE NORGÅRDEN

Design: Camilla Jarem, Simon Oldani, Cathrine Lie Hansen
Company: Harpun Euro RSCG
Country: Norway
Category: Fish, meat, poultry (fresh, deep-frozen, dried or canned)

GOLD PENTAWARD 2009

HALVORS TRADISJONSFISK

Design: Sandro Kvernmo, Bjørn Viggo Ottem
Company: Tank Design
Country: Norway
Category: Fish, meat, poultry
(fresh, deep-frozen, dried or canned)

SILVER PENTAWARD 2009

The insight for **The Saucy Fish Company** was that the consumer was frightened by the thought of cooking fish, that they didn't know what to do with it, or how to serve it. Elmwood went on to create a brand that demystified and reduced risk, communicating to consumers that it's safe, easy to buy and cook fish. Building on a trend towards more flavoursome, dynamic food, the company designed a range of fish and sauce combinations.

Die **Saucy Fish Company** erkannte, wie verunsichert Verbraucher sind, wenn sie Fisch zubereiten sollen, weil sie nicht wissen, wie er zu verarbeiten oder zu servieren ist. Elmwood schuf daraufhin eine Marke, die das Problem entmystifizierte und das Risiko senkte. Dem Verbraucher wird vermittelt, wie einfach Fisch zu kaufen, sicher zu verarbeiten und zuzubereiten ist. Das Unternehmen greift den Trend zu wohlschmeckender und dynamischer Nahrung auf und schafft eine Produktpalette mit Fisch- und Saucenkombinationen.

L'idée de départ pour **The Saucy Fish Company** était que le consommateur est intimidé à l'idée de cuisiner du poisson, il ne sait pas quoi en faire, ni comment le servir. Elmwood a créé une marque qui démystifie et réduit les risques, en faisant comprendre au consommateur qu'il n'aura aucun mal à acheter et cuisiner du poisson. Tirant parti des tendances « alimentation savoureuse et dynamique », The Saucy Fish Company a conçu cette gamme de poissons et sauces combinés.

THE SAUCY FISH COMPANY

Design Director: Ben Greengrass; *Account Director:* Simon Preece
Designer: Stephen Woowat; *Copywriter:* Natalie Woodhead
Project Manager: Jan Hirst
Company: Elmwood
Country: UK
Category: Fish, meat, poultry
(fresh, deep-frozen, dried or canned)

GOLD PENTAWARD 2010

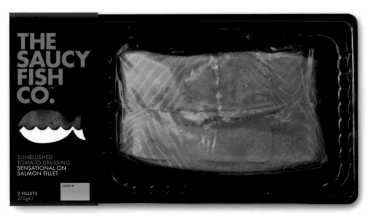
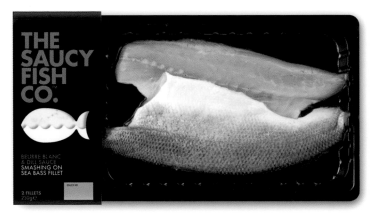

PRIOR
LITT AV EN KYLLING

Design: Caroline Dahlstrøm, Kristine Lillevik,
Andreas Kalleberg
Company: Dinamo Design
Country: Norway
Category: Fish, meat, poultry
(fresh, deep-frozen, dried or canned)

SILVER PENTAWARD 2010

KOBERG VILT

Creative Director: Ulf Berlin
Senior Designer: Cajsa Bratt
Illustration: Cajsa Bratt
Production Manager: Louise Stierna
Company: Designkontoret Silver KB
Country: Sweden
Category: Fish, meat, poultry
(fresh, deep-frozen, dried or canned)

SILVER PENTAWARD 2009

PAPANE

Design: Bogdan Dumitrache, Cristian Petre
Company: Brandient
Country: Romania
Category: Fish, meat, poultry
(fresh, deep-frozen, dried or canned)

BRONZE PENTAWARD 2009

DYBVIK

Art Director: Morten Throndsen
Design: Eia Gredal, Jarle Paulsen
Company: Strømme Throndsen Design
Country: Norway
Category: Fish, meat, poultry
(fresh, deep-frozen, dried or canned)

BRONZE PENTAWARD 2009

LE FISH

Design: Sue Aperghis
Company: Qurious
Country: Belgium
Category: Fish, meat, poultry
(fresh, deep-frozen, dried or canned)

BRONZE PENTAWARD 2009

BACKYARD FARMS

Art Director: Sam J. Ciulla
Designer: Shelley Scheer
Company: Ciulla Assoc.
Country: USA
Category: Fruit & vegetables
(fresh, deep-frozen, dried or canned)

GOLD PENTAWARD 2010

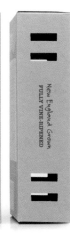

Backyard Farms was founded on the belief that everyone should be able to enjoy fresh, healthy, locally grown produce all year long delivered to grocery stores within a day of harvest. The brand name emphasises that produce is locally grown, and therefore the graphic identity and structure had to telegraph this brand personality. With a majority of products unpackaged in the produce category, the strategic mandate was to capture the attention of consumers with a fixed-weight package in this section of the grocery store. Other key considerations included the use of recycled post-consumer material, product protection, and a design that allowed consumers to see, touch, and smell the fresh produce.

Backyard Farms wurde mit der Überzeugung gegründet, dass alle Menschen frische, gesunde und örtlich hergestellte Produkte genießen sollten. Diese Produkte sollte man ganzjährig und spätestens einen Tag nach Ernte im Laden kaufen können. Der Markenname betont, dass das Produkt aus der örtlichen Umgebung stammt, und daher sollte dieser Aspekt durch den optischen Eindruck und die Packungsstruktur verdeutlicht werden. Die meisten Produkte aus dieser Kategorie werden unverpackt angeboten. Somit bestand der strategische Auftrag darin, die Aufmerksamkeit der Verbraucher in diesem Bereich des Lebensmittelhandels auf eine Packung mit festgelegtem Gewicht zu lenken. Außerdem sollten recycelte Materialien eingesetzt und das Produkt optimal geschützt werden. Für das Design war außerdem wichtig, dass die Verbraucher das frische Produkt gut sehen, berühren und riechen können.

Backyard Farms a été créée sur la conviction que chacun devrait pouvoir profiter de fruits et légumes frais, sains et produits localement, livrés tout au long de l'année dans les épiceries dès le lendemain de la récolte. Le nom de la marque souligne l'aspect de la production locale. L'identité visuelle et le graphisme devaient donc transmettre l'identité de cette marque. Dans la catégorie des fruits et légumes, la majorité des produits sont présentés sans emballage. La consigne stratégique était donc d'attirer l'attention des consommateurs avec un emballage à poids fixé dans cette partie du magasin. Il fallait également utiliser des matériaux recyclés, protéger le produit, et imaginer un emballage qui permettrait aux consommateurs de voir, toucher et sentir le produit frais.

HEINZ TOMATO RANGE

Design: David Pearman
Company: Cowan London
Country: UK
Category: Fruit & vegetables
(fresh, deep-frozen, dried or canned)

SILVER PENTAWARD 2010

BONDUELLE
PURE

Design: VanBerlo Communications team
Company: VanBerlo Communications
Country: The Netherlands
Category: Fruit & vegetables
(fresh, deep-frozen, dried or canned)

BRONZE PENTAWARD 2010

JEALOUS FRUITS
CANADIAN CHERRIES

Design: Bernie Hadley-Beauregard,
Laurie Millotte, Sarah King
Company: Brandever
Country: Canada
Category: Fruit & vegetables
(fresh, deep-frozen, dried or canned)

SILVER PENTAWARD 2009

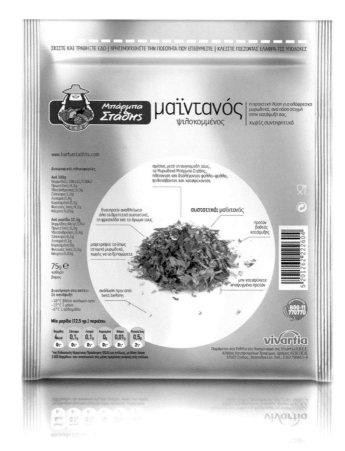

BARBASTATHIS
FROZEN HERBS

Design: Gregory Tsaknakis,
Ioanna Papaioannou,
George Drakopoulos, Tina Webb
Company: Mouse Graphics
Country: Greece
Category: Fruit & vegetables
(fresh, deep-frozen, dried or canned)

BRONZE PENTAWARD 2009

KINPACHI-MIKAN

Art Director: Koichi Sugiyama
Designer: Koichi Sugiyama
Company: Sugiyama Design
Country: Japan
Category: Fruit & vegetables
(fresh, deep-frozen, dried or canned)

SILVER PENTAWARD 2010

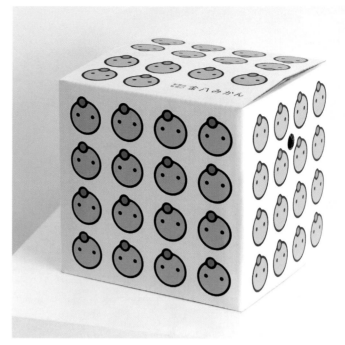

TRUE LEMON

Design: Mark Pursey, Reseigh Fooks
Company: Blue Marlin Brand Design
Country: UK
Category: Fruit & vegetables
(fresh, deep-frozen, dried or canned)

BRONZE PENTAWARD 2010

HEINZ TOMATO SOUPS

Design: Claire Parker, Joeri Florin, Olof Ten Hoorn, Stefan Hermsen, James McAllister
Company: Design Bridge Ltd.
Country: The Netherlands
Category: Soups, ready-to-eat dishes (fresh, deep-frozen, dry or canned)

GOLD PENTAWARD 2009

These new packs for the well-known **Heinz** tomato soup focus on one perfect tomato or a similar bunch of cherry tomatoes, combined with a big, bold branding exercise intended to achieve a "what you see is what you get" brand in consumers' minds. Soups typically focus on food shots of soup plates, or of rich ingredients, and come mostly in tins, cartons or bags.

Die neuen Verpackungen der weltbekannten **Heinz**-Tomatensuppen konzentrieren sich auf die perfekte Tomate oder das perfekte Bündel von Kirschtomaten. Verbunden mit einem umfassenden, mutigen Branding-Manöver zielen sie darauf ab, den Gedanken in den Köpfen der Verbraucher zu verankern, dass man bei dieser Marke genau das bekommt, was auf der Hülle gezeigt wird. Bei Suppen konzentriert man sich in der Darstellung üblicherweise auf Suppenteller oder die reichhaltigen Zutaten; sie werden meist in Dosen, Kartons oder Tüten verpackt.

Ces nouveaux emballages pour la célèbre soupe de tomate **Heinz** mettent en vedette une tomate ou une grappe de tomates-cerises parfaite. C'est un exercice de stratégie de marque audacieux et radical qui cherche à associer la marque à la notion de « ce que vous voyez, c'est ce que vous obtenez » dans l'esprit des consommateurs. En général, les soupes utilisent plutôt des photos d'assiettes de soupe ou d'ingrédients appétissants, et sont vendues en boîtes de conserve, en bricks ou en sachets.

365 SOUP

Design: VanBerlo Communications team
Company: VanBerlo Communications
Country: The Netherlands
Category: Soups, ready-to-eat dishes
(fresh, deep-frozen, dry or canned)

GOLD PENTAWARD 2010

LITTLE BUG

Art Director: Bob Hullinger
Design: Meegan Peery, Bill Kerr
Company: Brand Engine
Country: USA
Category: Soups, ready-to-eat dishes
(fresh, deep-frozen, dry or canned)

SILVER PENTAWARD 2009

LOKALE HELTER

Art Director: Morten Throndsen
Designer: Linda Gundersen
Typography: Richard Dawson
Company: Strømme Throndsen Design
Country: Norway
Category: Soups, ready-to-eat dishes
(fresh, deep-frozen, dry or canned)

SILVER PENTAWARD 2009

LAMB WESTON SUPREME

Design: Barbara van der Hoorn-van Noort, Bob Derksen
Company: Brandnew Design
Country: The Netherlands
Category: Soups, ready-to-eat dishes
(fresh, deep-frozen, dry or canned)

GOLD PENTAWARD 2008

TANOSHI

Design: Coconuts team; *Company:* Coconuts; *Country:* France
Category: Soups, ready-to-eat dishes
(fresh, deep-frozen, dry or canned)

BRONZE PENTAWARD 2009

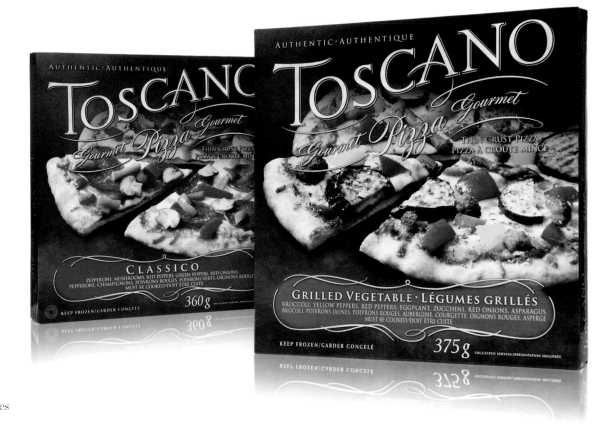

MCCAIN TOSCANO

Design: Dori Burchat
Company: Anthem Worldwide
Country: Canada
Category: Soups, ready-to-eat dishes
(fresh, deep-frozen, dry or canned)

BRONZE PENTAWARD 2009

FELIX ABBA

Design: David Pearman
Company: Cowan London
Country: UK
Category: Soups, ready-to-eat dishes
(fresh, deep-frozen, dry or canned)

BRONZE PENTAWARD 2010

The agency Millford Brand-id and Venco worked together on deciding the essential message behind communicating **Venco DropTwist**. The product offers a mature proposition that appeals to a broad target group, and unites different textures and special flavours in the licorice. They found it important to make sure that the consumer would not be overwhelmed by all kinds of different elements demanding attention. The choice made was for a bag of licorice that has a modern appeal to it, and the result was a clear design solution.

Gemeinsam erarbeiteten die Agentur Millford Brand-id und Venco die zentrale Botschaft, die mit **Venco DropTwist** vermittelt werden sollte. Die wohl überlegte Aussage des Produkts spricht eine groß angelegte Zielgruppe an. Es führt unterschiedliche Beschaffenheiten und spezielle Geschmacksvarianten bei der Lakritze zusammen. Es wurde als wichtig erachtet, die Verbraucher nicht mit verschiedenen Elementen zu überwältigen, die ihre Aufmerksamkeit verlangen. Die Wahl fiel auf eine Tüte Lakritz mit einem modernen Touch, und das Ergebnis war eine klare und eindeutige Designlösung.

L'agence Millford Brand-id et Venco ont travaillé ensemble sur le message de fond de la campagne pour **Venco DropTwist**. Ce produit à l'image adulte plaît à une large cible, et réunit différentes textures et différents goûts qui s'ajoutent au réglisse. La société voulait éviter que l'attention du consommateur ne soit noyée par trop d'éléments différents. Le choix s'est porté sur un sachet de bonbons au réglisse moderne, et le résultat est une solution de design claire.

VENCO DROPTWIST

Design: Danny Klein, Jeroen de Kok
Company: Millford Brand-id
Country: The Netherlands
Category: Confectionery & sweet snacks

GOLD PENTAWARD 2009

MONK'S

Design: Nicola Mincione
Company: RBA
Country: Italy
Category: Confectionery & sweet snacks

GOLD PENTAWARD 2008

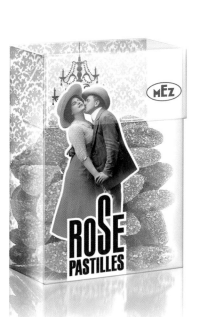

MEZ

Design: Gina Zafiraki, Vassiliki Argyropoulou
Company: Mouse Graphics
Country: Greece
Category: Confectionery & sweet snacks

SILVER PENTAWARD 2009

ABANICO
CHOCOLATS DE CRÉATION

Design: Sophie Schott
Company: Second Souffle
Country: France
Category: Confectionery & sweet snacks

SILVER PENTAWARD 2010

ROCKALETA

Design: Simon Thorneycroft, Nicholas Leebert
Company: Perspective Branding
Country: USA
Category: Confectionery & sweet snacks

SILVER PENTAWARD 2010

ZOKOKO

Design: Edouard Ball, Jon Clark, Jodi Hooker,
Frederico Hernandez, Thomas Finn
Company: Webb Scarlett deVlam Sydney
Country: Australia
Category: Confectionery & sweet snacks

BRONZE PENTAWARD 2010

NESTLÉ CLUB

Design: Stacey Ayers
Company: Cowan Design Sydney
Country: Australia
Category: Confectionery & sweet snacks

SILVER PENTAWARD 2009

NESTLÉ NOIR

Creative Director: Gary Oakley
Art Director: Dori Burchat
Senior Designer: Steve Van Rooy
Company: Anthem Worldwide
Country: Canada
Category: Confectionery & sweet snacks

BRONZE PENTAWARD 2010

NESTLÉ GRAND CHOCOLAT

Design: Gianni Rotta
Company: Raison Pure Design Group
Country: France
Category: Confectionery & sweet snacks

BRONZE PENTAWARD 2009

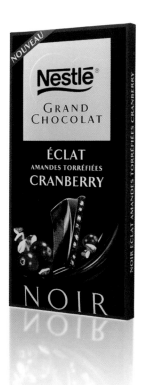

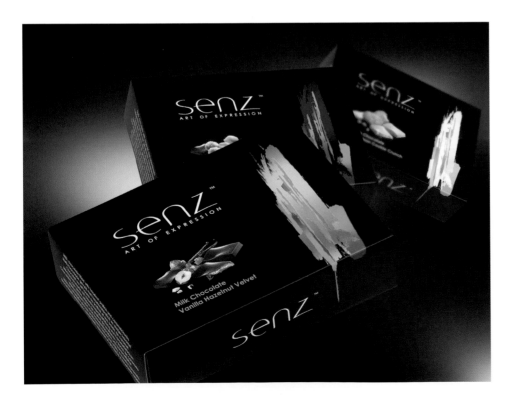

SENZ

Design: Sofan Man, Nayoun Kang
Company: Brandimage – Desgrippes & Laga
Country: China
Category: Confectionery & sweet snacks

BRONZE PENTAWARD 2009

TIC TAC
ORANGE & FRESH MINT
MULTI-PACKS

Creative Director: Linda McGregor
Lead Designer: Scott Tipping
Company: b2 Retail Solutions
Country: Canada
Category: Confectionery & sweet snacks

BRONZE PENTAWARD 2009

CLOETTA GOOD

Design: Identity Works design team
Company: Identity Works
Country: Sweden
Category: Confectionery & sweet snacks

BRONZE PENTAWARD 2010

The **Sultry Sally** potato chips range was new to the market, so it needed to have immediate cut-through, personality, and standout. The Vargas girls illustrations of the 1940s were used as a basis because, like the chips, they were high in flavour, had immediate character, and the figures of women from this era were slimmer as there was less fat in the diet. A plain matted foil was used for most of the pack surface, and by using colour, each flavour is distinguished with an individual feel and story through its pack design.

Die Kartoffelchips der Marke **Sultry Sally** kamen neu auf den Markt. Sie mussten also sofort durchschlagenden Erfolg haben, brauchten eine eigene Persönlichkeit und Alleinstellungsmerkmale. Die Illustrationen mit den Vargas Girls der 1940er-Jahre wurden als Grundlage verwendet, weil sie wie die Chips voller Geschmack sind und unmittelbar als Persönlichkeiten wirken. Außerdem waren die Frauen dieser Ära schlanker, weil ihre Ernährung fettärmer war. Für den Großteil der Verpackungsoberfläche wurde eine einfache, mattierte Folie eingesetzt. Die Farbgestaltung der Packungen verleiht jeder Sorte einen individuellen Touch und hebt sie durch eigene Geschichten voneinander ab.

La gamme de chips de pomme de terre **Sultry Sally** était nouvelle sur le marché. Il fallait donc qu'elle atteigne sa cible immédiatement en se démarquant et grâce à sa personnalité. Des illustrations de pin-ups Vargas des années 1940 ont été choisies comme base parce que, comme le produit, elles sont pleines de saveur, elles ont du caractère, et les silhouettes des femmes de cette époque étaient plus minces car leur régime contenait moins de graisse. La plus grande partie de la surface du sachet est occupée par de la feuille métallisée mate, et chaque parfum se distingue des autres grâce à la couleur employée et à un style et une histoire différents déclinés sur tout le paquet.

SULTRY SALLY

Creative Director: Tony Ibbotson
Illustration: Mark Sofilas
Artwork: Tanya Walker
Company: The Creative Method
Country: Australia
Category: Savoury snacks

GOLD PENTAWARD 2008

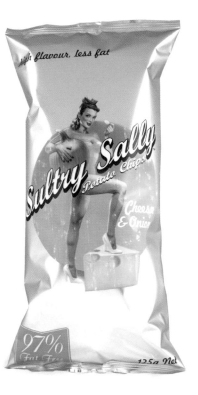

HAIRY BIKERS WORLD

Creative Director: Caz Hildebrand
Senior Designer: Sarah Carr
Designer: Laura Holden
Company: Here Design
Country: UK
Category: Savoury snacks

GOLD PENTAWARD 2010

KETTLE RIDGE

Design: Martin Grimer, Gavin Halford
Company: Blue Marlin Brand Design
Country: UK
Category: Savoury snacks

SILVER PENTAWARD 2010

ZWEIFEL
SECRETS

Design: Anete Melece
Company: ARD Design Switzerland
Country: Switzerland
Category: Savoury snacks

SILVER PENTAWARD 2009

NABISCO
WHEAT THINS

Design: Jeff Boulton; *Account Director:* Ben Blaber
Company: Davis; *Country:* Canada
Category: Savoury snacks

SILVER PENTAWARD 2010

FRITO-LAY
TRUENORTH

Creative Director: Todd Simmons
Design: Bill Darling, Masha Zolotarsky, Jodie Gatlin
Production Director: Beth Kovalsky
Production Manager: Michele Miller
Strategists: Christina O'Neal, Tina Mehta
Account Director: Jessica Chalifoux
Company: Wolff Olins
Country: USA
Category: Savoury snacks

BRONZE PENTAWARD 2009

BLOCKBUSTER MOVIE
MATINÉE POPCORN

Design: David Rogers, Rhian Moore, Sam Masters
Company: PureEquator Ltd.
Country: UK
Category: Savoury snacks

SILVER PENTAWARD 2009

QUAKER TORTILLAZ

Senior Designer: Robert Pearson
Illustration: Edward Griffin
Company: Haugaard Creative Group
Country: USA
Category: Savoury snacks

BRONZE PENTAWARD 2009

FutureBrand's key objective was to clearly position the brand in the Super Premium area, to determine and reflect the new brand essence and be strongly different from premium ice-cream competitors. The design principle was to create the most ice-cream super premium brand which would incarnate "The Art of Swiss Ice-Cream", born from a passion for gastronomy, combined with Swiss perfection.

FutureBrand hatte das Ziel gesetzt bekommen, die Marke eindeutig im Bereich der Super-Premiumprodukte zu positionieren und sie deutlich von den Konkurrenten auf dem Eiscreme-Markt unterscheidbar zu machen. Außerdem sollten die wesentlichen Merkmale dieser neuen Marke festgelegt und umgesetzt werden. Das Prinzip für das Design lautete: Es soll die maximale Super-Premiummarke für Eiscreme geschaffen werden. Diese Marke soll die „Eiscremekunst der Schweiz" verkörpern, die aus einer Leidenschaft für die Gastronomie geboren ist und mit Schweizer Perfektion kombiniert wird.

L'objectif essentiel de FutureBrand était de positionner clairement la marque en tant que « super premium », de définir et de communiquer sa nouvelle essence et de la différencier fortement de ses concurrents haut de gamme. Le principe du design était de créer la marque super premium la plus « crème glacée », qui incarnerait « l'art de la crème glacée suisse », né d'une passion pour la gastronomie et combiné à la perfection suisse.

MÖVENPICK
NESTLÉ SUPER PREMIUM

Design: Marie Thys
Company: FutureBrand
Country: France
Category: Pastry, biscuits, ice-cream, desserts, sugar

GOLD PENTAWARD 2009

MÖVENPICK®
THE ART OF SWISS ICE CREAM

SCOTTISH SINGLE MALT WHISKY & SHORTBREAD
SINGLE MALT WHISKY VON DEN SCHOTTISCHEN HIGHLANDS & SHORTBREAD
CREATION

MÖVENPICK®
THE ART OF SWISS ICE CREAM

ECUADOR GRAND CRU COCOA & GINGER
GRAND CRU KAKAO AUS ECUADOR & INGWER
CREATION

MÖVENPICK®
THE ART OF SWISS ICE CREAM

LAM DONG GREEN TEA & JASMINE FLOWERS
LAM DONG GRÜNTEE & JASMINBLÜTEN
CREATION

MÖVENPICK®
THE ART OF SWISS ICE CREAM

SUMATRA COCONUT & TOASTED SESAME
KOKOSNUSS AUS SUMATRA & CARAMELISIERTER SESAM
CREATION

MÖVENPICK®
THE ART OF SWISS ICE CREAM

VANILLA DREAM
VANILLE
CLASSICS

MÖVENPICK®
THE ART OF SWISS ICE CREAM

SWISS CHOCOLATE
SCHWEIZER SCHOKOLADE · CHOCOLAT SUISSE
CLASSICS

MÖVENPICK®
THE ART OF SWISS ICE CREAM

extra fruité
0,1%

RASPBERRY & STRAWBERRY
HIMBEER & ERDBEER · FRAMBOISE & FRAISE
DÉLICES DE FRUIT

MÖVENPICK®
THE ART OF SWISS ICE CREAM

4%
Fett/mat.gr./fat
100g

FOREST FRUIT
WALDBEEREN · FRUITS ROUGES
PLAISIR DE YOGHOURT

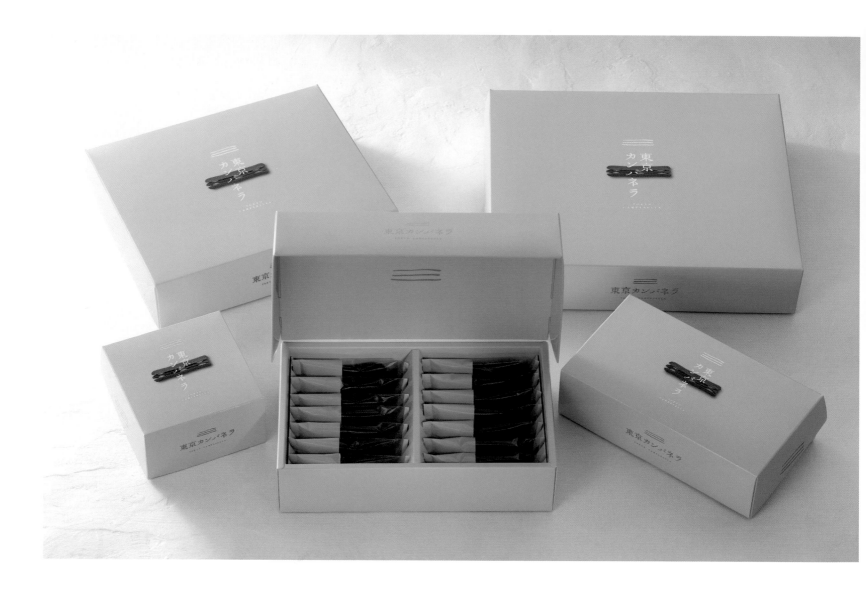

TOKYO CAMPANELLA

Design: Fumi Sasada
Company: Bravis International
Country: Japan
Category: Pastry, biscuits, ice-cream, desserts, sugar

GOLD PENTAWARD 2008

ZENKASHOIN "ZEN" CASTELLA

Art Director: Shigeno Araki
Designer: Toshiyuki Murayama, Mizuho Tada
Company: Shigeno Araki Design & Co.
Country: Japan
Category: Pastry, biscuits,
ice-cream, desserts, sugar

GOLD PENTAWARD 2010

GELATI SKY

Brand Strategist: Peter Singline
Creative Director: David Ansett
Design Director: Anton Drazevic
Designers: Lachlan McDougall, Cassandra Gill
Typography/Illustration: Lachlan McDougall, Cassandra Gill, Anton Drazevic
Copywriters: David Ansett, Peter Singline
Finish Artist: Rachel O'Brien
Company: Truly Deeply
Country: Australia
Category: Pastry, biscuits, ice-cream, desserts, sugar

SILVER PENTAWARD 2010

KAPITI

Creative Ditector: Jason Glassick
Client Manager: Anne Kernahan, Corinne Ang
Company: Design Bridge Ltd.
Country: UK
Category: Pastry, biscuits,
ice-cream, desserts, sugar

SILVER PENTAWARD 2010

CONNOISSEUR

Design: Asprey Creative team
Company: Asprey Creative
Country: Australia
Category: Pastry, biscuits, ice-cream,
desserts, sugar

SILVER PENTAWARD 2009

SUGARILLOS SUGAR STICKS

Design: Gregory Tsaknakis
Illustration: Ionna Papaioannou
Company: Mouse Graphics
Country: Greece
Category: Pastry, biscuits, ice-cream, desserts, sugar

BRONZE PENTAWARD 2010

EUROPEAN FOOD
PANDARO

Design: Somchana Kangwarnjit,
Chidchanok Laohawattanakul, Mathurada Bejrananda
Company: Prompt Design
Country: Thailand
Category: Pastry, biscuits, ice-cream, desserts, sugar

BRONZE PENTAWARD 2010

Creative Director: Anna Andersson
Company: Pulp
Country: France
Category: Pastry, biscuits, ice-cream, desserts, sugar

BRONZE PENTAWARD 2009

HONIG

Design: Rodrigo Cordova,
Angel Gonzalez, Sergio Enriquez
Company: Factor Tres
Country: Mexico
Category: Pastry, biscuits, ice-cream,
desserts, sugar

BRONZE PENTAWARD 2009

DELACRE TEA TIME

Design: Monique Jorge, Fabrice Wauthion
Company: JJM
Country: Belgium
Category: Pastry, biscuits, ice-cream,
desserts, sugar

BRONZE PENTAWARD 2009

Kameda Diet dessert, which was aimed at a female target group, took a very different approach from more usual diet products in its packaging. As every consumer understands "eating calories", the design solution was based on the impact of the 10 kcal, 25 kcal, and 0 kcal claims on every pack.

Das Dessert von **Kameda Diet** richtet sich an eine weibliche Zielgruppe und beschreitet im Vergleich zu geläufigeren Diätprodukten bei der Verpackung einen ganz anderen Weg. Da jeder Konsument versteht, was „Kalorien essen" bedeutet, basiert die Designlösung auf dem Effekt, den 10-kcal-, 25-kcal- und 0-kcal-Input bei jeder Packung klarzumachen.

Pour son packaging, le dessert **Kameda Diet,** qui s'adresse à une cible féminine, a adopté une démarche très différente de celle des produits de régime classiques. Comme chaque consommateur comprend le concept des calories absorbées, la solution de design s'est basée sur l'impact du nombre de calories déclaré sur chaque emballage, 10, 25 et 0 kcal.

KAMEDA DIET

Design: Emiko Shibasaki, Shizuka Nishiwaki
Company: Antenna Studio
Country: Japan
Category: Food trends (diet, weight control, health food, organic, fair trade, etc.)

GOLD PENTAWARD 2008

LIMA

Creative Director: Patrick De Grande
Designer: Jurgen Huughe
Food Design: Els Goethals
Company: Quatre Mains
Country: Belgium
Category: Food trends (diet, weight control,
health food, organic, fair trade, etc.)

BRONZE PENTAWARD 2009

EVERNAT

Design: Hélène Gendrillon,
Delphine Wibaux, Sandrine Morin
Company: Team Créatif
Country: France
Category: Food trends (diet, weight control,
health food, organic, fair trade, etc.)

SILVER PENTAWARD 2009

BACK TO NATURE

Creative Director: Ben Blaber
Lead Designer: Jeff Boulton
Company: Davis
Country: Canada
Category: Food trends (diet, weight control, health food, organic, fair trade, etc.)

SILVER PENTAWARD 2009

DOUTOR
PREMIUM BEANS SELECTION

Creative Director: Minoru Kitagawa
Art Director: Akihiro Nishizawa
Designer: Kanako Narita
Company: Eight Co., Ltd.
Country: Japan
Category: Limited editions,
limited series, event creations

GOLD PENTAWARD 2009

PRINGLES

Creative Director: David Stroud
Company: LPK
Country: UK
Category: Limited editions,
limited series, event creations

GOLD PENTAWARD 2010

KIT KAT
75TH ANNIVERSARY

Design: Abt Dylan
Company: ARD Design Switzerland
Country: Switzerland
Category: Limited editions,
limited series, event creations

SILVER PENTAWARD 2010

MONT BLANC
LIMITED EDITION

Design: Giovanni Rotta
Company: Raison Pure Design Group
Country: France
Category: Limited editions,
limited series, event creations

SILVER PENTAWARD 2010

Nisshin Oillio is a pure, domestically-produced canola oil, and a limited supply of it was produced to celebrate the 290th anniversary of a famous Japanese department store. The glass bottle was coated using an ancient spray-technique for porcelain ware, so that it feels like a porcelain bottle, suggesting that the oil is a relic of ancient Japan.

Nisshin Oillio ist ein reines Rapsöl aus einheimischer Produktion. Ein Teil davon wurde in begrenzter Auflage hergestellt, um den 290. Geburtstag eines berühmten japanischen Warenhauses zu feiern. Die Glasflasche wurde mittels einer altertümlichen Sprühtechnik für Porzellan bedeckt, damit sie sich wie eine Porzellanflasche anfühlt und somit den Eindruck vermittelt, das Öl sei ein Relikt des alten Japans.

Nisshin Oillio est une huile de colza pure produite au Japon. Une quantité limitée en a été produite pour célébrer le 290ᵉ anniversaire d'un grand magasin japonais renommé. La bouteille en verre a été recouverte à l'aide d'une technique ancienne de pulvérisation pour la vaisselle en porcelaine, afin de suggérer que l'huile est un vestige du Japon ancien.

NISSHIN OILLIO

Design: Hanae Yamamuro
Company: Deziro Co., Ltd.
Country: Japan
Category: Limited editions, limited series, event creations

GOLD PENTAWARD 2008

AGROVIL
ILIADA

Design: Gregory Tsaknakis,
Ioanna Papaioannou,
Vassiliki Argyropoulou
Company: Mouse Graphics
Country: Greece
Category: Limited editions,
limited series, event creations

SILVER PENTAWARD 2009

BOLLING COFFEE FORTNUM & MASON
300ᵀᴴ ANNIVERSARY COFFEE METAL TIN

Design: Fortnum and Mason
Company: Crown Speciality Packaging
Country: France
Category: Limited editions, limited series, event creations

BRONZE PENTAWARD 2009

KAHVE DÜNYASI
ISTANBUL 2010 CHOCOLATE TABLETS

Creative Director: Bülent Erkmen, Yesim Bakirküre
Designer: Bülent Erkmen
Company: BEK Tasarim & Ypsilon Tasarim
Country: Turkey
Category: Limited editions,
limited series, event creations

BRONZE PENTAWARD 2010

Oil Change is a premium olive oil flavoured with chilli, coriander, and lemon. To fit the garage character, the oils were packaged in the little oil bottles used for motor oil, and could be squeezed from them on to food. The illustrations on the bottles also suggest oil stains, and have the effect that when they are looked at through the bottle it's as if monsters are emerging from them. **The Deli Garage**, the maker of the product, also supports small and local manufacturers.

Oil Change (Ölwechsel) ist ein Premium-Olivenöl, das mit Chili, Koriander und Limone geschmacklich verfeinert wurde. Damit die Öle den gewünschten Werkstattcharakter bekommen, wurden sie in kleinen Fläschchen verpackt, wie sie auch für Motoröle verwendet werden. Das Öl spritzt man aus diesen Flaschen direkt auf die Lebensmittel. Die Illustrationen auf den Flaschen suggerieren Ölflecken. Wenn man durch die Flasche hindurch schaut, erzeugen sie außerdem den Eindruck, als würden sie Monster in sich tragen. **The Deli Garage** als Hersteller dieses Produkts unterstützt auch kleine und einheimische Erzeuger.

Oil Change (Vidange) est une huile haut de gamme parfumée au piment rouge, au romarin et au citron. Pour rester dans l'esprit « garage », les huiles ont été conditionnées dans de petites bouteilles similaires à celles utilisées pour l'huile de moteur. Ces bouteilles permettent de verser l'huile sur les aliments d'une simple pression de la main. Les illustrations évoquent également des taches d'huile et, lorsqu'on les regarde à travers la bouteille, on a l'impression de voir apparaître des monstres. **The Deli Garage**, qui produit ces huiles, soutient également les petits producteurs locaux.

THE DELI GARAGE
OIL CHANGE

Creative Director: Kathrin Oeding
Art Director: Reginald Wagner
Copywriter: Katharina Trumbach
Graphic Design: Jan Simmerl
Company: Kolle Rebbe
Country: Germany
Category: Distributors/ Retailers own brands

GOLD PENTAWARD 2009

Waitrose is a premium UK retailer with a reputation for innovation and bold branding. The objective for this series of packages created by Lewis Moberly was to find a cohesive style to link the products together as a family as well as a means of differentiating them. Each minimally designed pack carries bold tabloid-style text, and the seasonal herbs make an exclusive, and temporary appearance, with a splash of red in the headline.

Waitrose ist ein britischer Premium-Einzelhändler mit dem Ruf, beim Branding mutig und innovativ zu sein. Das Planziel für diese von Lewis Moberly gestaltete Verpackungsreihe war es, einen einheitlichen Stil zu finden, der die Produkte als Familie miteinander verknüpft, aber auch voneinander unterscheidbar macht. Jede mit geringstem Aufwand gestaltete Verpackung trägt einen schlagzeilenähnlichen Text in Fettdruck. Die Kräuter der Saison haben darin einen exklusiven und zeitlich begrenzten Auftritt, was durch eine rote Überschrift hervorgehoben wird.

Waitrose est une chaîne de magasins haut de gamme au Royaume-Uni, et est réputé pour son innovation et sa stratégie de marque audacieuse. L'objectif de cette série d'emballages créée par Lewis Moberly était de trouver un style cohérent pour établir un lien familial entre les produits tout en les différenciant. Chaque sachet minimaliste porte un texte dans le style des titres de tabloïds, et les herbes saisonnières font une apparition exclusive et temporaire, avec une touche de rouge dans le titre.

WAITROSE HERBS

Design Director: Mary Lewis
Design: Mary Lewis, Poppy Stedman
Copywriter: Mary Lewis
Company: Lewis Moberly
Country: UK
Category: Distributors'/Retailers' own brands

GOLD PENTAWARD 2008

ICA AB
TEAS RANGE

Design: Identity Works team
Company: Identity Works
Country: Sweden
Category: Distributors'/Retailers' own brands

SILVER PENTAWARD 2009

THE DELI GARAGE
MULTI NOODLES

Executive Creative Director: Stefan Kolle
Creative Director: Katrin Oeding (Kolle Rebbe, KOREFE)
Art Director: Reginald Wagner (Kolle Rebbe, KOREFE)
Graphic Design: Jan Hartwig, Paul Svoboda (Kolle Rebbe, KOREFE)
Copywriter: Till Grabsch (Kolle Rebbe, KOREFE)
Account Manager: Kristina Wulf (Kolle Rebbe)
Producer: Frank Witte (Produktionsbüro Romey von Malottky),
Stephan Gerlach (Kolle Rebbe), Philipp Christ, Natascha Harra-Frischkorn
Company: Kolle Rebbe GmbH
Country: Germany
Category: Distributors'/Retailers' own brands

GOLD PENTAWARD 2010

Design: CBX design team
Company: CBX New York
Country: USA
Category: Distributors'/Retailers' own brands

SILVER PENTAWARD 2010

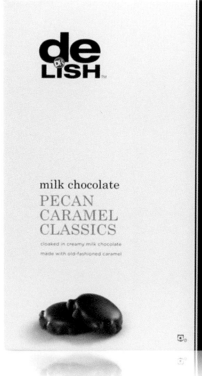

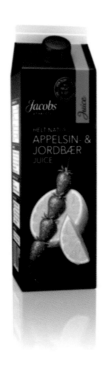

JACOBS UTVALGTE

Design: Morten Throndsen, Linda Gundersen
Company: Strømme Throndsen Design
Country: Norway
Category: Distributors'/Retailers' own brands

SILVER PENTAWARD 2010

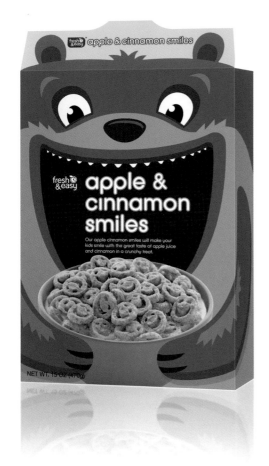

FRESH AND EASY

Creative Manager: Wesley Anson
Partner: Simon Pemberton
Company: Pemberton & Whitefoord
Country: UK
Category: Distributors'/Retailers' own brands

BRONZE PENTAWARD 2010

DELHAIZE MAINSTREAM

Creative Director: Dimitri Castrique
Art Director: Fabrice Kotulski
Company: Monalisa
Country: Belgium
Category: Distributors'/
Retailers' own brands

SILVER PENTAWARD 2009

TESCO

Creative Director: Spencer Buck
Designer: Karl Wills
Illustration: Gary Bullock
Company: Taxi Studio
Country: UK
Category: Distributors'/Retailers' own brands

BRONZE PENTAWARD 2009

MEGA PRIVATE LABEL

Design: Baruch creative team
Company: Baruch Naeh Creative Branding
Country: Israel
Category: Distributors'/Retailers' own brands

BRONZE PENTAWARD 2009

ICA

Creative Director: Ulf Berlin; *Designer:* Linus Östberg
Production Manager: Christine Schønborg
Company: Designkontoret Silver KB
Country: Sweden
Category: Distributors'/Retailers' own brands

BRONZE PENTAWARD 2010

WAITROSE
SMOKED SALMON

Creative Directors: David Turner & Bruce Duckworth
Design Director: Clem Halpin; *Designer:* Tanawat Pisanuwongse
Retouchers: Peter Ruane, Reuben James
Photographer: Andy Grimshaw; *Artwork:* Reuben James
Company: Turner Duckworth, London & San Francisco
Country: UK/USA
Category: Distributors'/Retailers' own brands

BRONZE PENTAWARD 2010

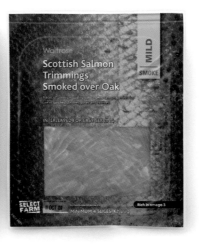

Best of the category

Clothing

Health care

body

Body care

Beauty

Distributors'/Retailers' own brands

Interview with
ADRIAN PIERINI

General Manager, Pierini Partners, Buenos Aires, Argentina
Member of the Pentawards Jury 2009/2010

How do you explain why a jury spread over 12 different countries around the world finally selected the same best designs?

I believe that this phenomenon has to do with a vision of design that has become more global. For a few years now, the way people communicate has transformed and improved a lot, and a consolidated tool like the Internet has made possible an aesthetic and cultural vision that is more general. This allows a unified judgement that wouldn't have been possible some time ago. Matching results between the members of the jury shouldn't surprise us. It should be seen as the natural consequence of a cultural integration that is in constant evolution.

How would you advise young people wishing to become a packaging designer?

Young professionals must understand that becoming a professional designer is not a simple task. It requires a lot of effort, practice, and above all love for what you do.

A packaging designer must know that his role will always debate between what's rational and aesthetic, emotional and commercial, between the satisfaction as a result of creation and the responsibility of generating profitability for your clients.

Those who work in strategic packaging design, like myself, have decided to take a much more analytical vision of our profession, looking for sense in every single resource used in order to accomplish the commercial goals settled. From this position, I would try to transmit to those initiating a career in design that there's a wonderful world to discover, an unlimited universe of shapes, fonts, and colours, but all of this will only make sense with criteria based on information and commitment.

Who impressed you the most in your professional life and why?

There were a lot of designers I loved when I was a student and that, without a doubt, settled the foundation of my current reality. Folon, Glaser, Fukuda were paradigms. Their plasticity, creativity, ability to synthesise and communicate encouraged me to create without boundaries, all pleasure and freedom. Of course, in the '90s the career of designer was new and just starting. Everything related to the rational part of design as we know it today was overlooked. It took years for designers like the American Primo Angeli or Australian Ken Cato to surprise me with high visual quality and a foundation able to combine logic, emotion, and functionality.

Like many Argentinians, your roots are in Europe. What do you think about French design these days?

It's sophisticated, elegant, and precise. French packaging design knew how to grow and become one of the most important referents of world packaging. From classic to outrageous, from elitist to mundane, French projects knew how to handle aesthetic codes with remarkable criteria without leaving functionality and commercial aspects to get overlooked.

I dare say there are several reasons why it has reached such a level of prestige: a rich cultural history, the joy and freshness of a people that made communication one of their most valuable assets. Last but not least, passion. That mobilising factor, so hard to find nowadays, but luckily it remains unaffected in France.

How would you comment on this packaging range: Living proof, Platinum 2009, Best of the category Body?

These packs very much deserve their Platinum Pentawards. They have a delicate balance that combines originality, warmth, sophistication, and also represent unquestionable innovation. An example of good taste, functional and modern, that delivers in respect of commercial goals and also represents a step forward in terms of aesthetic for this category.

Wie erklären Sie sich, dass eine Jury, deren Mitglieder kontinentüber-greifend aus zwölf Ländern stammen, sich schließlich auf dieselben besten Designs einigen konnte?

Ich glaube, dass dieses Phänomen mit einer Sicht auf das Designs zu tun hat, die globaler geworden ist. Die Art und Weise, wie Menschen miteinander kommunizieren, hat sich in den vergangenen Jahren verändert und deutlich verbessert. Das Internet hat sich als Instrument konsolidiert und gestattet eine ästhetische und kulturelle Vision, die allgemeiner und umfassender ist. Das erlaubt eine einheitliche Beurteilung, die noch vor einiger Zeit unmöglich gewesen wäre. Die übereinstimmenden Ergebnisse der Juroren sollten uns daher nicht überraschen. Man könnte sie als die natürliche Konsequenz einer kulturellen Integration betrachten, die einer fortwährenden Entwicklung unterliegt.

Was würden Sie jungen Menschen raten, die Verpackungsdesigner werden wollen?

Berufseinsteiger sollten wissen, dass es keine einfache Aufgabe ist, professioneller Designer zu werden. Es erfordert viel Mühe, praktische Erfahrung und vor allem Liebe zu dem, was man macht.

Ein Verpackungsdesigner muss sich darüber im Klaren sein, dass er in seiner Funktion immer wieder zwischen dem wird abwägen müssen, was rational und ästhetisch oder was emotional und kommerziell ist, zwischen seiner Zufriedenheit mit dem Ergebnis des Gestaltungsprozesses und seiner Verantwortung dafür, für seinen Kunden einen Vorteil zu erzielen.

Wer wie ich im Bereich der strategischen Verpackungsgestaltung arbeitet, hat sich für eine deutlich analytische Sicht auf unseren Beruf entschieden: Wir überprüfen jede einzelne Komponente, mit deren Hilfe die gesteckten kommerziellen Ziele erfüllt werden sollen, auf ihren Bedeutungsgehalt. So gesehen würde ich denen, die in der Designbranche Karriere machen wollen, vermitteln wollen, dass eine wunderbare Welt auf sie wartet, in der es ein unbegrenztes Universum von Formen, Fonts und Farben gibt, die aber nur dann ihren Sinn erfüllt, wenn man ihr Kriterien zugrunde legt, die auf Information und Hingabe basieren.

Wer hat Sie als Profi am meisten beeindruckt und warum?

Als ich noch Student war, gab es viele Designer, die ich verehrte, und das hat zweifellos die Basis meiner derzeitigen Realität gelegt. Folon, Glaser und Fukuda waren Paradigmen. Ihr Formverständnis, ihre Kreativität und ihre Fähigkeit,

etwas zusammenzuführen und zu kommunizieren, haben mich ermutigt, frei von irgendwelchen Grenzen schöpferisch tätig zu werden, aus purer Freude und in aller Freiheit. Natürlich war der Beruf des Designers in den 1990er-Jahren neu und stand gerade erst am Anfang. Alles, was zum rationalen Teil des Designs gehörte, wie wir es heute kennen, fiel unter den Tisch. Es hat Jahre gedauert, bis Designer wie der Amerikaner Primo Angeli oder der Australier Ken Cato mich mit hoher visueller Qualität und einer Grundlage überraschen konnten, die Logik, Emotion und Funktionalität kombiniert.

Wie viele Argentinier haben Sie Ihre Wurzeln in Europa. Was denken Sie über das französische Design heutzutage?

Es ist anspruchsvoll, elegant und präzise. Das französische Package Design hat es verstanden sich zu entwickeln und weltweit zu einem der wichtigsten Vorreiter in puncto Verpackung zu werden. Die französischen Projekte, seien sie klassisch oder außergewöhnlich, elitär oder banal, wussten, wie man mittels bemerkenswerter Kriterien mit ästhetischen Codes umgeht, ohne die Funktionalität und kommerzielle Aspekte hintenüber fallen zu lassen.

Ich will gerne glauben, dass es verschiedene Gründe gibt, warum es ein solches Maß an Prestige erreicht hat: seine reichhaltige kulturelle Geschichte, die Freude und Vorbehaltlosigkeit von Menschen, die Kommunikation zu einem ihrer wertvollsten Güter machen. Doch nicht zuletzt geht es hier um Leidenschaft. Dieser mobilisierende Faktor ist heutzutage ganz schwer zu finden, in Frankreich jedoch ist das zum Glück kein Problem.

Was können Sie zu dieser Verpackungsserie sagen: Living proof, Platin Pentaward 2009, Bestes in der Kategorie „Body"?

Diese Verpackungen sind zu Recht mit dem Platin Pentaward ausgezeichnet worden. Sie weisen eine feinfühlige Ausgewogenheit auf, die Originalität, Wärme und Raffinesse miteinander kombiniert. Außerdem stellen sie fraglos eine Innovation dar. Ein Stück guten Geschmacks, funktional und modern, das seinen Anspruch hinsichtlich kommerzieller Ziele erfüllt und innerhalb dieser Kategorie auch im Hinblick auf die Ästhetik einen Schritt nach vorn repräsentiert.

Interview with
ADRIAN PIERINI

Comment expliquez-vous qu'un jury issu de 12 pays différents des quatre coins du globe ait finalement sélectionné les mêmes meilleurs designs ?

Je pense que ce phénomène est lié à une vision de plus en plus mondialisée du design. Depuis quelques années, la façon dont les gens communiquent s'est transformée et s'est beaucoup améliorée, et l'instrument fédérateur qu'est l'Internet a engendré une vision esthétique et culturelle plus générale. Cela pose les bases pour un jugement unifié qui n'aurait pas été possible il y a quelque temps. La similarité des résultats obtenus par les différents membres du jury ne devrait pas nous surprendre. Il faut la voir comme une conséquence naturelle d'une intégration culturelle en évolution permanente.

Quels conseils donneriez-vous aux jeunes qui veulent devenir designer de packaging ?

Les jeunes qui débutent doivent comprendre que devenir un designer professionnel n'est pas chose facile. Cela demande beaucoup d'efforts, de l'entraînement, et surtout beaucoup de passion.

Un designer de packaging doit savoir qu'il devra toujours arbitrer entre le rationnel et l'esthétique, l'émotionnel et le commercial, entre la satisfaction issue du résultat de la création et la responsabilité de générer des profits pour ses clients.

Ceux qui travaillent dans le domaine du packaging stratégique, comme moi-même, ont décidé d'adopter une vision beaucoup plus analytique de notre métier, et recherchent du sens dans chaque ressource utilisée afin d'atteindre les objectifs commerciaux fixés. À partir de là, j'aimerais essayer de dire à ceux qui commencent leur carrière dans le design qu'il y a un monde merveilleux à découvrir, un univers infini de formes, de polices de caractères et de couleurs, mais tout cela ne prendra de sens qu'avec des critères basés sur l'information et l'engagement.

Dans votre parcours professionnel, qui vous a le plus marqué et pourquoi ?

J'ai aimé beaucoup de designers lorsque j'étais étudiant, et cela a sans aucun doute posé les fondations de ma réalité actuelle. Folon, Glaser, Fukuda ont été de véritables modèles. Leur plasticité, leur créativité, leur capacité à synthétiser et à communiquer m'ont encouragé à créer sans limites, pour le plaisir et en toute liberté. Bien sûr, dans les années 1990, le métier de designer en était à ses débuts. Tout ce qui a trait à la partie rationnelle du design tel que nous le connaissons aujourd'hui était ignoré. Il a fallu des années pour voir apparaître

des designers comme l'Américain Primo Angeli ou l'Australien Ken Cato, qui m'ont surpris avec une grande qualité visuelle et une base capable de combiner logique, émotion et fonctionnalité.

Comme de nombreux Argentins, vos racines sont européennes. Que pensez-vous du design français aujourd'hui ?

Il est sophistiqué, élégant et précis. Le design de packaging français a su évoluer et devenir l'une des références les plus importantes dans le monde du packaging. Classiques ou extravagants, élitistes ou terre-à-terre, les projets français ont su manier les codes esthétiques avec une intelligence remarquable sans pour autant négliger les aspects commerciaux et fonctionnels.

Il y a sans doute plusieurs raisons pour lesquelles le design français a atteint ce niveau de prestige : une histoire culturelle riche, l'enthousiasme et la fraîcheur d'un peuple qui a fait de la communication l'un de ses atouts les plus précieux. Enfin, il ne faut pas oublier la passion, ce facteur de mobilisation, si difficile à trouver de nos jours, mais qui reste heureusement intact en France.

Quel est votre commentaire sur cette gamme de packagings : Living proof, Platinum 2009, meilleur de la catégorie « Soin du corps » ?

Ces packagings ont tout à fait leur place dans les Pentawards Platinum. Ils font preuve d'un équilibre délicat qui combine originalité, chaleur et sophistication, et ils représentent également une innovation incontestable. C'est un exercice de bon goût, efficace et moderne qui fonctionne en termes d'objectifs commerciaux et représente également un pas en avant en termes d'esthétique pour cette catégorie.

For the **Living proof** range of packaging, Wolff Olins of New York dived deep into the world of beauty, ran diagnostic profiles of the competition, and went well beneath the skin of consumer needs to discover real insights. They observed that on many occasions the industry didn't pay attention to the basic needs of consistency, simplicity, confidence, truth, and responsibility. **Living proof, no frizz** is a line of silicone-free, hair-care straightening products. The design is very refined and sober, as too is the lettering. It draws inspiration from up-market cosmetics, and uses shiny white covers and a mouse-grey, matt background, thus differing from other hair products available on the market or in hairdressing salons.

Für die Verpackungsserie **Living proof** vertiefte sich Wolff Olins aus New York in die Welt der Schönheit, führte diagnostische Profile der Wettbewerbssituation durch und hinterfragte peinlich genau die Anforderungen der Verbraucher, um einen echten Erkenntnisgewinn zu erzielen. So stellte sich heraus, dass die Branche vielfach kaum auf grundlegende Bedürfnisse wie Konsistenz, Einfachheit, Vertrauen, Wahrheit und Verantwortung achtete. **Living proof, no frizz** ist eine silikonfreie Pflegelinie zum Glätten der Haare. Das Design ist wie die Beschriftung sehr edel und nüchtern. Es lässt sich von Kosmetikartikeln der gehobenen Preisklasse inspirieren und arbeitet mit glänzend weißen Deckeln und einem mausgrauen, mattierten Korpus. Dadurch unterscheidet es sich von den Haarprodukten, die im freien Handel oder in Friseursalons erhältlich sind.

Pour le packaging de la gamme **Living proof**, l'agence new-yorkaise Wolff Olins a plongé dans le monde de la beauté, a analysé les profils des concurrents et est allée bien au-delà de la surface des besoins des consommateurs pour découvrir de nouvelles perspectives. C'est ainsi que les designers ont remarqué que le secteur négligeait souvent les besoins de base en termes de cohérence, de simplicité, de confiance, de vérité et de responsabilité. **Living proof, no frizz** est une gamme de soins capillaires lissants sans silicone. Le design est très raffiné et sobre, tout comme la typographie. Il s'inspire des cosmétiques haut de gamme, et emploie des bouchons blancs brillants avec un fond gris souris mat, et se démarque ainsi des autres produits capillaires disponibles sur le marché ou dans les salons de coiffure.

LIVING PROOF
NO FRIZZ

Creative Director: Todd Simmons; *Design:* Tiziana Haug, Sung Kim
Production Director: Beth Kovalsky; *Production Manager:* Michele Miller
Copywriters: Mary Ellen Muckerman, Carmine Montalto
Strategist: Mary Ellen Muckerman; *Account Director:* Veronica Otto
Account Manager: Erin Roh
Company: Wolff Olins
Country: USA
Category: Best of the category Body

PLATINUM PENTAWARD 2009

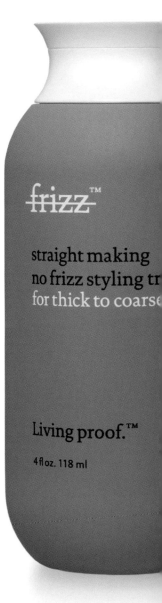

frizz™

straight making
no frizz styling spray
for fine to medium hair

Living proof.™

3.4 fl oz. 100 ml

frizz™ straight making
no frizz styling spray
for fine to medium hair

Living proof.™

frizz™ wave shaping
curl defining
no frizz styling treatment
for thick to coarse hair

Living proof.™

These **Schwarzkopf Professional OSiS**+ hairdressing gels are packaged in containers in boxes made of cardboard printed with different textures which exemplify the different results obtained: matt, strong, rough, light, gloss, and smooth. The project was intended to be simple, elegant, and precise, reflecting the professional quality of the products.

Diese **OSiS**+-**Haargels von Schwarzkopf** werden abgefüllt und dann in Kartons verpackt, auf denen in unterschiedlicher Beschaffenheit die jeweils zu erwartenden Ergebnisse veranschaulicht werden: matt, kräftig, rau, leicht, glänzend und glatt. Das Projekt sollte einfach, elegant und präzise sein und dabei die professionelle Qualität der Produkte widerspiegeln.

Ces gels de coiffage **Schwarzkopf Professional OSiS**+ sont conditionnés dans des pots présentés dans des boîtes en carton où les textures imprimées illustrent les résultats des produits : mat, fort, rugueux, léger, brillant et lisse. Le projet devait être simple, élégant et précis, pour refléter la qualité professionnelle des produits.

SCHWARZKOPF PROFESSIONAL
OSIS+ DESIGN MIX

Design: Andrea Gadesmann, Jordy Huisman, Martijn Doolaard
Company: Design Bridge Ltd.
Country: The Netherlands
Category: Best of the category Body

PLATINUM PENTAWARD 2008

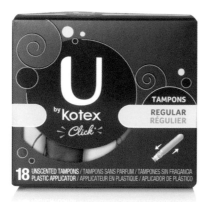
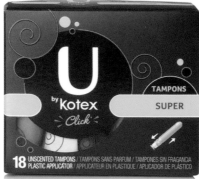
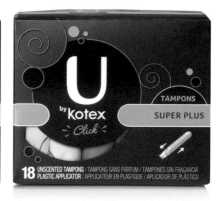

U BY KOTEX

Design: CBX design team
Company: CBX New York
Country: USA
Category: Best of the category Body

PLATINUM PENTAWARD 2010

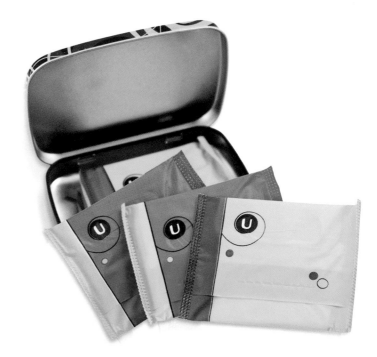

HERE! SOD T-SHIRT PACKAGING

Design: Somchana Kangwarnjit, Passorn Subcharoenpun, Chidchanok Laohawattanakul, Mathurada Bejrananda
Company: Prompt Design
Country: Thailand
Category: Clothing (clothing, shoes, underwear, hosiery, haberdashery, etc.)

GOLD PENTAWARD 2010

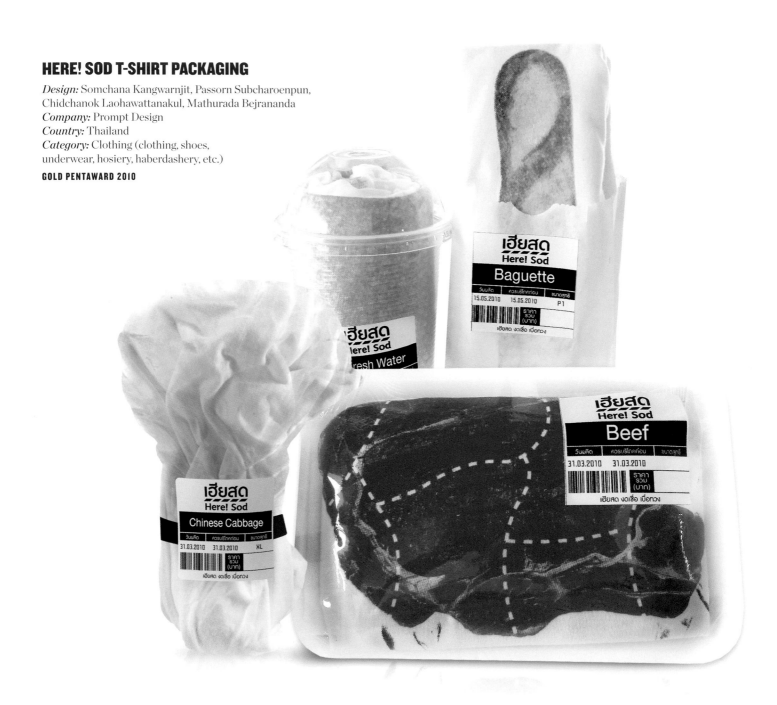

Here! Sod T-Shirt Packaging takes design clues from food packaging used to sell groceries and, as here, presents a new line of T-shirts sold in a simple and distinctive way to look like the food packaging found in supermarkets. Each shirt in the product line is sold in a different form of packaging to make them more eye-catching and to create a more engaging shopping experience.

Die von **Here! Sod T-Shirt** gestaltete Verpackung von T-Shirts greift das Design von Umverpackungen für Lebensmittel auf. Hier wird auf einfache, aber unverwechselbare Weise eine neue Produktlinie mit T-Shirts präsentiert, indem man sie wie Produkte aus dem Supermarkt aussehen lässt. Jedes T-Shirt dieser Kollektion wird in einer andersartigen Verpackungsform angeboten: Das fällt ins Auge und bietet eine unterhaltsame Kauferfahrung.

Here! L'emballage des tee-shirts **Here! Sod T-Shirt** s'inspire des emballages utilisés dans l'alimentation et, comme ici, présente une nouvelle ligne de tee-shirts avec simplicité et originalité, en leur donnant l'aspect des produits alimentaires que l'on trouve en supermarché. Chaque tee-shirt de la ligne est vendu dans un emballage différent, pour attirer l'œil et rendre le processus d'achat plus ludique.

ITO
KOBO ORIZA

Art Director: Hirokazu Kobayashi, Haruna Yamada
Designer: Hirokazu Kobayashi, Haruna Yamada, Satoko Manabe
Management: Riho Kokubu
Company: Spread Ltd.
Country: Japan
Category: Clothing (clothing, shoes, underwear, hosiery, haberdashery, etc.)

SILVER PENTAWARD 2010

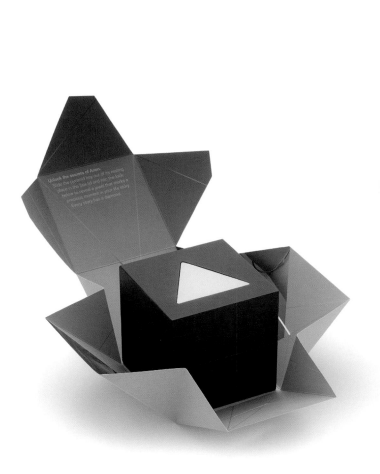

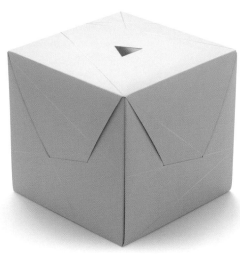

ANON

Creative Director: Natalie Chung
Creative Partner: Jonathan Ford
Designer: Will Gladden; *Strategy:* Georgia Levison
Copywriter: Sylvie Saunders
Company: Pearlfisher
Country: UK
Category: Clothing (clothing, shoes,
underwear, hosiery, haberdashery, etc.)

BRONZE PENTAWARD 2010

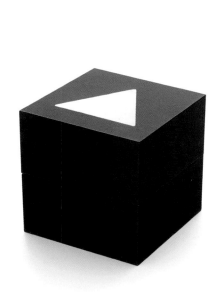

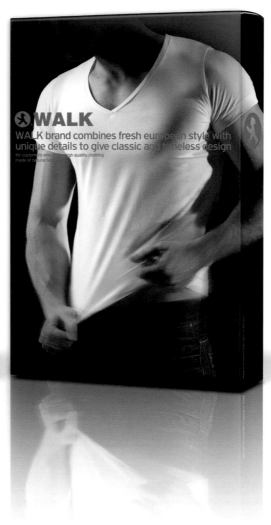
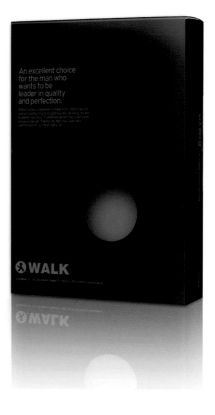

WALK SOCKS UNDERWEAR

Design: Gregory Tsaknakis
Illustration: Ionna Papaioannou
Company: Mouse Graphics
Country: Greece
Category: Clothing (clothing, shoes, underwear, hosiery, haberdashery, etc.)

BRONZE PENTAWARD 2010

DARKDESIGN PACKAGING FOR T-SHIRT COLLECTION

Design: Dima Zeibert, Larisa Mamleeva
Company: DarkDesignGroup
Country: Russia
Category: Clothing (clothing, shoes, underwear, hosiery, haberdashery, etc.)

SILVER PENTAWARD 2009

SPRUNK JANSEN

Design: Ping-pong design team
Company: Ping-pong Design
Country: The Netherlands
Category: Health care
(OTC, pharmaceuticals, vitamins,
optical, toilet paper, tissues,
feminine hygiene, diapers, etc.)

SILVER PENTAWARD 2009

RED DRY SKIN™
Relieves red, dry and itchy skin

SPRUNK-JANSEN®

FEMININE™
Spices up your love life

SPRUNK-JANSEN®

CHOLEVEL™
Maintains a healthy fat balance
in the blood

SPRUNK-JANSEN®

SOMINEX

Creative Director: Claire Robertshaw
Designer: Hannah Ferguson
Company: Design Bridge Ltd.
Country: UK
Category: Health care
(OTC, pharmaceuticals, vitamins, optical, toilet paper, tissues, feminine hygiene, diapers, etc.)

SILVER PENTAWARD 2010

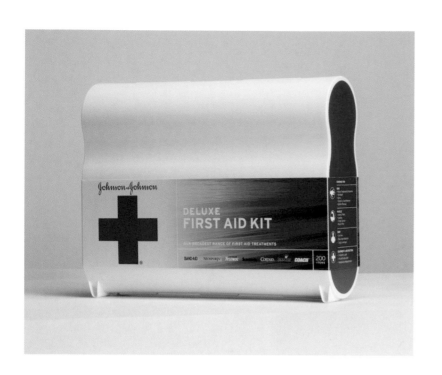

JOHNSON & JOHNSON
FIRST AID KIT

Design: Harry Allen
(Johnson & Johnson, Global Design Strategy Office)
Company: Harry Allen Design
Country: USA
Category: Health care
(OTC, pharmaceuticals, vitamins, optical,
toilet paper, tissues, feminine hygiene, diapers, etc.)

BRONZE PENTAWARD 2009

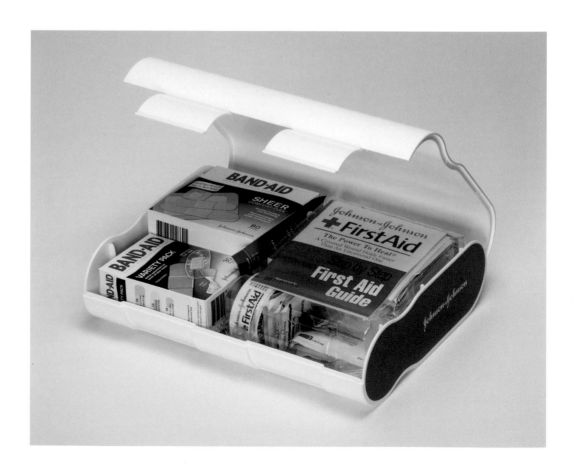

This project by Ciulla Associates for **Colgate** was targeted at consumers who needed portable oral care, and the package aimed to convey exactly such a portability and convenience platform: "Just Brushed Clean, Anytime, Anywhere." The design had to communicate core values of this demographic with connectivity to social need-states and interactivity behaviour at shelf.

Dieses Projekt von Ciulla Associates für **Colgate** richtet sich an Konsumenten, die ein mobiles Zahnpflege-set benötigen, und die Verpackung sollte exakt vermitteln, wie leicht tragbar und praktisch das Produkt ist: „Einfach sauber putzen – überall und jederzeit". Das Design sollte zentrale Werte der demographischen Zielgruppe ver-mitteln. Dabei sollte es sich mit dem sozialen Bedürfnis-status verbinden und das interaktive Verhalten am Regal berücksichtigen.

Ce projet de Ciulla Associates pour **Colgate** ciblait les consommateurs qui ont besoin d'accessoires d'hygiène buccale transportables, et l'emballage devait souligner ces aspects de portabilité et de commodité : « Des dents propres partout, tout le temps. » Le design devait commu-niquer les valeurs essentielles de ce public en les reliant aux besoins sociaux et à l'interactivité dans les rayons.

COLGATE
WISP

Art Director: Sam J. Ciulla
Designer: Julie Wineski
Company: Ciulla Assoc.
Country: USA
Category: Body care
GOLD PENTAWARD 2009

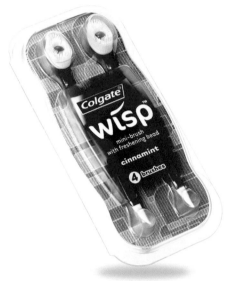

REXONA ANTIPERSPIRANT DEODORANT FOR MEN

Design: Adrian Pierini
Company: Pierini Partners
Country: Argentina
Category: Body care

GOLD PENTAWARD 2008

Pierini Partners designed the packaging for Quantum, **Rexona**'s latest deodorant, based on a futuristic and technological concept, using vivid lines, bright colours, and science-fiction-like graphic resources. The symmetrical structure and squared design try not only to communicate modernism and high efficiency, but also technology in its maximum expression. Moreover, the use of special ink applied to the aluminium hardware makes the pack glow and stand out, building in the consumer's mind an idea of science.

Pierini Partners gestalteten die Verpackung für das neue Deo von **Rexona** namens „Quantum". Das Design basiert auf einem futuristischen und technologischen Konzept und arbeitet mit lebhaften Linien, leuchtenden Farben und einer Science-Fiction-ähnlichen Bildsprache. Die symmetrische Struktur und das quadratische Design wollen nicht nur Modernität und höchste Effektivität vermitteln, sondern auch die Technologie optimal ausdrücken. Außerdem lässt der Einsatz einer speziellen Tinte, die auf dem Aluminiumkorpus aufgebracht wird, die Verpackung leuchten. Dadurch fällt sie auf und bringt in der Vorstellung des Konsumenten das Produkt zusätzlich in einen wissenschaftlichen Kontext.

L'agence Pierini Partners a conçu le packaging de Quantum, le dernier déodorant de **Rexona**, en se basant sur un concept futuriste et technologique avec des lignes fortes, des couleurs vives et une inspiration graphique qui puise dans l'univers de la science-fiction. La structure symétrique et le design carré n'essaient pas seulement de transmettre les notions de modernité et d'efficacité, mais également de technologie dans son expression la plus pure. Une encre spéciale appliquée sur le matériau aluminium fait briller l'objet et le rend plus visible, tout en introduisant l'idée de science dans l'esprit du consommateur.

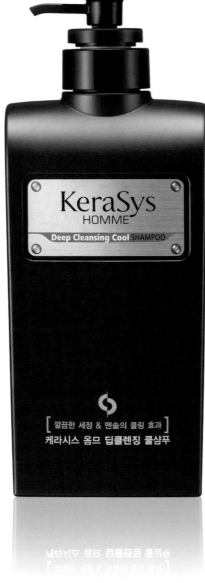

KERASYS HOMME

Design: Hyun-Keun Son, Hyun-Jin Koo
Company: Aekyung Industrial
Country: South Korea
Category: Body care

SILVER PENTAWARD 2009

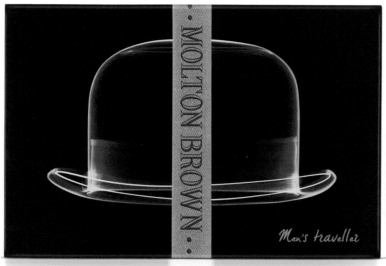
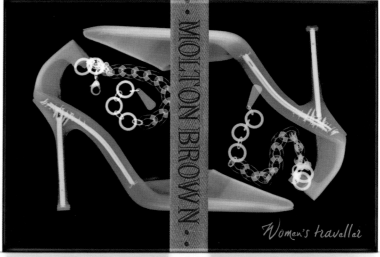

MOLTON BROWN
TRAVELLER

Design: Bronwen Edwards, Keely Jackman
Company: Brandhouse
Country: UK
Category: Body care

SILVER PENTAWARD 2010

REXONA
MEN

Design: Adrian Pierini
Company: Pierini Partners
Country: Argentina
Category: Body care

BRONZE PENTAWARD 2009

LIESE
IRON MAKE COLLECTION

Creative Director: Masako Hirasawa
Art Director/Designer: Akiko Saito
Designer: Yohei Shimura
Company: Kao Corporation
Country: Japan
Category: Body care

SILVER PENTAWARD 2010

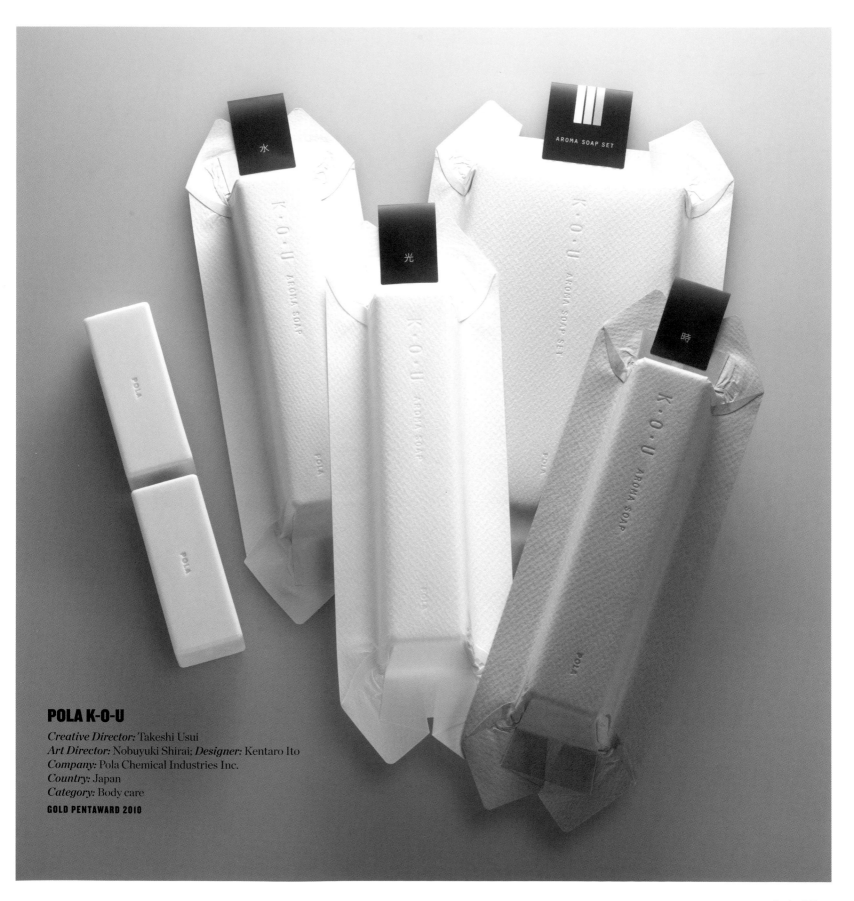

POLA K-O-U

Creative Director: Takeshi Usui
Art Director: Nobuyuki Shirai; *Designer:* Kentaro Ito
Company: Pola Chemical Industries Inc.
Country: Japan
Category: Body care

GOLD PENTAWARD 2010

LUCIDO-L DESIGNING POT

Design: Zenji Hashimoto
Company: Cloud8 Inc.
Country: Japan
Category: Body care

SILVER PENTAWARD 2009

UNILEVER
LUX

Creative Directors: Gustavo Piqueira, Marco Aurélio Kato
Company: Rex Design
Country: Brazil
Category: Body care

BRONZE PENTAWARD 2009

MAYBREEZE

Design: JooHyun Sohn, BoGyeong Jung (K-C Design), Woofer Design
Company: Yuhan-Kimberly; *Country:* South Korea
Category: Body care

BRONZE PENTAWARD 2010

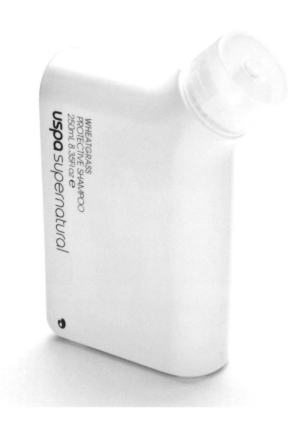

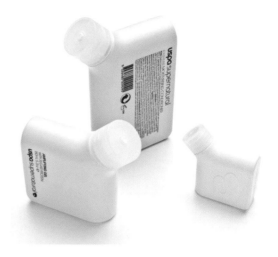

USPA

Design: Brenan Liston, Jonnie Vigar, Todd Gill, Mark Evans
Company: Container Ltd.; *Country:* Australia
Category: Body care

BRONZE PENTAWARD 2009

LEIF

Design: Brenan Liston, Jonnie Vigar, Mark Evans
Company: Container Ltd.; *Country:* Australia
Category: Body care

BRONZE PENTAWARD 2010

BOLT BARBER

Design: Simon Thorneycroft, Nicholas Leebert
Company: Perspective Branding
Country: USA
Category: Body care

BRONZE PENTAWARD 2010

DESIGN TEX

Design: Aoshi Kudo
Company: Communication Design Laboratory
Country: Japan
Category: Body care

BRONZE PENTAWARD 2010

EST

Art Director: Itsurou Yumoto
Designer: Akio Toyoda
Company: Kao Corporation
Country: Japan
Category: Beauty
(perfumes, cosmetics, make-up,
body decoration, etc.)

GOLD PENTAWARD 2009

AUBE

Art Director: Hideo Akiba
Designer: Hanae Yoshikiyo
Company: Kao Corporation
Country: Japan
Category: Beauty
(perfumes, cosmetics, make-up,
body decoration, etc.)

SILVER PENTAWARD 2009

KJÆR WEIS

Design: Marc Atlan
Company: Marc Atlan Design Inc.
Country: USA
Category: Beauty
(perfumes, cosmetics, make-up,
body decoration, etc.)

GOLD PENTAWARD 2010

The container form, crafted to articulate both instant action and translucence, portrays an image of clear stream-water flowing downwards. The flow of light generated by the overall silhouette prompts premonitions of whitening effects steeped in the sensation of sheer speed. The gentle bulge at the middle of the bottle, meanwhile, personifies the rich energy accumulated in the skin, and gives a pleasant sensation when taken in the hand. Moreover, the refillable container contributes to reducing the waste stream.

Die Behälterform vermittelt sowohl sofortige Einsetzbarkeit als auch Lichtdurchlässigkeit und transportiert das Bild von klarem, nach unten strömendem Wasser. Die Art, wie das Licht durch die gesamte Silhouette fällt, lässt an rasant wirksame Aufhellungseffekte denken. Die sanfte Auswölbung der Flaschenmitte verkörpert gleichzeitig die kraftvolle Energie, die sich in der Haut anreichert, und verleiht ein sehr angenehmes Gefühl, wenn man die Flasche in die Hand nimmt. Dass der Behälter nachfüllbar ist, trägt zur Abfallvermeidung bei.

La forme du flacon, conçue pour exprimer les notions d'action immédiate et de translucidité, représente un cours d'eau s'écoulant vers le bas. Le flux de lumière généré par la silhouette générale évoque l'effet blanchissant, et une sensation de vitesse fulgurante. Le léger renflement au milieu de la bouteille symbolise quant à lui la riche énergie accumulée dans la peau, et est agréable à prendre en main. De plus, le récipient rechargeable aide à réduire les déchets.

POLA WHITISSIMO

Creative Director: Takeshi Usui; *Art Director:* Takashi Matsui
Designers: Yushi Watanabe, Kanako Maruhashi, Momoko Usui
Company: Pola Chemical Industries Inc.
Country: Japan
Category: Beauty (perfumes, cosmetics, make-up, body decoration, etc.)

SILVER PENTAWARD 2010

AGLAIRA

Creative Director: Takeshi Usui
Art Director: Chiharu Suzuki
Design: Nobuyuki Shirai, Kazuhiko Kimishita, Emi Yabusaki
Company: Pola Chemical Industries Inc.
Country: Japan
Category: Beauty
(perfumes, cosmetics, make-up,
body decoration, etc.)

SILVER PENTAWARD 2009

HAKU

Design: Tetsuro Kanegae, Yoji Nobuto, Yuka Nagasaki
Company: Shiseido Co., Ltd.
Country: Japan
Category: Beauty (perfumes, cosmetics, make-up, body decoration, etc.)

SILVER PENTAWARD 2010

BOOTS ORIGINAL BEAUTY FORMULA

Design: Camilla Lilliesköld, Caroline Clark, Tone Skree
Company: Camilla Lilliesköld Design & Art Direction
Country: UK
Category: Distributors'/Retailers' own brands

SILVER PENTAWARD 2009

MINT

Design: Arimino Co., Ltd.; Another Report Co., Ltd.; Yasuo Kiuchi, XYZ Creation
Company: Arimino Co., Ltd.
Country: Japan
Category: Beauty (perfumes, cosmetics, make-up, body decoration, etc.)

BRONZE PENTAWARD 2010

LIESE
DESIGNING JELLY

Creative Directors: Mitsutoshi Yoshida, Naoto Katahira; *Art Director:* Masako Hirasawa
Design: Akiko Saito, Yohei Shimura
Company: Kao Corporation
Country: Japan
Category: Beauty
(perfumes, cosmetics, make-up, body decoration, etc.)

BRONZE PENTAWARD 2009

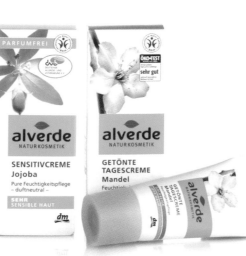

ALVERDE

Design: Simone Wössner, Knut Hartmann
Company: khdesign
Country: Germany
Category: Distributors'/Retailers' own brands

BRONZE PENTAWARD 2009

CACHAREL
JELLIES

Design: Kheireddine Sidhoum
Company: The Brand Union
Country: France
Category: Beauty (perfumes, cosmetics, make-up, body decoration, etc.)

BRONZE PENTAWARD 2010

ORIFLAME VERY ME

Creative Director: André Hindersson
Art Director: Cajsa Bratt
Production Designer: Monica Holm
Production Manager: Christine Schönborg
Company: Designkontoret Silver KB
Country: Sweden
Category: Beauty (perfumes, cosmetics, make-up, body decoration, etc.)

BRONZE PENTAWARD 2010

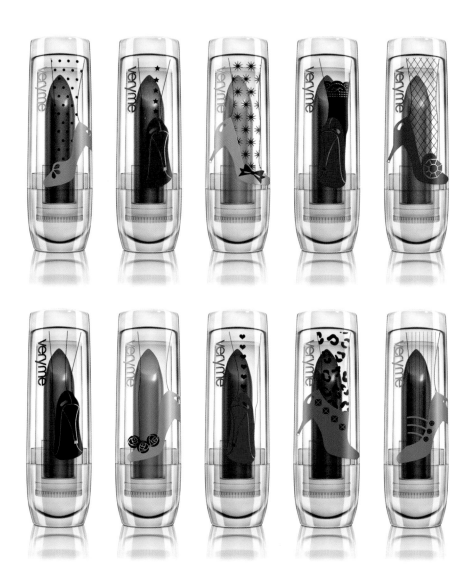

ORIFLAME VISIONS V*

Creative Director: André Hindersson
Senior Designer/Illustration: Cajsa Bratt
Project Manager: André Hindersson
Production Manager: Louise Stierna
Company: Designkontoret Silver KB
Country: Sweden
Category: Beauty
(perfumes, cosmetics, make-up, body decoration etc.)

BRONZE PENTAWARD 2009

Best of the category

Perfumes

Cosmetics

Spirits

Fine wines, champagne

luxury

Gourmet food

Casks, coffrets, gift boxes

Limited editions, limited series, event creations

Jewellery, watches, fashion garments

MARK COWAN

Chairman, Cowan Group of companies, Australia
Member of the Pentawards Jury 2008/2009/2010

How do you explain why a jury spread over 12 different countries around the world finally selected the same best designs?

Today, more than ever, the world is simply a global village. The aspirations of consumers in China are very similar to those of consumers in the USA and so on. So in reality it is not surprising that the judges came to similar conclusions about those pieces of communication that excelled in their rational messages and emotional connection.

Communication in its clearest form is rewarded and the barriers of individual languages are irrelevant.

Conversely, poor communication is pretty easy to mark down. Having said that, most of the entries were at least good or competent – the trick is to make good into great, and those that achieved that were rewarded.

How would you advise young people wishing to become a packaging designer?

To be successful in anything, you need passion. You need to love what you do. If you love to solve problems and feel you would enjoy using design to convince people of the benefit of a particular product, if you like Brands, if you are motivated to find the right big idea to communicate a proposition beautifully, then packaging design is a really good career choice. You will get a variety of different brands and categories on which to work. You will be given the opportunity to influence the big picture and really make a difference to the success of brands. It's also pretty cool that the medium is so public. It's good to go into a supermarket or local store and see your work is being chosen. From a personal perspective, I have been in packaging design for about 25 years and I am still as passionate about it as ever.

If you are thinking about a career in packaging design, don't just think about it. Do it – it's a great life and you get paid to do it.

Who impressed you the most in your professional life and why?

Everyone needs a mentor and mine was the man who founded Safeway in Australia. His name is Bill Pratt (now retired) and he pioneered so many retail initiatives in this country. He was a great inspiration to me, not just because of his many achievements and simple philosophy, but because of his manner. He was truly an old-fashioned gentleman whose word was his bond and while he could be ruthless, he was always fair. The last time I spoke to him I asked him about the tough times in retail. His response was that retail is always

tough, and to be successful you have to be better at it than the other retailers. A simple answer that sums up the secret to business success in any industry.

Your company, Cowan Design, is present in many countries around the world, but not in the USA. So how do you see design in the USA today?

US design is perfect for the US market, because it works. It is responsible and safe. It is typically very sound from a strategic and Brand viewpoint.

There are some wonderful design practices in the USA, which produce great work. I feel it is unfair to try to judge US work en masse as it is done by individuals for individual briefs and as per anywhere in the world, the final results vary from amazing to terrible.

"L'Or de Jean Martell" is a luxury packaging, what would you say about it?

A beautiful combination of materials and processes combine to surround the crystal-encased central drop. The final result is refined, elegant, and sophisticated.

From looking at it there is no doubt it holds a special cognac. I imagine if you were lucky enough to own a bottle, you would get as much pleasure from looking at it as you would from drinking it.

A wonderful result.

Wie erklären Sie sich, dass eine Jury, deren Mitglieder kontinentübergreifend aus zwölf Ländern stammen, sich schließlich auf dieselben besten Designs einigen konnte?

Heutzutage ist die Welt mehr denn je nichts weiter als ein globales Dorf. Die Erwartungen der Konsumenten in China ähneln stark denen der Konsumenten in den USA usw. Also überrascht es nicht wirklich, dass die Juroren bei Arbeiten der Kommunikation, die sich in ihren rationalen Botschaften und ihrer emotionalen Ansprache besonders hervortun, zu ähnlichen Schlussfolgerungen gekommen sind.

Kommunikation in ihrer reinsten Form wird belohnt, und Sprachgrenzen werden irrelevant.

Umgekehrt erkennt man auch ohne weiteres eine schlechte Kommunikation. Vor diesem Hintergrund sind die meisten eingereichten Beiträge zumindest gut oder kompetent. Der Trick besteht darin, aus Gutem Großartiges zu machen; wem das gelingt, der wird belohnt.

Was würden Sie jungen Menschen raten, die Verpackungsdesigner werden wollen?

Um erfolgreich zu sein, egal in welchem Bereich, braucht man Leidenschaft. Sie müssen das lieben, was Sie machen. Wenn Sie gerne Probleme lösen und es offenbar genießen, Menschen durch Gestaltung vom Vorteil eines bestimmten Produkts zu überzeugen, wenn Sie Marken mögen und wenn Sie motiviert sind, die passende große Idee zu finden, um eine Aussage ansprechend zu kommunizieren, dann ist Verpackungsdesign wirklich eine gute Karriereentscheidung. Sie werden eine Auswahl unterschiedlicher Marken und Kategorien kennenlernen, an denen Sie arbeiten können. Sie erhalten die Chance, den Gesamtzusammenhang zu beeinflussen und im Hinblick auf den Erfolg von Marken wirklich etwas zu bewirken. Außerdem ist es ganz schön cool, dass dieses Medium so öffentlich ist. Es ist toll, in den Supermarkt oder in ein Kaufhaus zu gehen und zu sehen, dass die eigenen Arbeiten gekauft werden. Ich persönlich bin schon seit 25 Jahren im Verpackungsdesign tätig und habe immer noch die gleiche Leidenschaft dafür wie eh und je.

Wenn Sie eine Karriere in der Verpackungsgestaltung erwägen, dann denken Sie nicht bloß darüber nach. Machen Sie es – das Leben mit diesem Beruf ist große Klasse, und Sie werden dafür auch noch bezahlt.

Wer hat Sie als Profi am meisten beeindruckt und warum?

Jeder braucht seinen Mentor, und meiner war der Mann, der in Australien Safeway gegründet hat. Sein Name ist Bill Pratt und er ist nun im Ruhestand. Er hat bei sehr vielen Einzelhandelsinitiativen in seinem Land Pionierarbeit geleistet. Für mich war er eine große Inspiration, nicht nur wegen seiner vielen Erfolge und seiner einfachen Philosophie, sondern aufgrund seiner Art. Er war wirklich ein altmodischer Gentleman, für den sein Wort bindend war, und obwohl er auch rücksichtslos sein konnte, war er immer fair. Als ich das letzte Mal mit ihm sprach, fragte ich ihn nach den harten Zeiten im Einzelhandel damals. Seine Antwort lautete, dass es im Einzelhandel immer hart ist; um erfolgreich zu sein, muss man besser sein als die anderen. Eine einfache Antwort, die das Geheimnis des geschäftlichen Erfolgs in jeder Branche zusammenfasst.

Ihre Firma Cowan Design ist in vielen Ländern weltweit vertreten, aber nicht in den USA. Was halten Sie nun vom heutigen amerikanischen Design?

Amerikanisches Design ist perfekt für den amerikanischen Markt, weil es funktioniert. Es ist verantwortungsbewusst und sicher. Aus strategischer und Markenperspektive ist es in der Regel sehr solide.

Es gibt einige wunderbare Designpraktiker in den USA, die ausgezeichnete Arbeiten abliefern. Ich habe das Gefühl, dass es unfair wäre, die US-amerikanischen Arbeiten *en masse* zu beurteilen, weil sie von Individuen aufgrund individueller Briefings gemacht werden. Und wie überall auf der Welt rangieren die Ergebnisse, die dabei herauskommen, zwischen erstaunlich und schrecklich.

„L'Or de Jean Martell" ist eine Luxusverpackung. Was können Sie darüber sagen?

Eine wunderschöne Verbindung von Materialien und Prozessen, um den zentralen Tropfen in Kristall einzufassen. Das Endergebnis ist raffiniert, elegant und sehr anspruchsvoll.

Allein schon vom Anblick her gibt es keinen Zweifel, dass sich darin ein ganz spezieller Cognac verbirgt. Wenn man das Glück hat, eine solche Flasche zu besitzen, dann hat man meiner Ansicht nach beim Anblick der Flasche genauso viel Freude, als wenn man daraus trinkt.

Ein wunderbares Ergebnis!

MARK COWAN

Comment expliquez-vous qu'un jury issu de 12 pays différents des quatre coins du globe ait finalement sélectionné les mêmes meilleurs designs ?

Aujourd'hui plus que jamais, le monde est tout simplement un village global. Les aspirations des consommateurs chinois ressemblent beaucoup à celles des consommateurs américains, etc. Alors en réalité, il n'est pas surprenant que les juges arrivent à des conclusions similaires sur les exercices de communication qui excellent à transmettre un message rationnel et à établir une connexion émotionnelle.

La communication sous sa forme la plus pure est récompensée et les barrières de la langue n'ont aucune importance.

Inversement, une communication de mauvaise qualité est toujours facile à repérer. Ceci étant dit, la plupart des candidatures étaient au moins bonnes ou satisfaisantes, mais le truc, c'est de prendre quelque chose de bon et de le rendre excellent, et c'est ceux qui sont arrivés à faire cela qui ont été récompensés.

Quels conseils donneriez-vous aux jeunes qui veulent devenir designer de packaging ?

Pour avoir du succès, dans quelque domaine que ce soit, il faut être passionné. Il faut aimer ce que l'on fait. Si vous aimez résoudre des problèmes et que vous pensez que vous aimerez utiliser le design pour convaincre les gens des avantages d'un certain produit, si vous aimez les marques, si vous aimez rechercher une bonne idée pour transmettre un message avec style, alors le design de packaging est vraiment un métier pour vous. Vous travaillerez sur différentes marques et catégories de produits. Vous aurez l'opportunité d'influencer le cours des choses et le succès de la marque. Le fait que ce support de communication soit très public est aussi assez plaisant. C'est gratifiant d'aller dans un supermarché ou un magasin de quartier et de voir des consommateurs choisir votre travail. D'un point de vue personnel, je travaille dans le design de packaging depuis 25 ans environ, et mon travail me passionne toujours autant.

Si vous envisagez de travailler dans ce secteur, ne vous contentez pas d'y réfléchir. Faites-le. C'est une vie formidable, et on vous paie pour la vivre.

Dans votre parcours professionnel, qui vous a le plus marqué et pourquoi ?

Tout le monde a besoin d'un mentor, et le mien était l'homme qui a fondé Safeway en Australie. Il s'appelle Bill Pratt (aujourd'hui il a pris sa retraite), et il est à l'origine de nombreuses initiatives innovantes dans le domaine des points de vente dans ce pays. Il m'a beaucoup inspiré, non seulement à cause de ses nombreux succès et de la simplicité de sa philosophie, mais aussi à cause de son attitude. C'était vraiment un gentleman à l'ancienne, il n'avait qu'une parole et, même s'il pouvait être impitoyable, il était toujours juste. La dernière fois que je l'ai rencontré, je lui ai demandé de me parler de l'époque où les temps étaient durs dans le commerce. Il m'a répondu que dans ce domaine les temps sont toujours difficiles, et que pour avoir du succès il faut être meilleur que les autres vendeurs. C'est une réponse simple qui résume le secret du succès commercial dans n'importe quel secteur.

Votre société, Cowan Design, est présente dans de nombreux pays du monde entier, mais pas aux États-Unis. Que pensez-vous du design américain aujourd'hui ?

Le design américain est parfait pour le marché américain, parce qu'il fonctionne. Il est responsable et sûr. En général, il est très solide du point de vue de la stratégie de marque.

Il y a aux États-Unis quelques agences de design fantastiques, qui font un excellent travail. Je trouve qu'il serait injuste d'essayer de juger le travail produit aux États-Unis en mettant tout dans le même panier, car il est réalisé par des individus, pour des missions individuelles et, comme partout dans le monde, les résultats finaux peuvent être admirables ou horribles.

« L'Or de Jean Martell » est un packaging de luxe, que pourriez-vous dire à son sujet ?

Une combinaison magnifique de matériaux et de processus sert d'écrin à la goutte centrale enchâssée dans le cristal. Le résultat final est raffiné, élégant et sophistiqué.

On voit au premier coup d'œil qu'il contient un cognac très particulier. J'imagine que si on a la chance d'en posséder une bouteille, on a autant de plaisir à la regarder qu'à en boire le contenu.

Un résultat admirable.

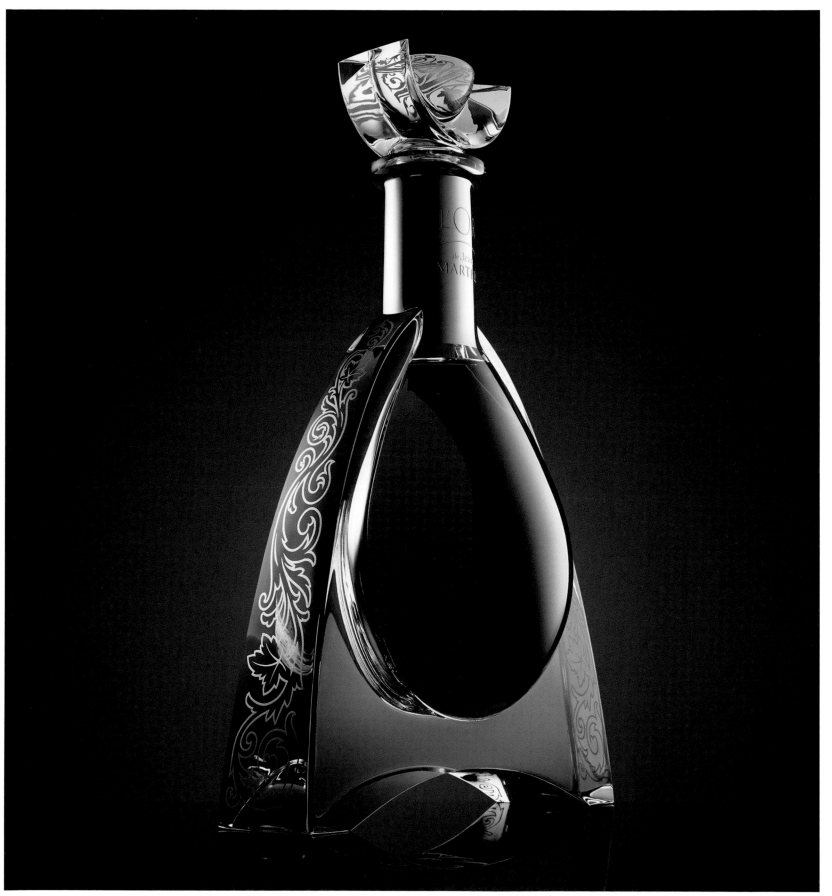

Created by Dragon Rouge Paris, **"L'Or de Jean Martell"** is a very luxuriously designed bottle for a rare cognac. With this conspicuously up-market product Martell pursues its development strategy in the luxury market to meet the demands of elite customers distributed in different cultural environments such as Russia and Asia. The bottle is the combination of creative and technical prowess, developed in cooperation with the Cristallerie de Sèvres. By building on the concept of perfect harmony as expressed through the "golden number" the agency imagined a bottle fashioned from pure crystal in which the precious liquid is concentrated in a single droplet suspended by an arch decorated with arabesques in gold. Produced in a very limited edition, each bottle is sold for €3,000.

„L'Or de Jean Martell" wurde von Dragon Rouge in Paris geschaffen und ist eine außergewöhnlich luxuriös gestaltete Flasche für einen seltenen Cognac. Mit diesem auffallenden Produkt für ein gehobenes Marktsegment treibt Martell seine Entwicklungsstrategie im Markt der Luxusgüter voran. Hier soll den Anforderungen der Elitekunden entsprochen werden, die in verschiedenen kulturellen Kontexten wie Russland und Asien leben. Die Flasche ist eine Kombination aus kreativem und technischem Können und wurde in Zusammenarbeit mit der Cristallerie de Sèvres entwickelt. Hier setzt man auf das Konzept einer perfekten Harmonie, wie beim „Goldenen Schnitt". Die Agentur stellte eine aus reinem Kristall gefertigte Flasche vor, in der die kostbare Flüssigkeit von einem einzigen Tropfen umschlossen wird, der unterhalb eines mit goldenen Arabesken dekorierten Bogens hängt. Jede Flasche erscheint in einer sehr begrenzten Auflage und kostet 3.000 Euro.

Créée par Dragon Rouge Paris, « L'Or de Jean Martell » est une bouteille au design extrêmement luxueux, pour un cognac rare. Avec ce produit ostensiblement très haut de gamme, Martell poursuit sa stratégie de développement sur le marché du luxe pour répondre aux besoins d'une clientèle d'élite qui évolue dans des environnements culturels divers, notamment en Russie et en Asie. La bouteille allie prouesse créative et technique, et a été développée en collaboration avec la Cristallerie de Sèvres. En partant du concept d'harmonie parfaite exprimé par le « nombre d'or », l'agence a imaginé une bouteille en cristal pur, où le précieux liquide est concentré en une seule goutte suspendue à une arche décorée d'arabesques en or. Chaque bouteille de cette édition très limitée est vendue 3 000 €.

PERNOD RICARD
L'OR DE JEAN MARTELL

Design: Angelique Lecussan
Company: Dragon Rouge
Country: France
Category: Best of the category Luxury

PLATINUM PENTAWARD 2009

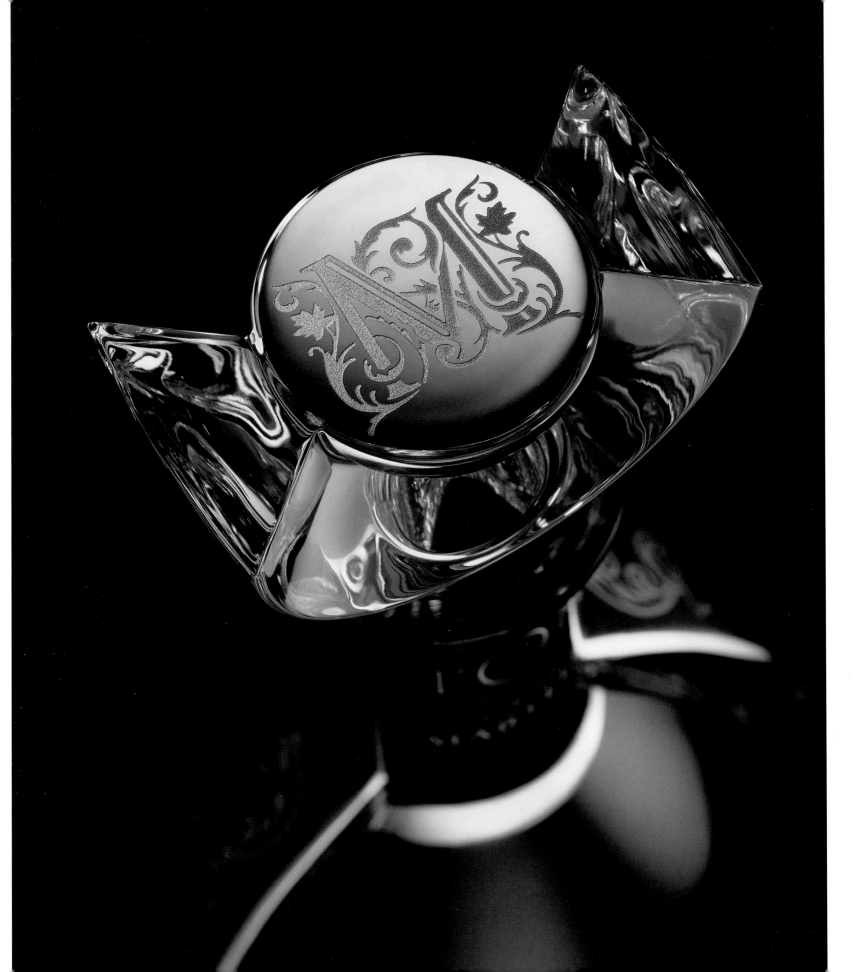

This project developed by Dentsu Kyushu was commissioned by **Yaoki** Sake and resulted in a very elegant bottle, with a white refined shape and a rounded base, allowing it to regain its vertical position by itself. The product is made from potatoes, and the packaging is made from the famous Arita porcelain, from the Japanese island of Kyushu. The message was drawn from an ancient proverb that says "If you fall down seven times, get up the eighth time".

Dieses von Dentsu Kyushu entwickelte Projekt wurde von **Yaoki** Sake in Auftrag gegeben und führte zu einer sehr eleganten Flasche mit einer raffinierten weißen Form und einer runden Basis. Aufgrund dieser Form stellt sie sich immer wieder von selbst auf. Das Getränk wird aus Kartoffeln hergestellt. Die Flasche besteht aus dem berühmten Arita-Porzellan von der japanischen Insel Kyushu. Die Botschaft leitet sich von dem alten Sprichwort ab: „Wenn du siebenmal hinfällst, stehe auch das achte Mal wieder auf."

Ce projet développé par Dentsu Kyushu a été commandé par **Yaoki** Sake et son résultat est une bouteille très élégante, aux formes raffinées, avec une base arrondie, et qui reprend sa position verticale toute seule. Ce Sake est obtenu à partir de pommes de terre, et la bouteille est fabriquée en porcelaine Arita, de l'île japonaise de Kyushu. Le message est tiré d'un proverbe ancien : « Si tu tombes sept fois, relève-toi la huitième fois ».

YAOKI

Designer: Tadashi Cho
Copywriter: Iku Nara
Planner: Shinji Kaneko
Company: Dentsu Kyushu Inc.
Country: Japan
Category: Best of the category Luxury

PLATINUM PENTAWARD 2008

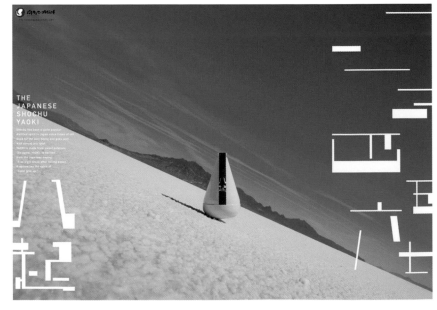

THE
JAPANESE
SHOCHU
YAOKI

Shochu has been a
quite popular disti-
lled spirit in Japan
since times of old.
YAOKI means to ri-
se again and again,
thus symbolizing
the spirit of
"never give up".

In order to continue to boost Van Cleef & Arpels' high-end image in the perfume industry in line with the famous jeweller's positioning, the objective of this new package was to pursue the story initiated in 2008 with Féerie in the gems perfume territory, with a new fragrance emphasising the universe of precious stones dear to **Van Cleef & Arpels**. For the design of this baroque bottle Brandimage – Desgrippes & Laga drew inspiration from the brand's heritage, taking up the luxurious shapes of a high-end jewellery ring and its rare tourmaline sparkle. Oriens was launched in March 2010 (in the US exclusively at Bergdorf Goodman and Neiman Marcus stores).

Um das Top-Image von Van Cleef & Arpels in der Parfümbranche zusammen mit seiner Positionierung als berühmte Juweliere weiter zu fördern, lautete der Auftrag bei dieser Verpackung, die 2008 im Bereich von Edelsteinen und Parfüms mit Féerie initiierte Story auszubauen. Dazu sollte ein neuer Duft das Universum kostbarer Steine betonen, an denen **Van Cleef & Arpels** besonders gelegen ist. Für das Design dieser barocken Flasche ließ man sich vom traditionellen Erbe dieser Marke inspirieren: Brandimage – Desgrippes & Laga griff die luxuriösen Formen eines Topklasse-Rings und das Funkeln seines seltenen Turmalins auf. Oriens kam im März 2010 auf den Markt (in den USA exklusiv in den Luxuskaufhäusern Bergdorf Goodman und Neiman Marcus).

Pour continuer à renforcer l'image haut de gamme de Van Cleef & Arpels sur le marché des parfums, en cohérence avec le positionnement du joaillier, l'objectif de ce nouvel emballage était de poursuivre le fil narratif né en 2008 avec Féerie sur le territoire des parfums bijoux, avec une nouvelle fragrance qui reprend l'univers des pierres précieuses, si cher à **Van Cleef & Arpels**. Pour concevoir ce flacon baroque, Brandimage – Desgrippes & Laga a tiré son inspiration de l'héritage de la marque, et lui a emprunté les formes voluptueuses d'une bague de luxe et l'éclat rare de la tourmaline. Oriens a été lancé en mars 2010 (aux États-Unis, exclusivement dans les magasins Bergdorf Goodman et Neiman Marcus).

ORIENS
VAN CLEEF & ARPELS

Design: Joël Desgrippes, Eric Douane
Company: Brandimage – Desgrippes & Laga
Country: France
Category: Best of the category Luxury

PLATINUM PENTAWARD 2010

Féerie by Van Cleef & Arpels was first launched in August 2008, and the perfume range was later extended with a new Eau de Toilette. The exclusive bottle, faceted like a precious stone, displays the colour of night and illuminates the heavenly mystery of the luxurious Van Cleef & Arpels perfumery. The package's most distinguished feature is its unexpected oversized silver cap bearing an iconic fairy resting delicately in a graceful, impish pose atop a moonflower.

Féerie, ein Parfüm von Van Cleef & Arpels, kam erstmals im August 2008 auf den Markt und wurde von einem neuen Eau de Toilette begleitet. Der exklusive Flakon, facettiert wie ein kostbarer Edelstein, stellt die Farbe der Nacht dar und erhellt das himmlische Geheimnis der Luxusparfümerie Van Cleef & Arpels. Die auffallendste Eigenschaft der Verpackung ist ihr unerwartet großer silberner Verschluss, der symbolisch eine Fee darstellt, die feingliedrig in einer eleganten und kecken Haltung auf einer Mondblume sitzt.

Féerie est un parfum de Van Cleef & Arpels. Initialement lancée en août 2008, la gamme s'est agrandie avec l'arrivée d'une nouvelle eau de toilette. Le flacon exclusif, taillé comme une pierre précieuse, est couleur nuit et illumine le divin mystère des parfums luxueux de Van Cleef & Arpels. La caractéristique la plus originale du packaging est un bouchon surdimensionné portant une fée gracieuse et espiègle assise sur une fleur de lune.

VAN CLEEF & ARPELS FÉERIE

Creative Director: Joël Desgrippes
Art Director/3D: Eric Douane
Art Director/2D: Sylvie Verdier
Company: Brandimage – Desgrippes & Laga
Country: France
Category: Perfumes

GOLD PENTAWARD 2009

PLAYBOY

Creative Director: Delphine Colin; *Art Director:* Charlotte Regnier
Senior Product Designer: Bertrand Bruyat; *Product Manager/3D:* Franz Ezin
Execution/Production: Tann Vindeoux; *Production Manager:* Armelle Pumir
Company: Logic Selectif
Country: France
Category: Perfumes

GOLD PENTAWARD 2010

EGOFACTO

General Partner: Chantale Coussaud
Creative Director: Françoise Bouchez
Art Directors: Pascal Morlighem, Laetitia Arrighi
Account Planner: Olivier Raymond
Photography: Michael Hirsch, Christel Vermaut
Company: Bayadères
Country: France
Category: Perfumes

SILVER PENTAWARD 2010

GIVENCHY
ANGE OU DÉMON

Design: Angela Summers, Vincent Villéger
Company: Villéger Summers Design
Country: UK
Category: Perfumes

GOLD PENTAWARD 2008

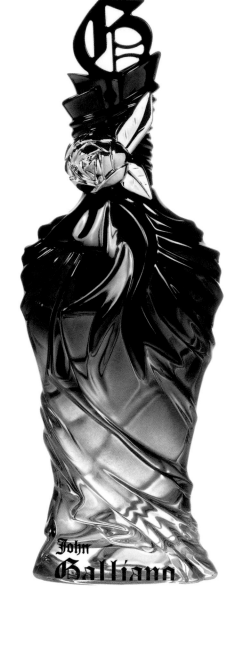

Villéger Summers Design received the brief from Givenchy to design a luxurious bottle, linking with its original design, and the main inspiration for it arose from the crystal chandelier. This refillable version is complemented by a chain of beads, and additional facets give an increased feeling of luxury. Originally meant to be disposable, the bottle was thought too good to throw away, prompting **Givenchy** to introduce a soft disposable refill. In this case, the challenge was that the graphics had also to provide a luxurious aspect for a format usually associated with lower-end products.

Givenchy gab Villéger Summers Design das Briefing an die Hand, einen luxuriösen Flakon zu gestalten und dabei eine Verbindung zum ursprünglichen Design herzustellen. Inspirieren ließ man sich dafür hauptsächlich von einem Kronleuchter. Diese nachfüllbare Version wird durch eine Glasperlenkette ergänzt. Außerdem bekommt das Gefäß durch zusätzliche Facetten noch ein sehr luxuriöses Flair. Eigentlich war diese Flasche als Einwegartikel gedacht, aber man fand, sie sei zu gut zum Wegwerfen. So sah **Givenchy** sich veranlasst, eine Soft-Nachfüllpackung anzubieten. Hier bestand die Herausforderung darin, bei einem Format, das man eher mit geringwertigen Produkten assoziiert, das äußere Erscheinungsbild ebenfalls erstklassig wirken zu lassen.

Givenchy a chargé Villéger Summers Design de concevoir une bouteille luxueuse qui devait établir un lien avec le design original, et la principale inspiration a été le chandelier en cristal. Cette version rechargeable est complétée par une chaîne de perles, et les facettes augmentent encore la sensation de luxe. À l'origine, la bouteille devait être jetable, mais elle a été considérée trop réussie pour finir à la poubelle, ce qui a poussé **Givenchy** à lui ajouter une recharge jetable dans un packaging souple. Dans ce cas, le défi était que le graphisme devait également transmettre la notion de luxe, sur un format qui est habituellement associé à des produits plus bas de gamme.

SELECTIVE BEAUTY
JOHN GALLIANO

Creative Director: Elie Papiernik
Creative Team: Katja Liebig, Guozheng Jiang,
Nathalie Pierre, Cécile Cazanova
Company: centdegrés
Country: France
Category: Perfumes

SILVER PENTAWARD 2009

PERRY ELLIS

Design: Denis Boudard
Company: QSLD Paris
Country: France
Category: Perfumes

BRONZE PENTAWARD 2009

KENZO
UNIDENTIFIED

Design: Ron Arad
Company: Kenzo Parfums
Country: France
Category: Perfumes

SILVER PENTAWARD 2009

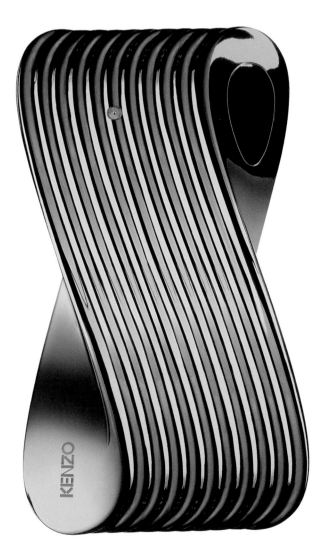

GIVENCHY
EAUDEMOISELLE

Design: Elie Papiernik, François Vesin
Photographer: Boris Ovini
Company: centdegrés
Country: France
Category: Perfumes

BRONZE PENTAWARD 2010

VALENTINO
PARFUM & EXQUISITE BODY MILK

Design: Ian Carnduff, NiCE Ltd. team
Company: NiCE Ltd.
Country: USA
Category: Perfumes

SILVER PENTAWARD 2010

OILILY

Design: Kareem Baqai,
Joost La Housse, Claire Morelli
Company: Brandnew Design
Country: The Netherlands
Category: Perfumes

BRONZE PENTAWARD 2010

SHANGHAI BOUQUET

Creative Director: Izumi Matsumoto (Shiseido Co., Ltd.)
Art Director: Yoji Nobuto (Shiseido Co., Ltd.)
Illustration: Takashi Yamaguchi
Company: Shiseido Co., Ltd.
Country: Japan
Category: Perfumes

BRONZE PENTAWARD 2009

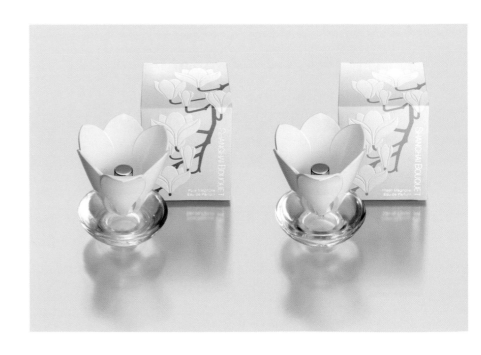

CHANTAL THOMASS
OSEZ-MOI !

Design: Sylvie de France
Company: Sylvie de France
Country: France
Category: Perfumes

BRONZE PENTAWARD 2009

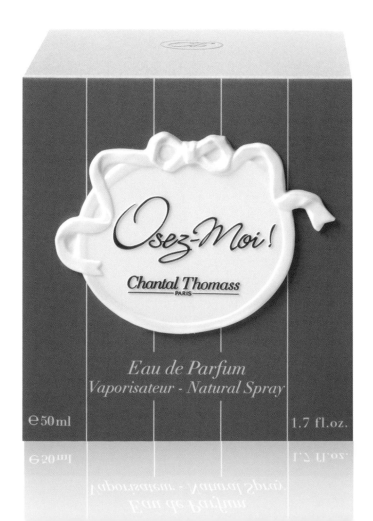

Menard's **Authent Cream** is the result of 50 years of cumulative development, including six years of state-of-the-art stem-cell research. The cream rejuvenates the skin by using a concept which focuses on stem cells, whose numbers decrease with age. The result is a product that exemplifies both "the origin of beauty" and "the future of beauty". At the base of the container, the raised surface emerges to symbolise the creation of a new cell, the gold sphere, separated from the past.

Die **Authent**-**Creme** von **Menard** ist das Ergebnis einer 50-jährigen Entwicklungsarbeit, zu der eine sechsjährige, hochmoderne Stammzellenforschung gehört. Die Creme verjüngt die Haut, indem sie nach einem auf Stammzellen basierenden Konzept arbeitet. Die Zahl der Stammzellen verringert sich mit zunehmendem Alter. Dieses Produkt veranschaulicht nun sowohl den „Ursprung der Schönheit" als auch die „Zukunft der Schönheit". Auf der Bodenfläche des Flakons ist die Oberfläche ein wenig erhaben, um die Kreation einer neuen Zelle zu symbolisieren: die goldene Kugel, die sich von der Vergangenheit ablöst.

La crème **Authent** de **Ménard** est le résultat de 50 ans de développement cumulés, dont six ans de recherche de pointe sur les cellules souches. Elle rajeunit la peau en utilisant un concept qui cible les cellules souches, dont le nombre baisse avec l'âge. Le résultat est un produit qui illustre à la fois « l'origine de la beauté » et « le futur de la beauté ». Le fond du présentoir du pot s'élève en son centre pour symboliser la création d'une nouvelle cellule, la sphère dorée, qui se détache du passé.

AUTHENT CREAM

Design: Shohei Yagi; *Assistant Designer:* Akira Okamoto
Company: Nippon Menard Cosmetic Co., Ltd.
Country: Japan
Category: Cosmetics
(make-up, body care, beauty products, etc.)

GOLD PENTAWARD 2009

SHISEIDO
BIO-PERFORMANCE

Creative Director: Katsuhiko Shibuya
Art Director: Eriko Hirato
Designer: Ippei Murata
Company: Shiseido Co., Ltd.
Country: Japan
Category: Cosmetics
(make-up, body care, beauty products, etc.)

GOLD PENTAWARD 2008

By employing advanced resin formation and vapour deposition technologies in the shape of this new packaging for **Pola B.A.** the result is a new, dynamic, and dazzling life created by cellular division. The container opens and closes with a unique screw mechanism, an engineering feat stemming from an ingenious combination of practical use and smart design. The inner container can be replaced, creating a stylish and welcome touch that preserves natural resources.

Bei der Gestaltung dieser neuen Verpackung für **Pola B.A.** wurden fortschrittliche Techniken der Kunstharzformung und Aufdampfverfahren eingesetzt. Das Produkt sorgt für ein neues, dynamisches und glanzvolles Leben, das durch Zellteilung geschaffen wird. Der Behälter wird mit einem einzigartigen Schraubverschluss geöffnet. Diese technische Meisterleistung kombiniert praktischen Nutzen und cleveres Design auf ausgeklügelte Weise. Der innere Behälter kann ausgetauscht werden und schafft somit eine stilvolle und willkommene Note, mit der natürliche Ressourcen bewahrt werden.

La forme de ce nouvel emballage pour **Pola B.A.** est le fruit de technologies de pointe dans le moulage de la résine et la vaporisation. Le résultat est une nouvelle vie dynamique et éclatante créée par division cellulaire. Le pot s'ouvre et se ferme grâce à un mécanisme à vis original, une prouesse technique qui opère une alliance ingénieuse entre commodité d'utilisation et conception intelligente. Le pot interne peut être remplacé, une touche élégante et bienvenue pour préserver les ressources naturelles.

POLA B.A. THE CREAM

Creative Director: Takeshi Usui; *Art Director:* Chiharu Suzuki
Designers: Haruyo Eto, Taishi Ono
Company: Pola Chemical Industries Inc.
Country: Japan
Category: Cosmetics
(make-up, body care, beauty products, etc.)

GOLD PENTAWARD 2010

IPSA
THE TIME RESET

Design: Aoshi Kudo, Shuichi Ikedalo, Helmut Schmid
Company: Communication Design Laboratory
Country: Japan
Category: Cosmetics
(make-up, body care, beauty products, etc.)

SILVER PENTAWARD 2009

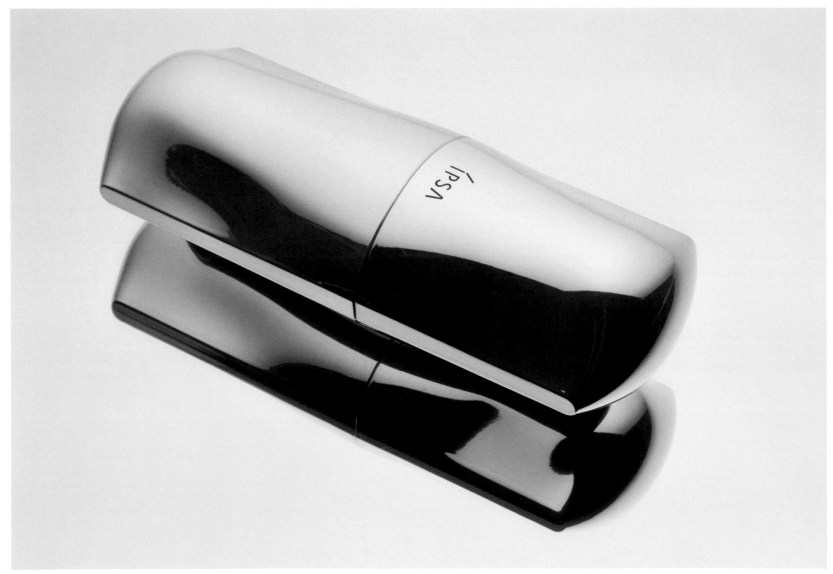

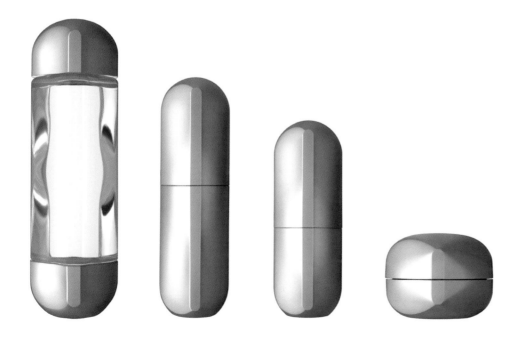

R'Pure created a new premium anti-ageing skin-care serum for **Guerlain**. Mixing technology and brand heritage to create a mythic product for the ultra-competitive market, the agency was inspired by one of the most essential life-forms in nature: the bee. Since its creation, Guerlain has used the bee as a symbol of the brand in its perfumes and fragrances. Given that one-third of human food supply depends on insect pollination, bees are a key factor in sustaining life and constitute a major type of pollinator in ecosystems. The agency developed unique packaging which translates the bee universe into reality, by adding a complementary element (Beehive) to an existing brand code (Bee).

R'Pure schuf für **Guerlain** ein neues Premium-Produkt: ein neuartiges Hautpflegeserum gegen Hautalterung. Die Agentur ließ sich von einer der grundlegendsten Lebensformen der Natur inspirieren: von der Biene. Seit seiner Entstehung hat Guerlain bei dieser Marke die Biene als Symbol für seine Parfüms und Duftstoffe eingesetzt. Wenn man bedenkt, dass ein Drittel der menschlichen Nahrungsversorgung auf Befruchtung durch Insekten beruht, sind Bienen ein zentraler Faktor für den Erhalt des Lebens. Sie dienen in unseren Ökosystemen als besonders wichtige Bestäuber. Die Agentur entwickelte eine charakteristische Verpackung, über die die Welt der Bienen in die Realität umgesetzt wird: Dem vorhandenen Code der Marke (die Biene) wird ein ergänzendes Element hinzugefügt, nämlich der Bienenstock.

R'Pure a créé un nouveau sérum anti-âge haut de gamme pour **Guerlain**. L'agence a allié la technologie et l'héritage de la marque pour créer un produit mythique sur un marché ultra concurrentiel, et s'est inspirée de l'une des formes de vie les plus essentielles dans la nature : l'abeille. Depuis sa création, Guerlain a utilisé l'abeille comme symbole de la marque pour ses parfums. Étant donné qu'un tiers des aliments consommés par les humains dépend de la pollinisation des insectes, et que les abeilles sont un agent majeur de pollinisation dans les écosystèmes, elles jouent un rôle clé pour la vie sur la planète. L'agence a imaginé un emballage original qui traduit l'univers des abeilles dans notre réalité, en ajoutant un élément complémentaire (la ruche) à un code qui existait déjà pour la marque (l'abeille).

GUERLAIN

Art Director: Sébastien Servaire; *Designer:* Candido De Barros
Account Manager: Virginie Bourgoin; *Illustration:* Yael Bibliowicz
Company: R'Pure Studio
Country: France
Category: Cosmetics
(make-up, body care, beauty products, etc.)
SILVER PENTAWARD 2010

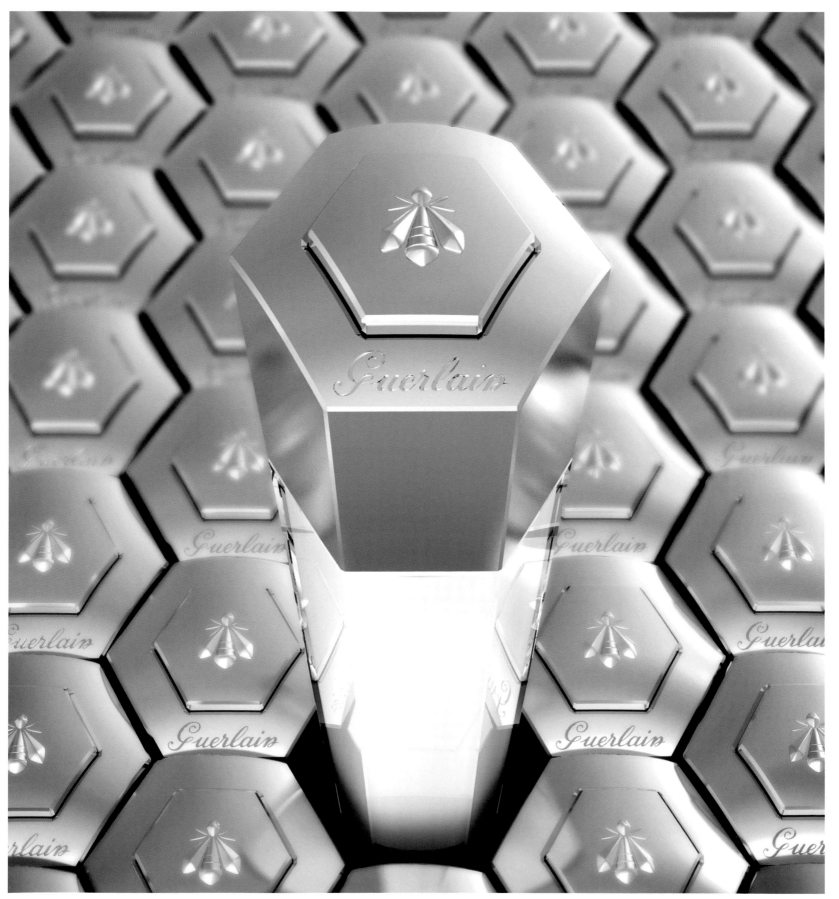

SOIGNE AGEDISCUSS

Design: CP Cosmetics Yoshinari & Associates
Company: CP Cosmetics
Country: Japan
Category: Cosmetics
(make-up, body care, beauty products, etc.)

SILVER PENTAWARD 2010

SULWHASOO

Design: BETC Design team
Company: BETC Design
Country: France
Category: Cosmetics
(make-up, body care, beauty products, etc.)

BRONZE PENTAWARD 2010

GIVENCHY
LE PRISME VISAGE PRODUCT

Design: Elie Papiernik, François Vesin, Marc Venot
Photographer: Eric Sauvage
Company: centdegrés
Country: France
Category: Cosmetics
(make-up, body care, beauty products, etc.)

BRONZE PENTAWARD 2010

ORIBE HAIR CARE

Design: Buero New York team
Company: Buero New York
Country: USA
Category: Cosmetics
(make-up, body care,
beauty products, etc.)

BRONZE PENTAWARD 2009

MED BEAUTY SWISS
CELL PREMIUM

Client: Med Beauty Swiss
Design: Righetti & Partner GmbH
Packaging Construction: Limmatdruck/Zeiler
Country: Switzerland
Category: Cosmetics
(make-up, body care, beauty products, etc.)

BRONZE PENTAWARD 2010

SYNERGIQUE

Creative Director: Katsuhiko Shibuya
Art Director: Chieko Yamamoto
Design: Chieko Yamamoto, Yuji Uneno, Yuka Nagasaki
Company: Shiseido Co., Ltd.
Country: Japan
Category: Cosmetics
(make-up, body care, beauty products, etc.)

SILVER PENTAWARD 2009

GRANAS

Creative Director: Eriko Hirato
Art Director: Chieko Yamamoto
Design: Ippei Murata, Asako Hase
Company: Shiseido Co., Ltd.
Country: Japan
Category: Cosmetics
(make-up, body care, beauty products, etc.)

BRONZE PENTAWARD 2009

EST
ETERNAL FLOW

Art Director: Saika Oohira
Company: Kao Corporation
Country: Japan
Category: Cosmetics
(make-up, body care,
beauty products, etc.)

BRONZE PENTAWARD 2009

Old Nassau Imports needed a bottle that would match the price range of this premium spirit. Through research and strategy it was determined that the package needed to delicately blend the rich heritage of Slovakia with a modern, simple, and pure aesthetic reflecting the quality product it contained. The strikingly simple form of the bottle provides a perfect canvas for small touches of rich detail, including hand-lettered Slovakian poems, the Slovakian crest, and the logo for **Double Cross** which is a modern take on the crest.

Old Nassau Imports suchte nach einer Flasche, die zum Preissegment dieser Premium-Spirituose passt. Recherchen und strategische Überlegungen ergaben, dass bei der Verpackung das kulturelle Erbe der Slowakei mit einer modernen, einfachen und klaren Ästhetik verschmelzen sollte, was dem darin enthaltenen qualitativ hochwertigen Produkt entspricht. Die erstaunlich einfache Form der Flasche bietet die perfekte Projektionsfläche für viele kleine Details, z. B. handschriftliche slowakische Gedichte, das slowakische Wappen und das Logo von **Double Cross** (eine moderne Umsetzung des Wappens).

Old Nassau Imports avait besoin d'une bouteille qui correspondrait à la fourchette de prix de ses alcools haut de gamme. Une étude stratégique a permis de conclure que le packaging devait trouver une alliance délicate entre le riche héritage de la Slovaquie et une esthétique simple, pure et moderne reflétant la qualité du produit. La forme extrêmement simple de la bouteille est une base parfaite pour de petites touches de détail très travaillées, notamment des poèmes slovaques calligraphiés à la main, le cimier slovaque, et le logo de **Double Cross,** une réinterprétation moderne de ce cimier.

DOUBLE CROSS

Art Director: Brian Adducci
Design: Brian Adducci, Dan Baggenstoss
Illustration: John Stevens
Company: Capsule
Country: USA
Category: Spirits
GOLD PENTAWARD 2009

DOMAINE DE CANTON

Design: John Cooper
Producer: Cameo Metal Products
Country: USA
Category: Spirits

GOLD PENTAWARD 2008

ONE KEY DRY GIN

Design: Branko Lukic, Steven Takoyama (NONOBJECT)
Company: One Key
Country: Serbia
Category: Spirits

GOLD PENTAWARD 2010

LEOPOLD RAFFIN

Design: Optima Design
Company: Maison René Laclie
Country: France
Category: Spirits
BRONZE PENTAWARD 2010

BRAASTAD

Design: Denis Boudard
Company: QSLD Paris
Country: France
Category: Spirits
SILVER PENTAWARD 2009

DIAGEO
JOHNNIE WALKER
THE JOHN WALKER

Design: Linea design team
Company: Linea Development
Country: France
Category: Spirits

SILVER PENTAWARD 2010

TENJIN-BAYASHI

Design: Uonuma Sake Brewery Co., Ltd.,
Kuroyanagi Jun
Company: Kuroyanagi Jun
Country: Japan
Category: Spirits

SILVER PENTAWARD 2010

GIN MARE

Design: Series Nemo team
Company: Series Nemo
Country: Spain
Category: Spirits
SILVER PENTAWARD 2010

TANTEO

Design: Lincoln Mayne
Company: Tanteo Spirits
Country: USA
Category: Spirits
SILVER PENTAWARD 2009

HENNESSY BLACK

Design: Pascal Viguier
Company: Curius
Country: France
Category: Spirits

BRONZE PENTAWARD 2009

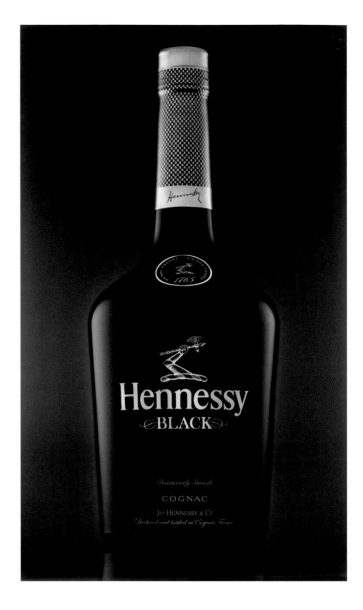

THE LONDON N°1

Design: Carles Graell
Company: CB'a Design Solutions
Country: France
Category: Spirits

BRONZE PENTAWARD 2010

IS VODKA

Design: VGS International Inc. team
Company: VGS International Inc.
Country: USA
Category: Spirits

BRONZE PENTAWARD 2009

La Pubilla (meaning first daughter born in a family) is part of the Premium range of cavas (sparkling wines) from Pere Ventura Cellars in Sant Sadurní, Catalonia, which is produced using the Champenoise method. Morera Design had to create a unique bottle that would reflect the attributes of the product, a meticulous, elegant, and fresh cava to suit the personality of a young woman. The selection of the unconventional and sleek curves in the bottle's shape, the bottle capsule featuring the profile of the daughter and the story behind "La Pubilla", are all elements chosen to communicate the concept of the product.

La Pubilla (Katalanisch für die erstgeborene Tochter einer Familie) gehört zur Premiumpalette des Cava-Schaumweins vom Weingut Pere Ventura im katalanischen Sant Sadurní. Dieser wird nach der Champagner-Methode produziert. Morera Design wollte eine einzigartige Flasche schaffen, die den Attributen des Produkts entspricht: ein akribisches, elegantes und frisches Cava, das zur Persönlichkeit einer jungen Frau passt. Um das Konzept des Produkts zu vermitteln, entschied man sich für die unkonventionellen und geschmeidigen Linien der Flaschenform, die Korkenhülle mit dem Profil des Mädchens und die „La Pubilla" zugrunde liegende Geschichte.

Le vin La Pubilla (terme qui désigne la première née dans une famille) fait partie de la gamme premium de cava (vin pétillant) des caves Pere Ventura à Sant Sadurní, en Catalogne, et est produit selon la méthode champenoise. Morera Design devait créer une bouteille originale pour refléter les attributs du produit, un cava soigné, élégant et frais, qui correspond à la personnalité d'une jeune femme. Les courbes originales et épurées de la bouteille, le médaillon décoré du profil de la jeune fille et l'histoire derrière « La Pubilla » sont les éléments choisis pour communiquer sur le concept du produit.

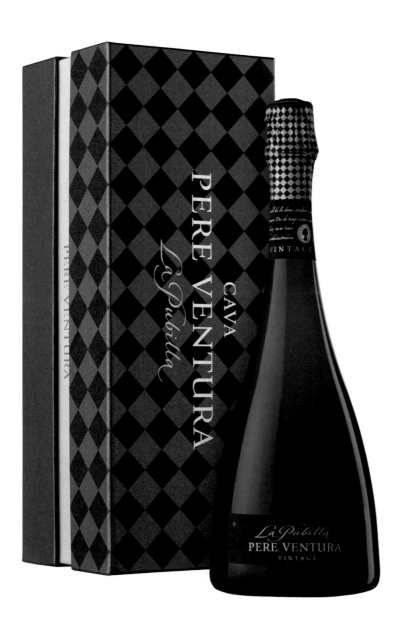

PERE VENTURA
LA

Design: Josep Maria Morera
Company: Morera Design
Country: Spain
Category: Fine wines, champagne
GOLD PENTAWARD 2008

OPUS ONE

Design: Weijie Kang
Company: EHO Package Design
Country: China
Category: Fine wines, champagne

GOLD PENTAWARD 2009

AFIP DIAMOND

Design: Wu Kuan Fu
Company: Shenzhen Excel Package Design Co., Ltd.
Country: China
Category: Fine wines, champagne

GOLD PENTAWARD 2010

NAKED KING

Design: Yiannis Charalambopoulos,
Alexis Nikou, Vagelis Liakos
Company: Beetroot
Country: Greece
Category: Fine wines, champagne

SILVER PENTAWARD 2010

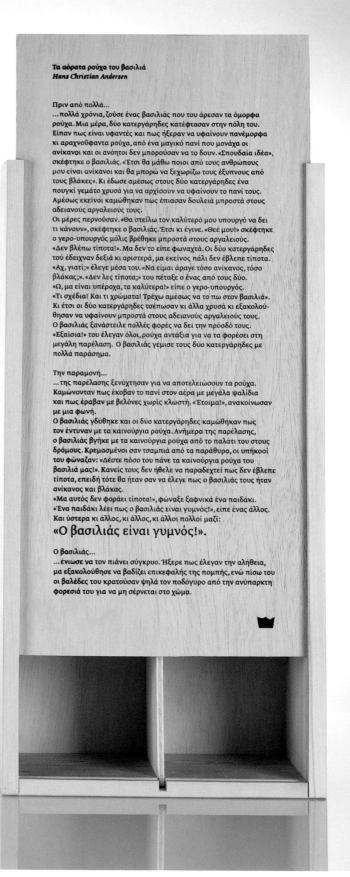

Τα αόρατα ρούχα του βασιλιά
Hans Christian Andersen

Πριν από πολλά...
... πολλά χρόνια, ζούσε ένας βασιλιάς που του άρεσαν τα όμορφα ρούχα. Μια μέρα, δύο κατεργάρηδες κατέφτασαν στην πόλη του. Είπαν πως είναι υφαντές και πως ήξεραν να υφαίνουν πανέμορφα κι αραχνοΰφαντα ρούχα, από ένα μαγικό πανί που μονάχα οι ανίκανοι και οι ανόητοι δεν μπορούσαν να το δουν. «Σπουδαία ιδέα», σκέφτηκε ο βασιλιάς. «Έτσι θα μάθω ποιοι από τους ανθρώπους μου είναι ανίκανοι και θα μπορώ να ξεχωρίζω τους έξυπνους από τους βλάκες». Κι έδωσε αμέσως στους δύο κατεργάρηδες ένα πουγκί γεμάτο χρυσά για να αρχίσουν να υφαίνουν το πανί τους. Αμέσως εκείνοι καμώθηκαν πως έπιασαν δουλειά μπροστά στους αδειανούς αργαλειούς τους.
Οι μέρες περνούσαν. «Θα στείλω τον καλύτερό μου υπουργό να δει τι κάνουν», σκέφτηκε ο βασιλιάς. Έτσι κι έγινε. «Θεέ μου!» σκέφτηκε ο γερο-υπουργός μόλις βρέθηκε μπροστά στους αργαλειούς. «Δεν βλέπω τίποτα!». Μα δεν το είπε φωναχτά. Οι δύο κατεργάρηδες τού έδειχναν δεξιά κι αριστερά, μα εκείνος πάλι δεν έβλεπε τίποτα. «Αχ, γιατί;» έλεγε μέσα του. «Να είμαι άραγε τόσο ανίκανος, τόσο βλάκας;». «Δεν λες τίποτα;» του πέταξε ένας από τους δύο. «Ω, μα είναι υπέροχα, τα καλύτερα!» είπε ο γερο-υπουργός. «Τι σχέδια! Και τι χρώματα! Τρέχω αμέσως να το πω στον βασιλιά». Κι έτσι οι δύο κατεργάρηδες τσέπωσαν κι άλλα χρυσά κι εξακολούθησαν να υφαίνουν μπροστά στους αδειανούς αργαλειούς τους. Ο βασιλιάς ξανάστειλε πολλές φορές να δει την πρόοδό τους. «Εξαίσια!» του έλεγαν όλοι, ρούχα αντάξια για να τα φορέσει στη μεγάλη παρέλαση. Ο βασιλιάς γέμισε τους δύο κατεργάρηδες με πολλά παράσημα.

Την παραμονή...
... της παρέλασης ξενύχτησαν για να αποτελειώσουν τα ρούχα. Καμώνονταν πως έκοβαν το πανί στον αέρα με μεγάλα ψαλίδια και πως έραβαν με βελόνες χωρίς κλωστή. «Έτοιμα!», ανακοίνωσαν με μια φωνή.
Ο βασιλιάς γδύθηκε και οι δύο κατεργάρηδες καμώθηκαν πως τον έντυναν με τα καινούργια ρούχα. Ανήμερα της παρέλασης, ο βασιλιάς βγήκε με τα καινούργια ρούχα από το παλάτι του στους δρόμους. Κρεμασμένοι σαν τσαμπιά από τα παράθυρα, οι υπήκοοί του φώναζαν: «Δέστε πόσο του πάνε τα καινούργια ρούχα του βασιλιά μας!». Κανείς τους δεν ήθελε να παραδεχτεί πως δεν έβλεπε τίποτα, επειδή τότε θα ήταν σαν να έλεγε πως ο βασιλιάς τους ήταν ανίκανος και βλάκας.
«Μα αυτός δεν φοράει τίποτα!», φώναξε ξαφνικά ένα παιδάκι. «Ένα παιδάκι λέει πως ο βασιλιάς είναι γυμνός!», είπε ένας άλλος. Και ύστερα κι άλλος, κι άλλος, κι άλλοι πολλοί μαζί:

«Ο βασιλιάς είναι γυμνός!».

Ο βασιλιάς...
... ένιωσε να τον πιάνει σύγκρυο. Ήξερε πως έλεγαν την αλήθεια, μα εξακολούθησε να βαδίζει επικεφαλής της πομπής, ενώ πίσω του οι βαλέδες του κρατούσαν ψηλά τον ποδόγυρο από την ανύπαρκτη φορεσιά του για να μη σέρνεται στο χώμα.

BLACKBIRD WINES

Design: Vanja Cuculic
Illustration: Tomislav Tomi
Company: Studio Cuculic
Country: Hungary
Category: Fine wines, champagne

SILVER PENTAWARD 2010

BUCCELLA WINES

Design: Uxus design team
Company: Uxus
Country: The Netherlands
Category: Fine wines, champagne

SILVER PENTAWARD 2009

LAURENT-PERRIER GRAND SIÈCLE

Design: Béatrice Mariotti, Yann Guitton, Pierre-Antoine Chèron
Company: Carré Noir
Country: France
Category: Fine wines, champagne

BRONZE PENTAWARD 2009

CHAMPAGNE LANSON ROSÉ

Design: Lanson
Producer: Sleever International
Country: France
Category: Fine wines, champagne

BRONZE PENTAWARD 2010

ESTERHAZY TESORO

Design: Alessandri Design
Company: Esterhazy Wein GmbH & Co.
Country: Austria
Category: Fine wines, champagne

BRONZE PENTAWARD 2010

STRATVS

Design: Salvatore Adduci
Company: Salvatore Adduci
Country: Spain
Category: Fine wines, champagne

SILVER PENTAWARD 2009

LE GRAND NOIR

Design: Kevin Shaw, Guy Pratt
Company: Stranger & Stranger Ltd.
Country: UK
Category: Fine wines, champagne

BRONZE PENTAWARD 2009

ARCTIC ICE BLUEBERRY WINE

Design: Wu Kuan Fu
Company: Shenzhen Excel Package Design Co., Ltd.
Country: China
Category: Fine wines, champagne

BRONZE PENTAWARD 2010

TEXTUAL

Design: Mariano Gioia, Sebastián Yanez
Typography: Mariano Gioia
Company: YG Yanez Gioia Design
Country: Argentina
Category: Fine wines, champagne

BRONZE PENTAWARD 2010

The **Black Pearl** is a design cooling-box for the world's first super-premium caviar which protects it from external conditions, cools it during transportation, and with its look presents it in a stylish manner. It's a reference to the black pearl of the Pacific Ocean, the rarest of all pearls. The Black Pearl is produced in Switzerland and Germany, and can carry optionally one or two caviar tins. The conventional caviar tins of the same brand are then placed in a secondary sphere, a pearl-like shaped package.

Black Pearl ist eine Designer-Kühlverpackung für den weltweit ersten Super-Premium-Kaviar. Der Kaviar wird dadurch vor äußeren Einwirkungen geschützt, beim Transport gekühlt und sehr elegant präsentiert. Diese Verpackung spielt auf die schwarze Perle aus dem Pazifik an, die seltenste aller Perlen. Black Pearl wird in Deutschland und der Schweiz produziert und kann optional eine oder zwei Kaviardosen enthalten. Die herkömmlichen Kaviardosen derselben Marke werden dann in eine zusätzliche Sphäre gesetzt – eine perlenförmige Verpackung.

La **Black Pearl** est une boîte réfrigérante pour le caviar super premium le plus précieux au monde, qui le protège des conditions extérieures, le refroidit pendant le transport, et le présente avec style. C'est une référence à la perle noire de l'Océan Pacifique, la plus rare de toutes les perles. Elle est fabriquée en Suisse et en Allemagne, et peut contenir au choix une ou deux boîtes de caviar. Les boîtes de caviar classiques de la même marque sont placées dans une sphère secondaire, un récipient en forme de poire.

ZWYERCAVIAR
THE BLACK PEARL

Design: Roger Zwyer, Alexander Zwyer, Roger Dejakum
Company: ZwyerCaviar
Country: Switzerland
Category: Gourmet food

GOLD PENTAWARD 2009

TAISHAN
EMPEROR LOVE OOLONG TEA

Design: Jennifer Tsai, Brenda Chang
Company: Proad Identity
Country: Taiwan
Category: Gourmet food

GOLD PENTAWARD 2008

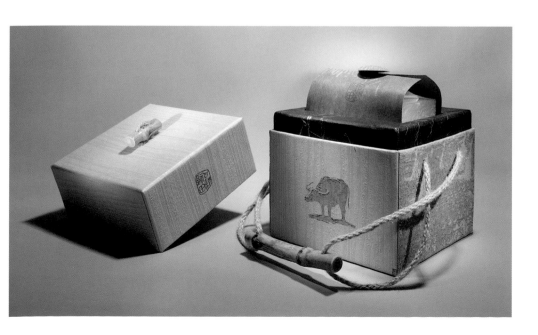

BLESSING CULTIVATED

Design: Jennifer Tsai, Janice Kao, Brenda Chang
Company: Proad Identity
Country: Taiwan
Category: Gourmet food

SILVER PENTAWARD 2009

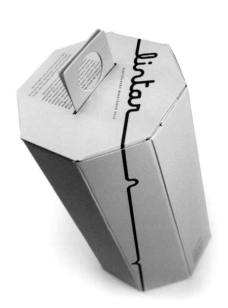

LINTAR OLIVE OIL

Design: Izvorka Juric
Company: Tridvajedan Ltd.
Country: Hungary
Category: Gourmet food

GOLD PENTAWARD 2010

The brand and packaging design of **Lintar** olive oil are inspired by the shape of the funnel and pouring. The Maline font aims to express the oil pouring on the surface and creating the name. The visual identity of this product is both traditional and contemporary, which is particularly evident in the specific combination of colours and shapes. The dark-brown glass bottle is hand painted in a very light yellow-green tone and text elements are printed on the surface. The label, with basic information about the product, is attached to the bottle handle, and other information is printed on a cardboard box with a finger handle. The name Lintar derives from the Greek word for "funnel" and is the old name for the Kastela Gulf, the geographical origin of the oil.

Für das Design der Marke und der Verpackung von **Lintar** Olivenöl ließ man sich durch die Form eines Trichters und das Gießen des Öls inspirieren. Die Schriftart Maline soll vermitteln, wie das Öl auf eine Oberfläche gegossen wird und so der Name entsteht. Die visuelle Identität dieses Produkts ist gleichermaßen traditionell und modern, was besonders bei der speziellen Kombination aus Farben und Formen deutlich wird. Die dunkelbraune Glasflasche ist mit einer sehr hellen, gelbgrünen Tönung handbemalt, und die Textelemente werden auf die Oberfläche aufgedruckt. Ein Etikett mit wichtigen Informationen über das Produkt wird am Flaschengriff angebracht. Auf dem Flaschenkarton mit einem Loch zum Tragen finden sich weitere Infos zum Produkt. Der Name Lintar stammt vom griechischen Wort für „Trichter" ab und ist der alte Name für den Golf von Kaštela (Kroatien), dem geografischen Ursprung des Öls.

La marque et l'emballage de l'huile d'olive **Lintar** sont inspirés de la forme d'un entonnoir. La police de caractères Maline représente l'huile qui coule sur la surface, et dessine son nom. L'identité visuelle de ce produit est traditionnelle et contemporaine à la fois, ce qui est particulièrement évident dans la combinaison de couleurs et de formes. La bouteille en verre brun foncé est peinte à la main dans un vert-jaune très clair, et le texte est imprimé à la surface. L'étiquette, portant les informations de base sur le produit, est attachée à l'anse de la bouteille, et les autres informations sont imprimées sur la boîte en carton, dotée d'une poignée étudiée pour y passer un doigt. Le nom Lintar vient du terme grec signifiant « entonnoir », et est l'ancien nom du golfe de Kastela, le lieu d'origine de cette huile.

WOMERSLEY

Design: Barry Gillibrand; *Typography:* Roger Akroyd
Marketing: Katherine Greenwood; *Illustration:* Petra Borner
Company: Mayday
Country: UK
Category: Gourmet food

SILVER PENTAWARD 2010

1/2 lb

of mango in this
MANGO CHUTNEY

LEMON
CURD .J

1/3 lb

of mixed mustard seeds in this
MUSTARD

a pinch of
ROSE
MARY
sea salt

CHILLI
SEA
SALT

4

of French
FRENCH B

THE JME FOOD RANGE

Creative Director: Shaun Bowen
Copywriter: Sylvie Saunders
Design: Sarah Pidgeon, Natalie Chung
Senior Digital Artwork: Henry Preston
Digital Artwork: Lucy Milne
Account Director: Beth Marcall
Account Manager: Erin Tucker
Realisation Manager: Tracy Sutton
Company: Pearlfisher
Country: UK
Category: Gourmet food

SILVER PENTAWARD 2009

TRIKALINOS
GREY MULLET BOTTARGA

Creative Director: Minos Zarifopoulos
Photographer: Stavros Kostakis
Company: Office Communication Consultants
Country: Greece
Category: Gourmet food

BRONZE PENTAWARD 2009

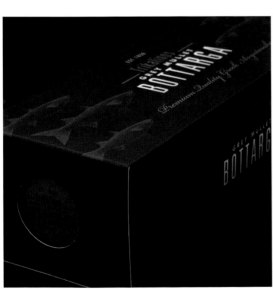

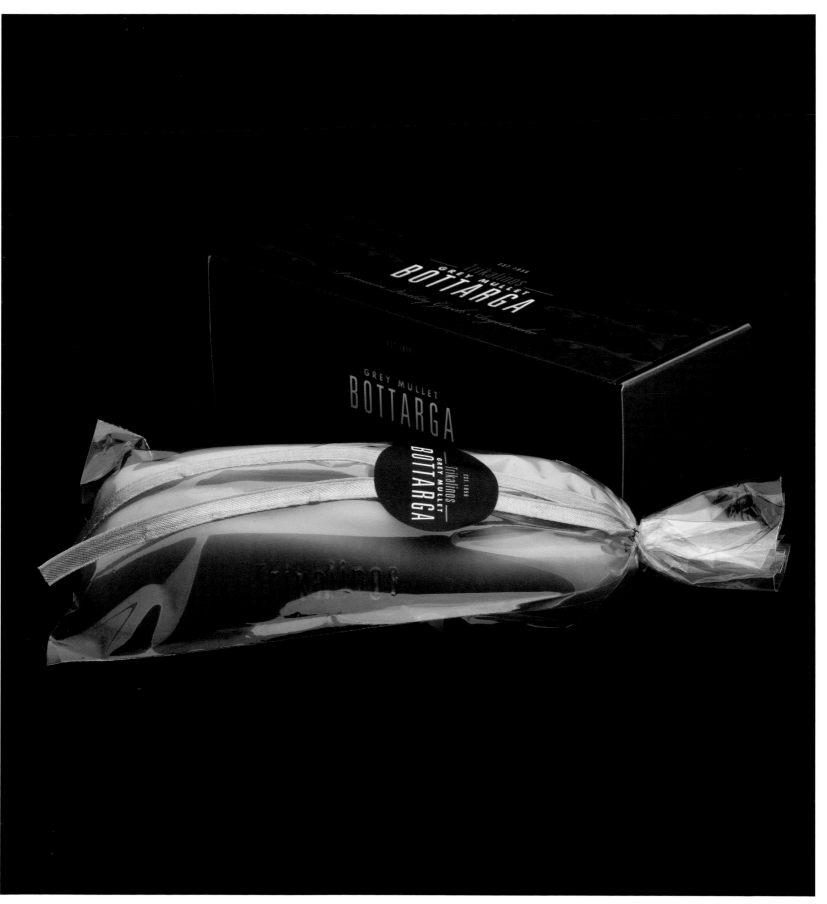

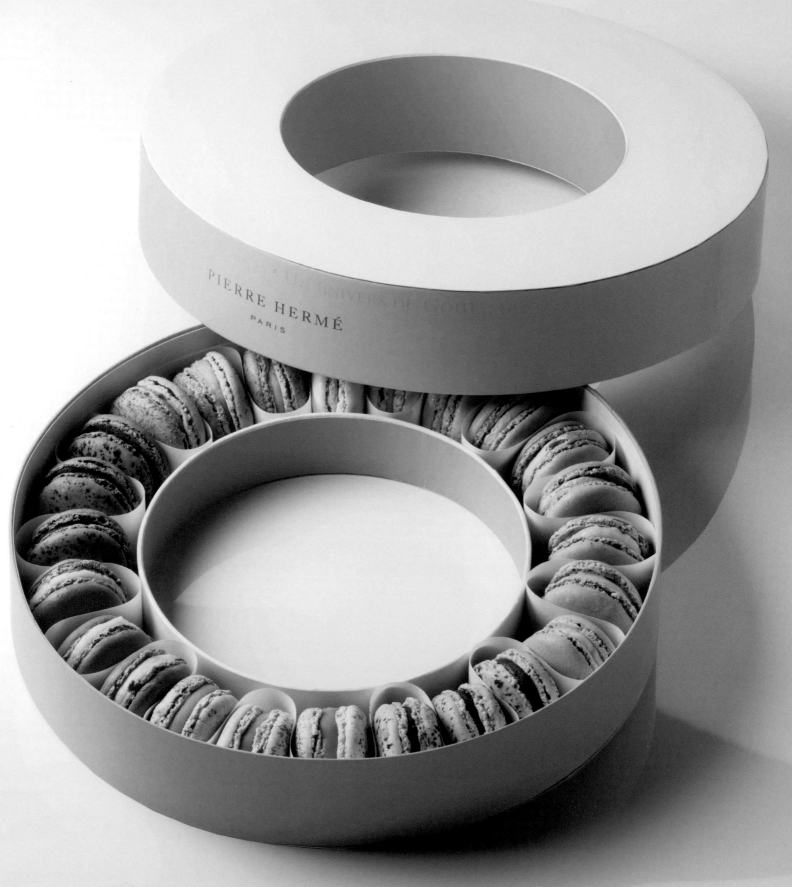

PIERRE HERMÉ
PARIS

PIERRE HERMÉ PACKAGING FOR 24 MACARONS

Design: Agnès Cambus,
Manuel Bonnemazou
Company: BonnemazouCambus
Country: France
Category: Gourmet food
SILVER PENTAWARD 2010

TOKYO PASTELLO

Design: Bravis International team
Company: Bravis International
Country: Japan
Category: Gourmet food
BRONZE PENTAWARD 2009

Auberginenkaviar
Caviar d'aubergine

Panforte

Mandeltuille
Tuile d'amande

Zitronenconfit
Citron confit

Gemüseessenz
Essence de légumes

Safranessenz
Essence au safran

ANDREAS CAMINADA

Design: Remo Caminada and team: Remo Arpagaus,
Donat Caduff, Arno Camenisch, Gion Mathias Cavelty,
Michel & Anita Decurtins, Michael Häne,
Marietta Jemmy, Claudio Spescha
Company: Remo Caminada
Country: Switzerland
Category: Gourmet food

BRONZE PENTAWARD 2010

HALLERTAU
HEROIC RANGE

Design: Ryan Henderson, Alicia Christie
(Degree Design), Cleve Cameron (Toot Group)
Illustration: Evan Purdie; *Sculptor:* Eden Small
Company: Degree Design
Country: New Zealand
Category: Gourmet food

SILVER PENTAWARD 2010

RICE CASTLE

Design: Jennifer Tsai
Company: Proad Identity
Country: Taiwan
Category: Gourmet food

BRONZE PENTAWARD 2010

DOM RUINART
THE INVERSION GIFT BOX

Design: François Takounseun,
Gérald Galdini, Gabriel Brouste
Company: Partisan du Sens
Country: France
Category: Limited editions,
limited series, event creations

GOLD PENTAWARD 2009

The **Inversion** gift box is a black monolith made of lacquered wood, from which emerges an uncommon type of embossment, with the characteristic curves of two champagne flutes and the merest suggestion of a Dom Ruinart bottle, as if sculpted in the box itself. Only the badge of **Dom Ruinart**, accented in gold, is distinctly visible. The contents are revealed by simply sliding the lid that turns upside-down and opens on to a mirrored interior in which stand two engraved flutes and a bottle of Dom Ruinart 1998.

Die Geschenkpackung **Inversion** stellt einen schwarzen Monolith aus lackiertem Holz dar. Unter dem Holz zeichnen sich die charakteristischen Formen zweier Champagnerflöten und, in leichter Andeutung, einer Flasche Dom Ruinart ab, als drängte es sie aus der Kiste. Eine solche Reliefarbeit hat es bisher selten gegeben. Lediglich das mit Gold betonte Emblem von **Dom Ruinart** ist eindeutig erkennbar. Der Inhalt eröffnet sich, wenn man den Deckel um die eigene Achse dreht. Er stellt sich dann kopfüber und gibt den Zugang zum verspiegelten Inneren frei, in dem zwei gravierte Flöten und eine Flasche Dom Ruinart 1998 stehen.

Le coffret-cadeau **Inversion** est un bloc noir en bois laqué à la surface duquel affleure un relief très original, avec les courbes caractéristiques de deux flûtes à champagne et une bouteille de Dom Ruinart à peine suggérée, comme si elle était sculptée dans la boîte. Seul l'écusson de **Dom Ruinart**, rehaussé d'or, est distinctement visible. Pour révéler le contenu de la boîte, il suffit de faire glisser son couvercle, qui se renverse et s'ouvre sur l'intérieur en image inversée avec deux flûtes gravées et une bouteille de Dom Ruinart 1998.

DOM RUINART

Design: Gérard Galdini, François Takounseun
Company: Partisan du Sens
Country: France
Category: Casks, coffrets, gift boxes

SILVER PENTAWARD 2010

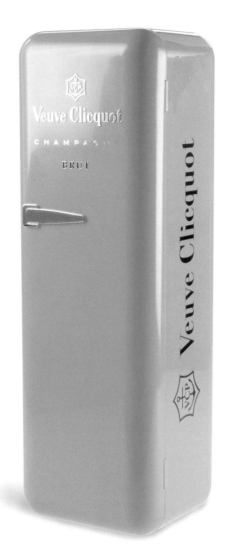

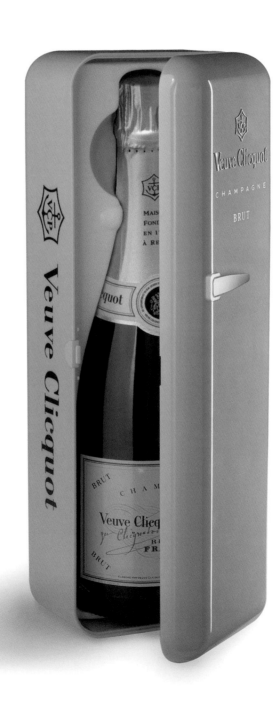

VEUVE CLICQUOT

Design: Denis Boudard (QSLD)
Development/Production: DAPY
Company: DAPY – DO International
Country: France
Category: Casks, coffrets, gift boxes

GOLD PENTAWARD 2010

MOËT & CHANDON

Art Director: Sébastien Servaire
Designer: Candido De Barros
Account Manager: Clara Gaillères
Illustration: Yael Bibliowicz
Photographer: Arnaud Guffon
Developer/Manufacturer: Jean-David Curiel
Company: R'Pure Studio (Creation),
Virojanglor (Manufacturing)
Country: France
Category: Casks, coffrets, gift boxes

SILVER PENTAWARD 2010

LOUIS XIII
RARE CASK

Design: BETC Design team
Company: BETC Design
Country: France
Category: Casks, coffrets, gift boxes

SILVER PENTAWARD 2010

The **Rare Cask** packaging is definitely considered a part of the product experience itself, during purchasing, drinking, and sharing. This laced-up, metallic-stitched exclusive packaging works like a safe. Lights appear when the two halves are slid apart like curtains, revealing the beautifully illuminated Baccarat-crystal carafe displayed in a jewellery case with a pattern-engraved mirror behind. The lily-flower quadrilobe pattern has been especially designed to be the Rare Cask's trademark. The central feature is to keep **Louis XIII** as the cognac's cultural reference, the height of luxury in drinking. It was essential for Louis XIII to indicate the sheer scarcity of Rare Cask by taking the iconic Louis XIII packaging and turning it into a piece of art. Each carafe in this collection limited to only 786 pieces is customised with its own engraved serial number to emphasise its uniqueness.

Bei **Rare Cask** gehört die Verpackung bei Erwerb und Genuss wesentlich zur Produkterfahrung dazu. Diese exklusive Umhüllung mit ihren Verzierungen aus Metall gleicht einem Tresor: Werden die beiden Hälften wie Vorhänge auseinander gezogen, erstrahlt die wunderschöne Karaffe aus Baccarat-Kristall im Licht und zeigt sich wie in einer Schmuckschatulle vor einem mit eingravierten Mustern geschmückten Spiegel. Das vierblättrige Lilienmuster ist speziell als Markenzeichen für Rare Cask gestaltet worden. Als zentrale Eigenschaft soll **Louis XIII** als kulturelle Referenz für Cognac und als höchste Luxusklasse beim Trinkgenuss bewahrt werden. Louis XIII verdeutlicht die außergewöhnliche Seltenheit von Rare Cask damit, dass die symbolträchtige Verpackung von Louis XIII in ein Kunstwerk verwandelt wird. Jede Karaffe dieser auf nur 786 Stücke begrenzten Kollektion trägt ihre eigene Seriennummer, was ihre Einzigartigkeit unterstreicht.

L'emballage de **Rare Cask** est sans aucun doute considéré comme faisant partie intégrante du produit, au moment de l'acheter, de le boire, et de le partager. Cet emballage exclusif, lacé de mailles métalliques, fonctionne comme un coffre-fort. Lorsque les deux moitiés s'écartent comme un rideau, les lumières qui s'allument révèlent une magnifique carafe en cristal de Baccarat présentée dans un écrin, adossée à un miroir gravé. Le motif de la fleur de lis a été dessiné tout spécialement pour devenir l'emblème du Rare Cask. L'intention est de conserver à **Louis XIII** sa place de cognac de référence, de sommet du luxe dans la culture de l'alcool haut de gamme. Il était essentiel d'indiquer la rareté extrême du Rare Cask en faisant de l'emballage emblématique de Louis XIII une véritable œuvre d'art. Dans cette collection limitée à seulement 786 unités, chaque carafe porte un numéro de série gravé qui souligne son caractère unique.

DIAGEO
TEQUILA DON JULIO 1942

Design Directors: Tosh Hall and JB Hartford
Executive Creative Director: Richard Brandt
Client Managers: Pamela Mazzocco, Sam Gardner
Company: Landor Associates
Country: USA
Category: Limited editions,
limited series, event creations

GOLD PENTAWARD 2010

COINTREAU
CATHERINE MALANDRINO
EDITION

Design: BETC Design,
Catherine Malandrino, Arthus Bertrand
Company: Rémy Cointreau
Country: France
Category: Limited editions,
limited series, event creations

SILVER PENTAWARD 2009

The **Catherine Malandrino** limited-edition bottle of this Cointreau is a mix of tradition and modernity, urban and romantic, a bridge between Paris and New York. The design succeeds in playing on the most feminine emblem of the US, the Statue of Liberty, haloed with the stars of the American flag. The Cointreau silhouette remains unchanged, but is now fully dressed up to the cap of the bottle with a very refined metal fishnet, like a lacework of finely chased metal that embraces the bottle like the finest "dentelle". The project has turned the iconic Cointreau bottle, unchanged for 135 years, into a glamour icon and a chic accessory, giving the brand a modernity never previously seen.

Die „Limited Edition" von **Catherine Malandrino** für Cointreau ist eine Mischung aus Tradition und Moderne, aus urban und romantisch, eine Brücke zwischen Paris und New York. Das Design schafft es, erfolgreich mit dem femininsten Symbol der USA zu spielen: der Freiheits-statue. Sie ist von einem Glorienschein aus den Sternen der amerikanischen Flagge umgeben. Die Silhouette der Cointreauflasche bleibt unverändert, aber nun zieht sich bis zum Verschluss ein sehr feines metallenes Netz hoch, sodass die Flasche wirkt, als wäre sie von allerfeinster Spitze umhüllt. Mit diesem Projekt wird die Cointreau-Flasche – als Ikone seit 135 Jahren unverändert – in ein glamouröses Symbol und schickes Accessoire verwandelt. Das verleiht der Marke eine bisher ungeahnte Modernität.

La bouteille de Cointreau en édition limitée **Catherine Malandrino** est un mélange de tradition et de modernité, urbain et romantique, un pont jeté entre Paris et New York. Le design joue avec succès sur l'emblème le plus féminin des États-Unis, la Statue de la Liberté, auréolée des étoiles du drapeau américain. La forme de la bouteille reste intacte, mais est entièrement revêtue jusqu'au bouchon d'un filet métallique très raffiné, comme une dentelle de métal finement ciselée qui épouse délicatement les parois de verre. Le projet a transformé la célèbre bouteille de Cointreau, qui n'a pas changé depuis 135 ans, en icône glamour et en accessoire chic, et a conféré à la marque une modernité qu'elle n'avait encore jamais connue.

CLAN CAMPBELL
PACO RABANNE

Design: Paco Rabanne
Company: TBWA\Consulting
Country: France
Category: Limited editions,
limited series, event creations

SILVER PENTAWARD 2009

MERUS WINES
MERUS WINERY 10TH ANNIVERSARY

Design: Uxus design team
Company: Uxus
Country: The Netherlands
Category: Limited editions,
 limited series, event creations

SILVER PENTAWARD 2010

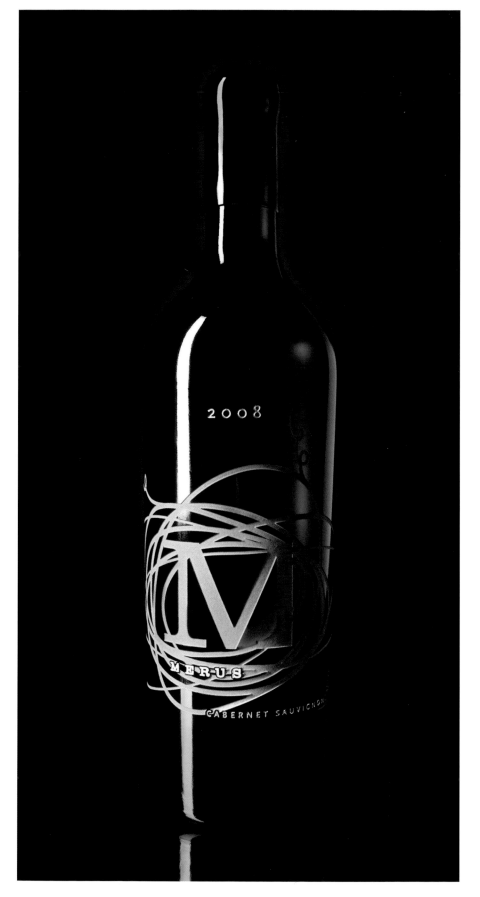

CHRISTIAN AUDIGIER

Art Direction: Barry Sutton
Producer: Sleever International
Country: France
Category: Limited editions,
limited series, event creations

SILVER PENTAWARD 2009

346

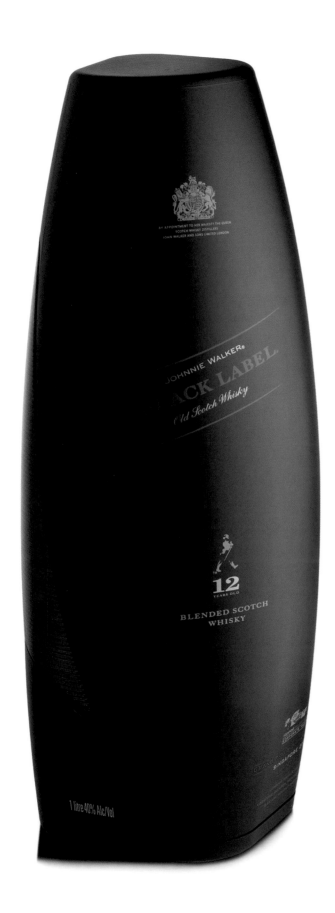

DIAGEO
JOHNNIE WALKER – F1

Managing Director: Anthony Dowler
Company: MW Luxury Packaging
Country: UK
Category: Limited editions,
limited series, event creations

BRONZE PENTAWARD 2009

REMY MARTIN
REMY COINTREAU

Design: Barbé Agency – David LaChapelle
Producer: Sleever International
Country: France
Category: Limited editions,
limited series, event creations

BRONZE PENTAWARD 2009

REMY MARTIN
COEUR DE COGNAC

Design: Gérard Galdini, François Takounseun
Company: Partisan du Sens
Country: France
Category: Limited editions,
limited series, event creations

SILVER PENTAWARD 2010

LE POÈTE

Design: Eriko Misawa
Company: Shiseido Co., Ltd.
Country: Japan
Category: Limited editions,
limited series, event creations

GOLD PENTAWARD 2009

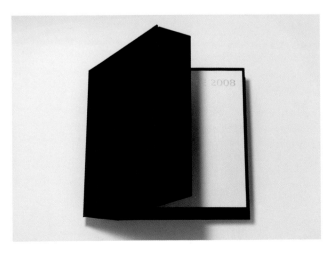

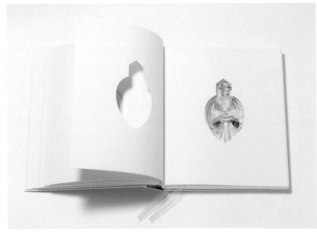

LE POÈTE

Design: Eriko Misawa
Company: Shiseido Co., Ltd.
Country: Japan
Category: Limited editions,
limited series, event creations,
SILVER PENTAWARD 2010

PARFUMS JEAN-PAUL GAULTIER
SOLID PERFUME JEWEL TINS

Design: Crown Speciality Packaging team
Producer: Crown Speciality Packaging
Country: France
Category: Limited editions,
limited series, event creations

SILVER PENTAWARD 2009

VIKTOR & ROLF
ANTIDOTE

Design: Sebastien Servaire
Company: R'Pure Studio
Country: France
Category: Limited editions,
limited series, event creations

BRONZE PENTAWARD 2009

LOLITA LEMPICKA AU MASCULIN

Design: Sylvie de France
Company: Sylvie de France
Country: France
Category: Limited editions,
limited series, event creations

GOLD PENTAWARD 2008

To celebrate their tenth anniversary and to illustrate their innovative spirit since their conception, Parfums Lolita Lempicka launched a Collector's Edition of their masculine fragrance: **Lolita Lempicka au Masculin**. Conceived in partnership with Sylvie de France, this innovative design uses for the first time on the cosmetic market the "fabric overmoulding" technology set up by MT Packaging (Alcan Group). This creation returns to the fragrance's origins and the symbolism of the line's emblematic tree: "beneath the rough and rugged protective bark, the unexpected softness of the Lolita Lempicka Man".

Aus Anlass ihres 10. Geburtstages und um den innovativen Geist seit ihrer Entstehung zu illustrieren veröffentlichten Parfums Lolita Lempicka eine Sammlerausgabe des maskulinen Duftes **Lolita Lempicka au Masculin**. Dieses gemeinsam mit Sylvie de France entwickelte Design arbeitet auf dem Kosmetikmarkt erstmalig mit der Technologie des „Fabric Overmoulding", bei dem im Formgussverfahren mehrere Teile nacheinander kombiniert werden. Es wurde von MT Packaging (Alcan Group) entwickelt. Diese Kreation kehrt zu den Ursprüngen des Duftes zurück und zur Symbolik des sinnbildlichen Baumes der Produktlinie: „Unter der rauen und zerfurchten schützenden Rinde findet sich die unerwartete Weichheit von Lolita Lempicka Man".

Pour fêter son dixième anniversaire et illustrer l'esprit d'innovation dont elle a fait preuve dès sa naissance, la marque de parfums Lolita Lempicka a lancé une édition collector de son parfum pour homme: **Lolita Lempicka au Masculin**. Conçu en collaboration avec Sylvie de France, ce design innovant emploie pour la première fois sur le marché des cosmétiques la technique de « surmoulage textile » mise au point par MT Packaging (Alcan Group). Cette création opère un retour aux origines de ce parfum et au symbolisme de l'arbre emblématique de la gamme : « sous l'écorce protectrice rugueuse et dure, la douceur inattendue de l'homme Lolita Lempicka ».

HUGO BOSS
HUGO MAN

Design: Karim Rashid
Company: Karim Rashid Inc.
Country: USA
Category: Limited editions, limited series, event creations

GOLD PENTAWARD 2010

MANDOM
THE 80TH ANNIVERSARY
FRAGRANCE

Box Design: Forme Design Office Inc.
Design: Hirai Yuko, Imahori Atsuko
Bottle: Able Design Planning
Art Director: Hanamura Kenji
Designer: Shigeta Motoe
Company: Forme Design Office Inc.
Country: Japan
Category: Limited editions, limited series, event creations

SILVER PENTAWARD 2009

ALTO MILANO
LUXURY SOCKS

Design: William Raineri
Company: Raineri Design
Country: Italy
Category: Jewellery, watches, fashion garments

SILVER PENTAWARD 2009

Best of the category
Household maintenance
Home improvement
Electronic
Non-electronic
Automobile products
B2B products

other markets

Brand identity programmes
Distributors'/Retailers' own brands
Pet products
Entertainment
Miscellaneous
Self-promotion

BRUCE DUCKWORTH

Founding partner and Creative Director
Turner Duckworth London & San Francisco
Member of the Pentawards Jury 2009/2010

How do you explain why a jury spread over 12 different countries around the world finally selected the same best designs?

Great design must have clarity of thought, be appropriately executed, and have a clear point of difference. On top of all that, it should be something that makes me viscerally respond, "I wish I'd done that!"

When judging, you see so many designs that are over-worked and complicated in their design or message. It is such a relief to see simple, strong ideas-based work that cuts through the normality. Wherever you are in the world, the cream always floats to the top of the coffee.

How would you advise young people wishing to become a packaging designer?

Concentrate on good ideas, there's nothing better. Think of packages like small posters on the shelf, think of simple, big ideas then reduce them down to fit on a pack. Packaging is often just the start of an identity that gets applied across all sorts of applications from Brand stores to websites. Make sure your design comes to life off the packaging, as well as on it.

Who impressed you the most in your professional life and why?

Hypgnosis, the album cover design group of the '70s, got me wanting to be a designer in the first place, I still love their album cover ideas for Pink Floyd and the rest. I always wanted to design an album cover. It took me until I was 45 years old to do our first one!

Bob Gill is the greatest ideas Graphic Designer ever. He introduces witty ideas and doesn't rely on complex execution for them to work. His work is as inspirational today as it ever was.

Marcello Minale (of Minale Tattersfield, where David Turner and I met) was a hugely impressive character. He had a larger-than-life personality, witty ideas and was great fun to be around. David Turner and I actually refer to him as the Spiritual Chairman of our company because of his attitude to design, business, and the importance he placed on a balanced life.

Mary Lewis of Lewis Moberly is a class above most designers. Her aesthetic judgement, intelligence, and perfectionist tendencies make everything she touches a joy to behold.

My father, who has always run his own companies, is great for giving me perspective and a common-sense approach to business matters.

The person that inspires me most is my business partner David Turner. David makes me think harder and push ideas further, he is my conscience to do great design. He thinks of ideas that I wish I'd thought of, genuinely big ideas which lead to really interesting ground-breaking work. Most importantly, he doesn't take himself too seriously and for the last 17 years we have had a lot of fun.

Japan is known for its package design like the UK, where you come from. How do you see their take on design over the last years as a foreigner?

I'm always envious of Japanese design, it seems that Japanese designers have an innate sense of style, an appreciation of simplicity of form and preciousness of typography. Unfortunately I can't actually read the Japanese so I have no idea if it's a good idea or funny, etc., but the graphic style of the work does appeal in a way that most Western design doesn't compare.

Concerning a Platinum winner from 2009: a Greek cement packaging showing a sophisticated lady... What do you think about it?

Cement with a picture of a beautiful woman on it. I've never seen it before, it's irreverent and fun and the most interesting cement bag I've ever seen! I'm sure builders love it.

Wie erklären Sie sich, dass eine Jury, deren Mitglieder kontinentübergreifend aus zwölf Ländern stammen, sich schließlich auf dieselben besten Designs einigen konnte?

Herausragendes Design muss eine Klarheit im Denken besitzen, entsprechend ausgeführt werden und deutliche Unterscheidungsmerkmale aufweisen. Obendrein sollte es etwas sein, von dem ich gefühlsmäßig sagen würde: „Das hätte ich auch total gerne gemacht!"

In einer Jury begegnen einem so viele Designs, die überstrapaziert oder in ihrer Gestaltung beziehungsweise ihrer Botschaft zu kompliziert sind. Was für eine Erleichterung, wenn man dann auf einfache Arbeiten trifft, die auf starken Ideen beruhen und sich von der Normalität abheben. Die Sahne schwimmt immer oben auf dem Kaffee, das gilt überall auf der Welt.

Was würden Sie jungen Menschen raten, die Verpackungsdesigner werden wollen?

Konzentriert euch auf gute Ideen – etwas Besseres gibt es nicht. Stellt euch Verpackungen wie kleine Plakate im Regal vor. Denkt euch einfache, große Ideen aus und reduziert sie dann, damit sie auf eine Packung passen. Die Verpackung ist oft nur der Ausgangspunkt einer Identität. Sie kann in allen möglichen Bereichen eingesetzt werden, von Brandstores bis zu Websites. Achtet darauf, dass euer Design ohne, aber auch mit Verpackung lebendig wird.

Wer hat Sie als Profi am meisten beeindruckt und warum?

Die Designgruppe Hypgnosis, die in den 1970ern Plattencover gestaltete, war für mich überhaupt der Grund, Designer zu werden. Ich mag ihre Ideen für die Cover von Pink Floyd und all die anderen immer noch. Ich wollte schon immer einmal eine Plattenhülle gestalten, aber ich musste erst 45 Jahre alt werden, bevor wir unser erstes Cover machen konnten!

Bob Gill ist der Grafikdesigner mit den großartigsten Ideen überhaupt. Er führt pfiffige Ideen ein und verlässt sich nicht auf eine komplexe Ausführung, damit sie funktionieren. Seine Arbeiten sind heute immer noch so inspirierend wie eh und je.

Marcello Minale (von Minale Tattersfield, wo ich David Turner traf) war ein höchst beeindruckender Mensch. Er hatte eine überlebensgroße Persönlichkeit und geistreiche Ideen; es machte einfach Spaß, in seiner Nähe zu sein. David Turner und ich bezeichnen ihn als den „spirituellen Vorsitzenden"

unserer Firma wegen seiner Einstellung zum Design, zum Geschäft und wegen der Bedeutung, die er einem ausgewogenen Leben beimaß.

Mary Lewis von Lewis Moberly gehört im Vergleich zu den meisten anderen Designern zu einer ganz eigenen Klasse. Ihr ästhetisches Urteilsvermögen, ihre Intelligenz und ihre Neigung zum Perfektionismus machen alles, was sie anpackt, zu einer wahren Augenweide.

Ich finde meinen Vater, der immer seine eigenen Firmen geleitet hat, deswegen großartig, weil er mir Perspektiven aufzeigt und sagt, wie man geschäftliche Angelegenheiten mit gesundem Menschenverstand angeht.

Die Person, die mich am meisten inspiriert, ist mein Geschäftspartner David Turner. David bringt mich dazu, noch mehr nachzudenken und Ideen weiter voranzutreiben. Er ist mein Gewissen, das es mir erlaubt, gutes Design zu machen. Er denkt sich Sachen aus, auf die ich auch liebend gerne gekommen wäre, wirklich großartige Ideen, die zu interessanten, bahnbrechenden Arbeiten führen. Doch am wichtigsten ist, dass er sich selbst nicht allzu ernst nimmt; wir hatten in den letzten 17 Jahren eine Menge Spaß.

Japan ist ähnlich wie Großbritannien, von wo Sie stammen, für sein Verpackungsdesign sehr bekannt. Wie beurteilen Sie als Ausländer den japanischen Ansatz beim Design der letzten Jahre?

Auf japanisches Design bin ich immer neidisch. Bei japanischen Designern ist der Sinn für Stil scheinbar angeboren. Sie würdigen die Einfachheit von Formen und die Kostbarkeit der Typographie. Leider kann ich kein Japanisch und habe deswegen auch keine Ahnung, ob etwas eine gute Idee oder lustig ist oder so, aber der grafische Stil der Arbeit ist doch auf eine Weise ansprechend, mit der die meisten westlichen Designs nicht gleichziehen können.

Nehmen wir einen Platin-Gewinner aus dem Jahre 2009: Eine griechische Zementpackung zeigt eine wunderschöne Dame... Was halten Sie davon?

Zement mit dem Bild einer wunderschönen Frau darauf. Das habe ich vorher noch nie gesehen. Es ist respektlos, macht Spaß und ist der interessanteste Zementsack, den ich je gesehen habe! Ich bin sicher, dass die Bauarbeiter das lieben.

Interview with
BRUCE DUCKWORTH

Comment expliquez-vous qu'un jury issu de 12 pays différents des quatre coins du globe ait finalement sélectionné les mêmes meilleurs designs ?

Un bon design doit illustrer une pensée claire, être exécuté de façon appropriée et être différent des autres. En plus de tout cela, il faut que ce soit quelque chose qui me fasse penser spontanément : « J'aurais aimé en être l'auteur ! »

Lorsqu'on fait partie du jury, on voit des quantités de projets dont le design ou le message est trop élaboré et compliqué. C'est un tel soulagement de voir des travaux basés sur des idées simples et fortes, qui ne sont pas soumis à la normalité. Où que l'on soit dans le monde, la fine fleur se détache toujours du reste.

Quels conseils donneriez-vous aux jeunes qui veulent devenir designer de packaging ?

De se concentrer sur de bonnes idées, il n'y a rien de mieux. Il faut voir les emballages comme de petites affiches sur les rayons, trouver des idées simples mais grandes et les réduire de façon à ce qu'elles tiennent sur un emballage. Le packaging n'est souvent que le point de départ d'une identité qui est appliquée sur toutes sortes de supports, des boutiques de marque jusqu'aux sites web. Faites en sorte que votre design prenne vie sur le packaging, mais aussi au-delà.

Dans votre parcours professionnel, qui vous a le plus marqué et pourquoi ?

C'est Hypgnosis, le groupe de designers de pochettes d'albums des années 1970, qui m'a donné envie d'être designer. J'aime toujours leurs idées de pochettes pour les Pink Floyd et les autres groupes de cette époque. J'ai toujours voulu créer une pochette d'album. J'ai dû attendre d'avoir 45 ans pour que nous fassions la première !

Le graphiste qui a les meilleures idées est Bob Gill. Il n'a pas besoin d'une réalisation complexe pour que ses idées brillantes fonctionnent. Son travail continue d'inspirer aujourd'hui comme par le passé.

Marcello Minale (de Minale Tattersfield, où j'ai rencontré David Turner) a été un personnage très marquant. Il avait une personnalité hors normes, des idées brillantes, et il était très drôle. David Turner et moi l'avons en fait nommé président spirituel de notre entreprise, à cause de son attitude envers le design et les affaires, et de l'importance qu'il accordait à mener une vie équilibrée.

Mary Lewis, de Lewis Moberly, est un cran au-dessus de la plupart des designers. Ses critères esthétiques, son intelligence et sa tendance au perfectionnisme font de tout ce qu'elle touche un plaisir pour les yeux.

Mon père, qui a toujours dirigé ses propres entreprises, m'a donné une perspective et une vision pleine de bon sens des aspects commerciaux.

La personne qui m'inspire le plus est mon associé, David Turner. Il m'oblige à pousser ma réflexion et mes idées plus loin, il est ma conscience pour faire du bon design. Il a des idées que j'aurais aimé avoir, des idées vraiment grandes qui mènent à un travail véritablement intéressant et innovant. Mais, et c'est le plus important, il ne se prend pas trop au sérieux et nous nous sommes beaucoup amusés ces 17 dernières années.

Le Japon est connu pour ses emballages, tout comme le Royaume-Uni, votre pays. En tant qu'étranger, que pensez-vous de leur interprétation de l'emballage ces dernières années ?

Je suis toujours jaloux du design japonais. Il semble que les designers japonais aient un sens inné du style, une appréciation de la simplicité des formes et de la beauté de la typographie. Malheureusement, je ne sais pas lire le japonais et je ne sais donc pas si l'idée est bonne, ou drôle, etc. Mais le style graphique a un charme qui échappe à une grande partie du design occidental.

Le lauréat du prix Platinum de l'édition 2009 est un packaging grec pour du ciment, illustré par l'image d'une élégante... Qu'en pensez-vous ?

Du ciment avec une belle femme dessus. Je n'avais jamais vu ça avant, c'est irrévérencieux et drôle, et c'est le sac de ciment le plus intéressant que j'aie jamais vu ! Je suis sûr que les maçons adorent.

Mouse Graphics in Athens created a surprising design for this range of **Petrocoll** cement bags that completely broke the mould in the field of construction. The agency's aim was to create a design for the product that would radically change the packaging compared to what all the competitors used, and thus get the brand much talked about. The design features elegant, non-provocative female figures, that does not resemble traditional cement bags, and therefore stands out both at the point of sale and on construction sites.

Mouse Graphics aus Athen überraschte mit seinem Design einer Reihe von **Petrocoll**-Zementsäcken, das im Bereich des Bauwesens völlig aus dem Rahmen fiel. Die Agentur wollte für das Produkt eine Gestaltung schaffen, die verglichen mit dem, was von der Konkurrenz bereits im Umlauf war, die Verpackung radikal verändert und so die Marke verstärkt ins Gespräch bringt. Die Gestaltung arbeitet mit eleganten, nicht-aufreizenden weiblichen Figuren. Es erinnert nicht an traditionelle Zementsäcke und hebt sich somit sowohl in den Verkaufsräumen als auch auf den Baustellen besonders hervor.

L'agence athénienne Mouse Gaphics a créé un design surprenant pour cette gamme de sacs de ciment **Petrocoll,** qui brise complètement le moule dans le secteur de la construction. Elle voulait créer un design qui transforme-rait complètement le packaging par rapport à ce que les concurrents utilisent, et ainsi faire parler de la marque. Les sacs sont illustrés de personnages féminins élégants, non provocants, et ne ressemblent pas aux sacs de ciment traditionnels. Ils se démarquent donc sur le point de vente, mais aussi sur les chantiers.

PETROCOLL SPATULA PUTTY

Design: Aris Pasouris
Company: Mouse Graphics
Country: Greece
Category: Best of the category
Other markets

PLATINUM PENTAWARD 2009

SPARK

Design: Young Soo, Park Hyun Kyun,
Son Kwang Pil, Choi
Company: Aekyung Industrial
Country: South Korea
Category: Best of the category Other markets

PLATINUM PENTAWARD 2008

The **Spark** laundry detergent box speaks a universal language thanks to the creative washing-machine shape and there is no need for further explanation to the consumer. They can immediately recognise the type of product and its use and furthermore can see how much of it is left in the box, making re-purchase easier. This package is also multi-use and can be filled again with a refill.

Der Karton für das Waschmittel **Spark** ist dank der kreativen Waschmaschinenform universell verständlich, und der Konsument braucht keine weiteren Erläuterungen. Er kann sofort den Typ des Produkts erkennen und wie es verwendet werden soll. Weil er auch immer sehen kann, wie voll die Box noch ist, wird der Nachkauf noch einfacher. Außerdem ist die Verpackung wiederverwendbar und kann aufgefüllt werden.

La boîte de lessive **Spark** parle une langue universelle grâce à sa forme créative de machine à laver, et le consommateur n'a pas de besoin d'autres explications. Il reconnaît immédiatement le type de produit et son utilisation. De plus, le hublot lui permet de voir le niveau de produit qui reste dans la boîte, ce qui facilite le réachat. Cette boîte est également réutilisable, et peut être remplie grâce à une recharge de lessive.

The Wild Bag Box is the packaging for **out_of_ark**, a bag collection with three basic models and 15 different motifs featuring animals from five continents. The Crossover bags are transported in the escape-proof Wild Bag Box – as is fitting for wild bags. The Wild Bag Box is thus intended to be more than just simple packaging, as it becomes part of the story and affirms the vitality of the products. The lively contents are kept safe, but are still clearly visible through the bars. The corrugated board, the basic material of the packaging, is left in its natural state.

Die Taschenkollektion **out_of_ark** erscheint in drei Grundmodellen und mit 15 unterschiedlichen Motiven von Tieren aus fünf Kontinenten und wird in der Wild Bag Box verpackt. Die Crossover-Taschen werden in der ausbruchssicheren Wild Bag Box transportiert – für „wilde Taschen" sehr angemessen. Die Wild Bag Box ist somit mehr als bloße Verpackung, sie ergänzt die mit dem Produkt erzählten Geschichte und bekräftigt dessen Vitalität. Die „lebhaften" Inhalte werden sicher transportiert, sind aber durch die Stäbe immer noch gut sichtbar. Das Grundmaterial der Verpackung ist unbehandelte Wellpappe.

La Wild Bag Box est l'emballage de **out_of_ark**, une collection de sacs avec trois modèles de base et 15 motifs différents représentant des animaux des cinq continents. Les sacs Crossover sont transportés dans la cage de la Wild Bag Box, ce qui est tout à fait approprié pour des sacs sauvages. La Wild Bag Box est donc plus qu'un simple emballage, car elle fait partie intégrante de l'histoire racontée au consommateur, et renforce la notion de produit vivant. Son contenu plein de vie est en sécurité, mais est bien visible derrière les barreaux. Le carton ondulé, un matériau de base dans l'emballage, est laissé à l'état brut.

OUT_OF_ARK

Design: Joseph Poelzelbauer, Simone Poelzelbauer
Company: Identis GmbH
Country: Germany
Category: Best of the category Other markets

PLATINUM PENTAWARD 2010

Lucibel is a new brand of compact fluorescent lights, entering the French and European market. For the naming, branding, and packaging, the agency nouvelœuvre created an aspirational brand and a strong and easy segmentation for consumers (wattage/colour strategy), an eco-designed and striking pack in recycled paper, very different from plastic blisters.

Lucibel ist eine neue Marke kompakter Leuchtstoffröhren für den französischen und europäischen Markt. Hinsichtlich Namensgebung, Branding und Verpackung schuf die Agentur nouvelœuvre eine begehrenswerte Marke, eine wirkungsvolle, aber einfache Segmentierung für die Verbraucher (die Wattzahl wird anhand von Farben kenntlich gemacht) und ein auffallendes Ökodesign aus Recyclingpapier, das sich stark von den Sichtverpackungen aus Kunststoff unterscheidet.

Lucibel est une nouvelle marque d'ampoules fluorescentes qui fait son entrée sur les marchés français et européens. Pour le nom, la stratégie de marque et le packaging, l'agence nouvelœuvre a créé une marque ambitieuse et une segmentation facile pour les consommateurs (stratégie watt/couleur), et un packaging écologique en papier recyclé qui se fait remarquer, très différent des blisters en plastique.

LUCIBEL

Design: Cédric Francois, Marie Laporte, Laurent Fontaine, Marco Savary, Paul Vickers
Company: nouvelœuvre
Country: France
Category: Household maintenance (detergents, cleaning products and utensils, batteries, light bulbs, etc.)

GOLD PENTAWARD 2009

GAUSS

Design: Alexey Lavrentiev, Max Tushakaev,
Vasily Gubin, Ilya Soloviov
Company: Fastway. Ideas that rock!
Country: Russia
Category: Household maintenance
(detergents, cleaning products and utensils,
batteries, light bulbs, etc.)

SILVER PENTAWARD 2009

  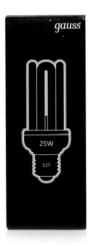   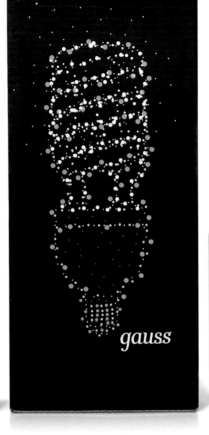 

CARE&S

Creative Direction/Design/Product Development: Jonas Lundin
Trend Analyst/Concept Development: Magdalena Bjurenstedt Adaktusson
Project Management: Frida Berggren
Company: LA+B, Love for Art and Business
Country: Sweden
Category: Household maintenance
(detergents, cleaning products and utensils, batteries, light bulbs, etc.)

SILVER PENTAWARD 2009

ARIEL
EXCEL GEL

Creative Director: Will Davis, Studio Davis
Development Director: David McNeill, Studio Davis
Senior Design Manager: Paul Scott, Procter & Gamble
Design Associate Director: Richard Moore, Procter & Gamble
Company: Studio Davis
Country: UK
Category: Household maintenance
(detergents, cleaning products and utensils,
batteries, light bulbs, etc.)

GOLD PENTAWARD 2010

SOONSAEM BUBBLE

Design: Karim Rashid
Company: Aekyung Industrial
Country: South Korea
Category: Household maintenance
(detergents, cleaning products and utensils,
batteries, light bulbs, etc.)
SILVER PENTAWARD 2010

SKIP

Creative Director: Gustavo Piqueira
Design: Gustavo Piqueira, Ingrid Lafalce
Assistant Designers: Danilo Helvadjian,
Leonardo Rodrigues, Lilian Meireles
Company: Casa Rex
Country: Brazil
Category: Household maintenance
(detergents, cleaning products and utensils,
batteries, light bulbs, etc.)
SILVER PENTAWARD 2010

CLOROX

Art Director: Bob Hullinger
Design: Meegan Peery, Bob Hullinger
Company: Brand Engine
Country: USA
Category: Household maintenance
(detergents, cleaning products
and utensils, batteries, light bulbs, etc.)

BRONZE PENTAWARD 2009

TIDE
TOTALCARE

Design: Brian Rice (Principal Design Manager, Global Fabric Care, Procter & Gamble)
Creative Director: Dale Doyle (Landor Cincinnati)
Client Director: Noelle Flood (Landor Cincinnati)
Senior Client Manager: Rebecca Moses (Landor Cincinnati)
Company: Procter & Gamble
Country: USA
Category: Household maintenance
(detergents, cleaning products and utensils, batteries, light bulbs, etc.)

BRONZE PENTAWARD 2009

ALL DETERGENT

Design: Stuart Harvey Lee,
Jochen Schaepers (Prime Studio),
Vincent Masotta, Keith Colacioppo (Sun Products)
Graphic Design: Raison Pure
Company: Prime Studio Inc.
Country: USA
Category: Household maintenance
(detergents, cleaning products
and utensils, batteries, light bulbs, etc.)

BRONZE PENTAWARD 2009

TRIOL

Design: Igor Palichev, Ramil Sharipov
Company: DarkDesignGroup
Country: Russia
Category: Home improvement
(paint, tools, gardening products, D.I.Y. etc.)
& decoration (furniture, equipment, etc.)

SILVER PENTAWARD 2010

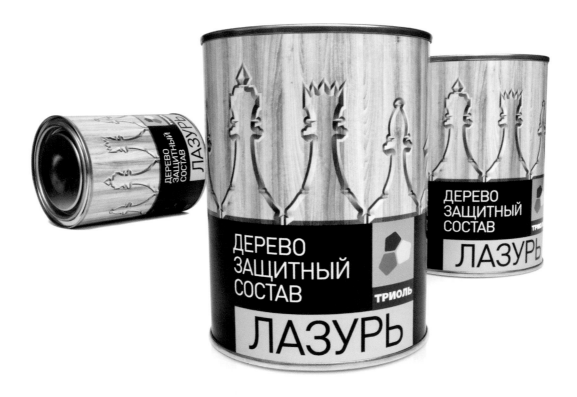

TIKKURILA
OPTIVA

Creative Director/Art Director: Aleksander Koczy
Company: SaltPepper Brand Design
Country: Poland
Category: Home improvement
(paint, tools, gardening products, DIY, etc.)
& decoration (furniture, equipment, etc.)

SILVER PENTAWARD 2010

STAS

Design: Cristina Poncu, Marius Ursache
Company: Grapefruit
Country: Romania
Category: Home improvement
(paint, tools, gardening products, DIY, etc.)
& decoration (furniture, equipment, etc.)

SILVER PENTAWARD 2009

Silver Cross produces nursery products such as prams, push-chairs, strollers, travel seats, and high chairs. The agency Love have developed a new brand approach for Silver Cross, moving them away from being perceived as a 'manufacturer of prams' to being a brand that understands what it's like being a parent. The concept for the packaging was developed from the insight that although parents see boxes as something to throw away, kids see them as a new toy... a boat, a house, a hat. The new designs encourage parents to recycle boxes and use them to feed their children's imaginations.

Silver Cross stellt Produkte für Kinder her, z. B. Kinderwagen, Buggys, Kindersitze und Kinderstühle. Die Agentur Love hat einen neuen Ansatz entwickelt, der Silver Cross davon wegbewegen soll, nur als „Kinderwagenhersteller" wahrgenommen zu werden. Stattdessen soll das Unternehmen als Marke etabliert werden, die weiß, was es bedeutet, Eltern zu sein. Beim Verpackungskonzept berücksichtigte man die Erkenntnis, dass Kartons für Eltern zwar Wegwerfartikel sind, Kinder darin aber neue Spielzeuge sehen: ein Boot, ein Haus oder einen Hut. Die neuen Designs ermuntern die Eltern, die Kartons zu recyceln und sie zu nutzen, um die Fantasie ihrer Kinder anzuregen.

Silver Cross fabrique des produits de puériculture, notamment des landaus, des poussettes, des sièges de voiture et des chaises hautes. L'agence Love a imaginé une nouvelle approche pour Silver Cross, afin de leur faire quitter le rôle de « fabricant de landaus » et de leur faire adopter celui de marque qui comprend ce que c'est que d'être parent. Le concept du packaging a été développé à partir de l'idée que bien que les parents voient les boîtes en carton comme des déchets à jeter, les enfants les voient comme un nouveau jouet...un bateau, une maison, un chapeau. Ces emballages encouragent les parents à recycler les cartons et à les utiliser pour nourrir l'imagination de leurs enfants.

SILVER CROSS UK LIMITED

Design: Emma Morton, Adam Rix, Simon Griffin
Company: Love
Country: UK
Category: Home improvement (paint, tools, gardening products, DIY, etc.) & decoration (furniture, equipment, etc.)

GOLD PENTAWARD 2008

NEWTON'S SEEDS

Design: Monique Pilley, Nigel Kuzimski
Company: Curious Design
Country: New Zealand
Category: Home improvement
(paint, tools, gardening products, DIY, etc.)
& decoration (furniture, equipment, etc.)

SILVER PENTAWARD 2009

LINENS
ARZU KAPROL HOME LINE

Design: Orhan Irmak design team
Company: Orhan Irmak Tasarim
Country: Turkey
Category: Home improvement
(paint, tools, gardening products, DIY, etc.)
& decoration (furniture, equipment, etc.)

BRONZE PENTAWARD 2009

Audiovox Accessories' research indicated younger customers purchased ear buds for their personal music-players as fashion accessories. With this in mind, JDA, Inc. Retail Ready Design set out to create a package directed to attracting this youthful customer. Changing completely the norms for this category, they strove for fun, edgy, unique, full-of-personality packaging designs.

Die Recherchen von **Audiovox Accessories** legen nahe, dass junge Kunden Ohrhörer für ihre eigenen Musik-abspielgeräte wie Modeaccessoires kaufen. Die Agentur JDA, Inc. Retail Ready Design berücksichtigte das und gestaltete eine Verpackung, die jugendliche Kunden direkt ansprechen sollte. Die Normen in dieser Kategorie wurden komplett verändert, und man legte die Verpackung in einer fröhlichen, auffälligen und unverwechselbaren Gestaltung mit ganz eigener Persönlichkeit an.

L'étude réalisée par **Audiovox Accessories** indiquait que les jeunes clients achetaient des écouteurs pour leur lecteur de musique personnel comme s'il s'agissait d'accessoires de mode. C'est avec cette idée à l'esprit que JDA, Inc. Retail Ready Design a commencé à créer un packaging conçu pour attirer ce profil de clients jeunes. L'agence a complètement bouleversé les normes de cette catégorie, et a parié sur des concepts drôles, tendance, uniques et pleins de personnalité.

AUDIOVOX ACCESSORIES CORP. EARBUDEEZ

Creative Director: David Jensen
Art Director: Jerome Calleja
Designer: Dean Kojima
Company: JDA, Inc. Retail Ready Design
Country: USA
Category: Electronic (computers, printers, consumables, software, etc.)

GOLD PENTAWARD 2009

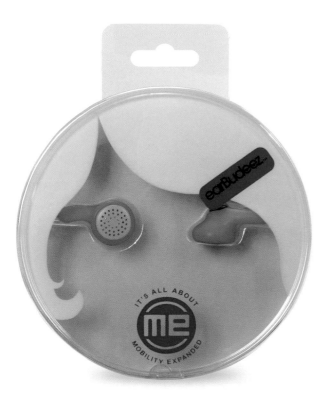

R-Design was approached by **WH Smith** to redesign the Art and Artist Materials predominantly bought by budding amateur artists and students. There were over 19 lines including sketchbooks, paint tubes, watercolour tins, pens, and pencils. The solution was to focus and inspire not only by how one paints and draws but also by conveying the artist's thoughts by choosing relevant artist's sayings. This was achieved by commissioning several different illustrators to use the sayings with the relevant use of materials.

R-Design bekam von **WH Smith** den Auftrag, Artikel des Künstlerbedarfs neu zu gestalten, die überwiegend von ambitionierten Hobbykünstlern und von Kunststudenten gekauft wurden. Es gab mehr als 19 Produktlinien, darunter Skizzenblöcke, Farbtuben, Tuschkästen, Federn und Zeichenstifte. Die Lösung bestand darin, sich nicht nur darauf zu konzentrieren und davon inspirieren zu lassen, wie jemand zeichnet und malt, sondern auch die Gedanken von Künstlern zu vermitteln, indem man die Verpackungen durch passende Zitate von Künstlern schmückt. Dafür bekamen verschiedene Illustratoren den Auftrag, diese Zitate umzusetzen und dabei relevante Materialien zu verwenden.

WH Smith a demandé à R-Design de revoir le design de ses fournitures artistiques, en général achetées par des artistes amateurs en herbe et des étudiants. Il y avait plus de 19 lignes de produits, notamment des carnets de croquis, des tubes de peinture, des boîtes d'aquarelle, des stylos et des crayons. La solution était d'inspirer les clients non seulement en évoquant la façon de peindre et de dessiner, mais aussi grâce à la pensée artistique, en reprenant des citations d'artistes. Plusieurs illustrateurs ont été chargés de travailler sur ces citations à l'aide du produit concerné.

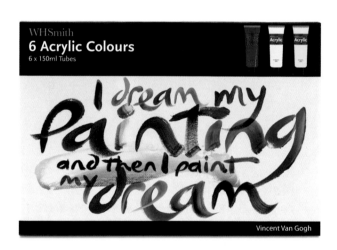

WH SMITH
ART AND ARTIST MATERIALS

Design: Steve Sheffield,
Dave Richmond, Peter Horridge
Company: R-Design Ltd.
Country: UK
Category: Non-electronic
(paper, writing materials, stationery, etc.)

GOLD PENTAWARD 2008

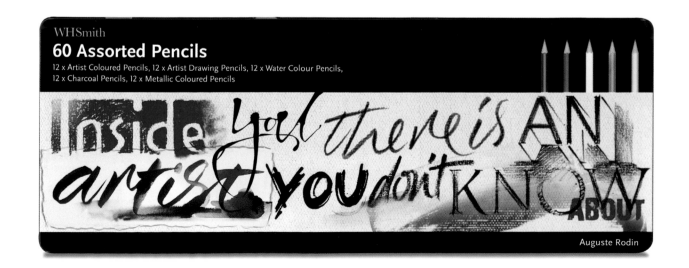

BIC TRIUMPH ROLLER BALL PENS

Creative Director: Daniel Dittmar
Design Leader: Anna Rubino
Conceptual Design Development: John Waski Design
Company: BIC Consumer Products
Country: USA
Category: Non-electronic
(paper, writing materials, stationery, etc.)

SILVER PENTAWARD 2009

Slice collaborates with world-renowned designers, such as Yves Béhar, Karim Rashid, and Michael Graves, to design and create award-winning cutting tools for the home and office. The products, many of which utilise ceramic cutting technology, are unusual, sharp, and safe. After creating a new logo for **Slice**, the range developed a graphic system that utilised a 40-degree angular "slice" – echoing the logo – that could be implemented in different ways across the packaging system to create an iconic and memorable packaging system. This allowed for consistent graphic application across varying formats, and varying budget considerations.

Slice arbeitet mit weltbekannten Designern wie Yves Béhar, Karim Rashid und Michael Graves zusammen, um preisgekrönte Schneidwerkzeuge für Heim und Büro zu schaffen. Die Produkte sind sehr scharf, sicher und fallen ins Auge. Viele von ihnen verwenden eine Keramik-schneidtechnik. Nach Erstellen eines neuen Logos für **Slice** wurde ein visuelles System entwickelt, bei dem die Verpackungen im Winkel von 40 Grad angeschnitten sind. Damit wird das Logo aufgegriffen, und bei den Verpackungen kann dieses Anschneiden auf verschiedene Weise implementiert werden, um ein symbolträchtiges Verpackungssystem mit hohem Wiedererkennungs-wert zu schaffen. Außerdem erlaubt es einen optisch einheitlichen Einsatz bei unterschiedlichen Formaten und verschiedenen Budgets.

Slice collabore avec des designers de renom inter-national, comme Yves Béhar, Karim Rashid et Michael Graves, pour concevoir et réaliser des outils coupants primés à usage domestique et professionnel. Les produits, dont beaucoup ont un tranchant en céramique, sont originaux, aiguisés et sûrs à utiliser. Après la création d'un nouveau logo pour **Slice**, la gamme a été dotée un système graphique articulé autour d'une « tranche » (« slice » en anglais, pour reprendre le logo) qui peut être utilisée de différentes manières dans les emballages pour créer un système d'emballage emblématique et mémorable. Cela donne une cohérence graphique sur différents formats, et pour différents budgets.

MAPED

Design: Caracas design team
Company: Caracas
Country: France
Category: Non-electronic
(paper, writing materials, stationery, etc.)

BRONZE PENTAWARD 2010

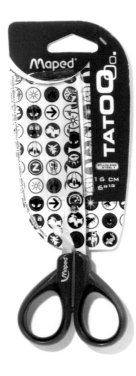

SLICE

Design: Tom Crabtree, Joshua Swanbeck, Eileen Lee
Company: Manual
Country: USA
Category: Non-electronic
(paper, writing materials, stationery, etc.)

GOLD PENTAWARD 2010

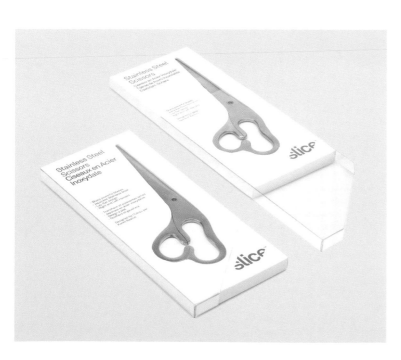

MICHELIN
MOUNTAIN BIKE TYRES

Design: Sébastien Canu, Lorenzo Santangelo,
Florent Soissons, Claire Bourlange
Company: Japa
Country: France
Category: Automobile products
(oils, car care, spare parts, etc.)

SILVER PENTAWARD 2010

PEWAG
SNOX

Strategy: Georg Wagner
Product Design: Stefan Arbeithuber
Brand Design: Tina Feiertag, Maria Hell
Copywriter: Mathias Miller-Aichholz
Company: Spirit Design/Innovation and Branding
Country: Austria
Category: Automobile products
(oils, car care, spare parts, etc.)

BRONZE PENTAWARD 2009

Over the years, Coke's packaging had become covered in drips and bubbles, emulating the fizzy refreshment inside. As a generic approach, every other soft drink could also do the same. So **Coca-Cola** asked Turner Duckworth offices in London and San Francisco to create a visual identity system in line with Coke's "21st Century refreshment" strategy. They responded by removing extraneous elements to reveal that only Coke can have the Spencerian script and the ribbon design creating emotional resonance with the fewest possible elements.

Im Laufe der Zeit bekam die Verpackung von Coke immer mehr Tröpfchen und Bläschen, die die darin enthaltene sprudelnde Erfrischung nachahmen sollten. Doch einen solch allgemeinen Ansatz kann man auch bei jedem anderen Erfrischungsgetränk finden. Also beauftragte **Coca-Cola** die Büros von Turner Duckworth in London und San Francisco, ein System für die visuelle Identität zu schaffen, das zur Coke-Strategie einer „Erfrischung des 21. Jahrhunderts" passt. Turner Duckworth entfernten dafür überflüssige Elemente. So wurde deutlich, dass nur Coke mit dieser Kursivschrift, der Spencerian Script, und dem Ribbon Design, also den geringstmöglichen Elementen, für emotionale Resonanz sorgt.

Au cours des années, le packaging de Coca-Cola s'était couvert de gouttes et de bulles pour imiter la boisson pétillante qu'il contenait. Toutes les autres marques de soda pouvaient adopter la même démarche générique. Alors **Coca-Cola** a demandé aux agences de Turner Duckworth de Londres et San Francisco de créer un système d'identité visuelle cohérent avec la stratégie « boisson rafraîchissante du XXIᵉ siècle » de la marque. Ils ont répondu en éliminant tous les éléments étrangers, pour révéler que seul Coca-Cola peut créer une résonance émotionnelle avec ses lettres spencériennes et son ruban, et le moins d'éléments supplémentaires possible.

COCA-COLA IDENTITY

Creative Directors: David Turner, Bruce Duckworth
Design Director: Sarah Moffat
Design: Jonathan Warner, Radu Ranga, Josh Michels, Rebecca Williams, Chris Garvey
Company: Turner Duckworth, London & San Francisco
Country: UK/USA
Category: Brand identity programmes

GOLD PENTAWARD 2009

THE DELI GARAGE

Executive Creative Director: Stefan Kolle; *Creative Director:* Katrin Oeding (Kolle Rebbe, KOREFE)
Art Director: Reginald Wagner (Kolle Rebbe, KOREFE); *Graphic Design:* Jan Hartwig, Jan Simmerl,
Paul Svoboda, Santa Gustina (Kolle Rebbe, KOREFE); *Copywriters:* Lorenz Ritter (Kolle Rebbe),
Till Grabsch, Katharina Trumbach, Madelen Gwosdz (Kolle Rebbe, KOREFE)
Producer: Frank Witte (Produktionsbüro Romey von Malottky); Stephan Gerlach (Kolle Rebbe)
Company: Kolle Rebbe GmbH
Country: Germany
Category: Brand identity programmes

GOLD PENTAWARD 2010

T.D.G. VERTRIEBS UG & CO. KG
STOP THE WATER WHILE USING ME!

Executive Creative Direction: Stefan Kolle
Creative Direction: Katrin Oeding
Art Direction: Christian Doering, Reginald Wagner
Concept/Graphic Design/Typography: Ana Magalhaes
Copywriter: Till Grabsch; *Photographer:* Imke Jansen
Artbuying: Emanuel Mugrauer
Producer: Produktionsbüro Romey von Malottky
Company: Kolle Rebbe GmbH
Country: Germany
Category: Brand identity programmes

SILVER PENTAWARD 2010

NAKASEI

Creative Director: Youichirou Ideura
Art Director: Akihiro Nishizawa
Designer: Kanako Narita
Company: Eight Co., Ltd.
Country: Japan
Category: Brand identity programmes

SILVER PENTAWARD 2009

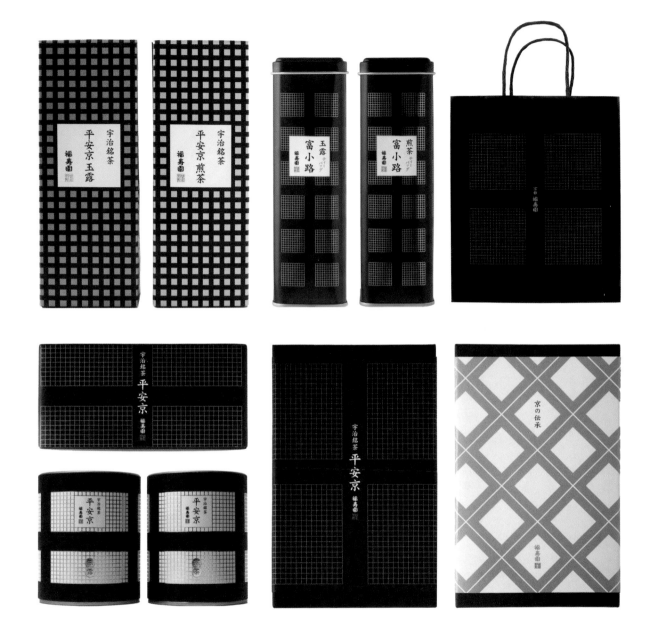

FUKUJUEN

Design: Takashi Kanome, Ichiro Tokudome,
Kazushige Oue, Kikuko Oue
Company: Kanome Design Office
Country: Japan
Category: Brand identity programmes
SILVER PENTAWARD 2009

SUSHIMANIA

Creative Director: Irinel Ionescu
Photographer: Sorin Iacob
DTP: Danubiu Birzu
Artwork: Oliwer Iovanovici, Aaron Balasz
Company: Ampro Design
Country: Romania
Category: Brand identity programmes

BRONZE PENTAWARD 2009

LIZ EARLE
BEAUTY CO. LTD.
IDENTITY

Creative Directors: David Turner, Bruce Duckworth
Design: Bruce Duckworth, Paula Talford, Mark Waters
Photographer: David Bookbinder
Company: Turner Duckworth, London & San Francisco
Country: UK/USA
Category: Brand identity programmes

BRONZE PENTAWARD 2009

INOUY

Design: Clement Eloy
Company: Feel Addicted
Country: France
Category: Pet products
(food and accessories)

BRONZE PENTAWARD 2010

FRISKIES
DRY CAT FOOD

Design: Bill Kumke, Mike Dillon, Nate Berra, Sandy Zub
Company: Nestlé Purina Petcare USA
Country: USA
Category: Pet products (food and accessories)

SILVER PENTAWARD 2010

Challenged with creating an engaging packaging piece for **Metallica**'s ninth studio album, **Death Magnetic**, Turner Duckworth offices in London and San Francisco developed an iconic, three-dimensional CD package using a conspicuous, sunken-grave image and an innovative, layered die cut. The end product shows dirt being sucked down towards a coffin, which lies low in a deepening pit. The classic Metallica logo was re-worked and a signature typographic style created. As well as this, a design kit including logos, imagery, and graphics was distributed to the band's record companies to use as promotional material around the world, ensuring this album was truly one of a kind.

Als sie vor der Herausforderung standen, eine spannende Verpackung für das neunte **Metallica**-Studioalbum **Death Magnetic** zu schaffen, entwickelten die Büros von Turner Duckworth in London und San Francisco eine symbolträchtige, dreidimensionale CD-Hülle. Dafür bedienten sie sich des sehr auffälligen Bildes eines eingesunkenen Grabes und einer innovativen mehrschichtigen Stanzung. Das Endprodukt zeigt, wie Schmutz von einem Sarg angezogen wird, der in einer tiefen Grube liegt. Das klassische Metallica-Logo wurde überarbeitet und mit einer auffälligen Typographie umgesetzt. Obendrein wurde ein Design-Kit mit Logos, Bildern und Grafiken an die Plattenfirmen der Band weitergegeben, das als Promotion-Material weltweit eingesetzt werden sollte, um zu verdeutlichen, wie einzigartig dieses Album ist.

Confrontés au défi de créer une pochette originale pour le neuvième album studio de **Metallica**, **Death Magnetic**, les bureaux de Turner Duckworth de Londres et San Francisco ont imaginé une pochette de CD tridimensionnelle emblématique à l'aide d'une image de tombe creusée et d'une technique innovante de découpe par couches. Le produit final montre de la terre aspirée vers un cercueil qui repose dans une tombe profonde. L'agence a retravaillé le logo classique de Metallica et a créé un style typographique propre au groupe. Un kit de design comprenant les logos, les visuels et les graphismes a également été distribué aux maisons de disques du groupe à travers le monde afin qu'elles l'utilisent pour leurs supports promotionnels, et fassent ainsi de cet album un objet réellement exceptionnel.

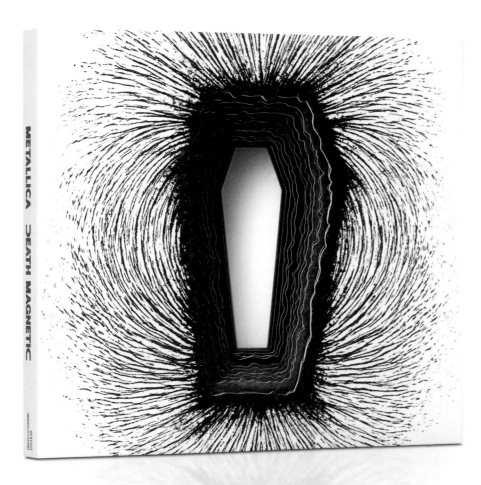

METALLICA
DEATH MAGNETIC DIGI CD

Creative Directors: David Turner, Bruce Duckworth
Design Director: Sarah Moffat
Design: Emily Charette, Marty O'Connor, Jamie McCathie
Design Assistant: Brian Labus
Retouch: Peter Ruane, Craig Snelgrove
Photography: Anton Corbijn, Robert Daly, Andy Grimshaw, Britt Hull, Gavin Hurrell, Mike Kemp, Harper Reed, Tom Schierlitz, Craig Snelgrove, David Turner, Missouri State Highway Patrol
Artwork: Craig Snelgrove
Company: Turner Duckworth, London & San Francisco
Country: UK/USA
Category: Entertainment
(sport, music, photography, phones, games, toys, etc.)

GOLD PENTAWARD 2009

PUMA
PING PONG PADDLE CASE

Design: Johan Liden, Tyler Askew
Company: Aruliden
Country: USA
Category: Entertainment
(sport, music, photography, phones, games, toys, etc.)

SILVER PENTAWARD 2009

This project aimed for a full global redesign of packaging for **Burton Snowboards**, including outerwear, thermal, glove hangtags, boot and binding boxes, and accessory packaging. Illustrations by Travis Millard vary based on the body part associated with each product and with the target demographics. Characters scattered throughout the imagery also depict ways to re-use the box, aligning with Burton's commitment to sustainability.

Dieses Projekt legt es auf eine umfassende globale Neugestaltung sämtlicher Verpackungen für **Burton Snowboards** an. Dazu gehören Thermo- und Oberbekleidung, Anhängeetiketten, Kartons für Stiefel und Bindungen sowie die Verpackungen für Accessoires. Die Illustrationen von Travis Millard variieren je nach Zielgruppe und je nachdem, für welchen Körperteil das Produkt gedacht ist. Über die gesamte Bildgestaltung verteilte Figuren verweisen außerdem darauf, wie man den Karton wiederverwenden kann. Das entspricht der Selbstverpflichtung von Burton, sich für Nachhaltigkeit zu engagieren.

Pour ce projet, il s'agissait de revoir complètement le design du packaging des **snowboards Burton,** y compris les boîtes pour les vestes et pantalons, les vêtements thermiques, les gants, les chaussures et les fixations, ainsi que le packaging des accessoires. Les illustrations de Travis Millard se déclinent en fonction de la partie du corps qui est associée à chaque produit et du public ciblé. Des personnages dispersés dans les images montrent également des façons de réutiliser la boîte, une démarche cohérente avec l'engagement de Burton sur le terrain de la durabilité.

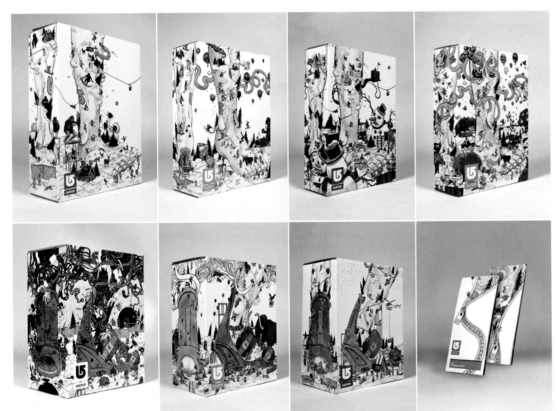

BURTON SNOWBOARDS

Creative Director: Alex Lowe
Design: Adam Weiss
Production Artist: Stew Brinegar
Company: Burton
Country: USA
Category: Entertainment
(sport, music, photography, phones, games, toys, etc.)

GOLD PENTAWARD 2008

POKÉMON TRADING CARD GAME TIN RANGE

Design: Kumi Okada
Producer: Crown Speciality Packaging
Country: France
Category: Entertainment
(sport, music, photography, phones, games, toys, etc.)

BRONZE PENTAWARD 2009

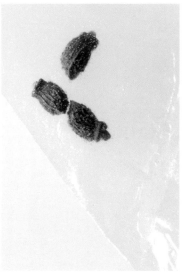

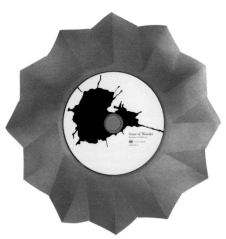

SENSE OF WONDER

Client: OBN Co./Yamaha A&R, Inc.
Creative Director: Hirokazu Kobayashi
Art Director: Hirokazu Kobayashi
Design: Hirokazu Kobayashi, Haruna Yamada,
Satoko Manabe
Photographer: Takashi Mochizuki, Ooki Jingu
Company: Spread Ltd.
Country: Japan
Category: Entertainment
(sport, music, photography, phones, games, toys, etc.)

BRONZE PENTAWARD 2009

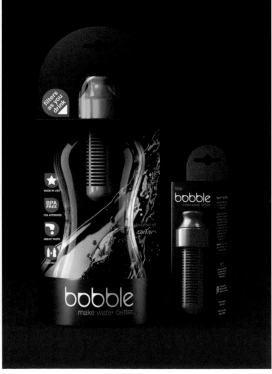

BOBBLE PACKAGING

Design: Chris Stern,
Katie Eaton, Craig Hench
Company: Safari Sundays
Country: USA
Category: Miscellaneous

GOLD PENTAWARD 2010

IIAMO

Design: Karim Rashid
Company: Karim Rashid Inc.
Country: USA
Category: Miscellaneous

SILVER PENTAWARD 2010

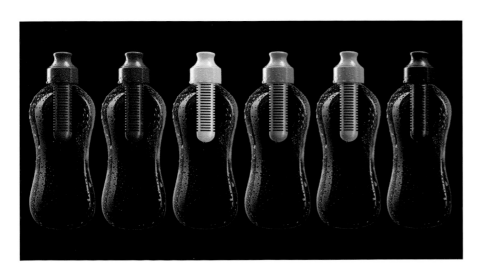

BOBBLE BOTTLE

Design: Karim Rashid
Company: Move Collective LLC
Country: USA
Category: Miscellaneous

BRONZE PENTAWARD 2010

FTD

Design: James Pietruszynski, Stephanie Crair
Company: Optima Soulsight
Country: USA
Category: Miscellaneous

SILVER PENTAWARD 2009

AMPRODESIGN
DESIGN PORTFOLIO MINI DISK

Creative Director: Irinel Ionescu
Art Director/3D: Mario Teodoru; *DTP:* Birzu Danubiu
Company: Ampro Design; *Country:* Romania
Category: Miscellaneous

BRONZE PENTAWARD 2010

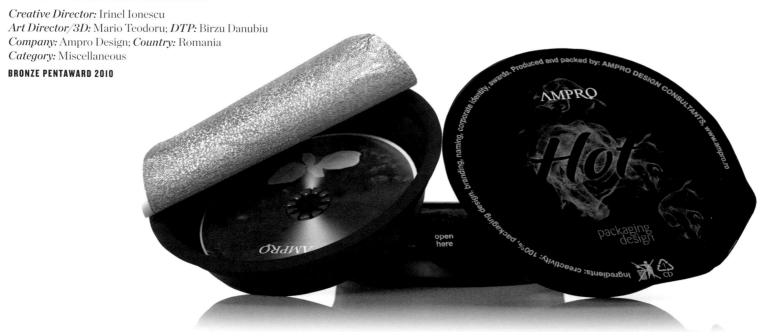

LUCKY STRIKE

Design: Pete Serjeant, Ben Cox
Company: G2 Hamburg
Country: Germany
Category: Miscellaneous

SILVER PENTAWARD 2009

NANA'S GREEN TEA TUMBLERS

Art Director: Akihiro Nishizawa
Design: Akihiro Nishizawa, Etsuko Sanada, Wakako Shibata
Company: Eight Co., Ltd.
Country: Japan
Category: Miscellaneous

SILVER PENTAWARD 2010

AERO

Design: Tony Sanders, Brian Coleman, Tim Austen
Company: Beyond Design Inc.
Country: USA
Category: Miscellaneous

BRONZE PENTAWARD 2010

TUNA PARTY INVITE
SUSTUNABILITY INVITATION

Creative Director: Stan Church
Illustration: Tom Davidson
Company: Wallace Church Inc.
Country: USA
Category: Self-promotion

SILVER PENTAWARD 2009

PENTAWARDS JURY

GÉRARD CARON
France, Chairman of the International Jury
+ Regarded as the founder of marketing design in France and Europe. + Set up Carré Noir in 1973 (today a member of the Publicis group). + Co-founder and former president of PDA (Pan-European Brand Design Association). + Author of many publications, organiser of conferences and seminars. + Designed the most complete website for design www.admirabledesign.com. + He has created no fewer than 1,200 brand identities and 13,000 package designs.

MICHAEL AIDAN
France, Danone Waters
+ Graduated in marketing from ESCP, Paris, in 1988. + Brand Manager at P&G and YSL international perfumes division. + Account & Marketing Director at Cato Gobé & Associates, New York. + Marketing Manager from 1993 to 2006, responsible for major brands at Pepsico (Lays, Pepsi-Cola, Tropicana). + VP Marketing at Danone Waters. + Lecturer in master classes at ESCP-EAP and HE.

OLEG BERIEV
Russia, Mildberry Brand Building Solutions
+ Born in 1967, started his career in marketing in 1990. + His career spans being head of sales for an import/export company to being vice-president of marketing of one of the largest Russian companies. + Set up the Mildberry agency in 1999, the first Russian packaging-design agency and currently the leader on the Russian market with branches in Brussels, London, and Milan.

STANLEY CHURCH
USA, Founder, Managing Partner, and Executive Creative Director of Wallace Church in New York
+ Graduate and former faculty member of Parsons School of Design. + Member of the Art Directors' Club, AIGA, Type Directors' Club, and Design Management Institute. + Judge in national and international design competitions. + Guest speaker at different organisations around the USA. + Winner of several Awards: at the Art Directors' Club, AIGA, ADLA, the Advertising Club of New York's ANDY, the CLIO Gold & Silver, and at Pentawards.

MARK COWAN
Australia, Founder, Managing Director of Cowan, Australia
+ Started his career in the Safeway Head Office in Melbourne as a grocery buyer and special projects marketer. + This led to Mark becoming a keen judge of packaging communication and accurately predicting success rates of new launches. + In 1987, Mark launched Cowan, a consumer brand communications company. + Cowan is now the largest consumer brand design agency in Australia. + Offices in Melbourne, Sydney, London, Auckland, Shanghai, Beijing, and Ho Chi Minh City. + Clients include blue chip FMCG brands such as Coca-Cola, Arnotts, Yoplait, Heinz, Nestlé, and Uncle Toby.

BRUCE DUCKWORTH
United Kingdom, Founding partner of Turner Duckworth, London & San Francisco
+ Bruce established Turner Duckworth in 1992 with David Turner, specialising in brand identity and packaging. + Based in London, Bruce is jointly responsible with David Turner for the creative output of both studios for clients as varied as the Coca-Cola Company, Homebase, Shaklee, Johnson & Johnson, and Metallica. + Over 200 international design awards including: Cannes Festival Inaugural Design Lions – Grand Prix 2008, D&AD Silver Award, DBA Design Effectiveness Award, Clio Awards,

Design Week Awards, LIAA, Pentawards, FAB Awards – Agency of the Year 2008, Creativity Awards, EPICA, Graphis. + Judging stints: ADC New York's 87th Annual Design jury, D&AD Awards, Design Week Awards, LIAA Royal Society of Arts Student Design Awards, Pentawards 2009/2010. + Lectures/Speeches: numerous lectures at art colleges and universities/British Council, Design Council, International Institute of Research, The Design Show.

MARTIN GRIMER
United Kingdom, Global Creative Director, Blue Marlin
+ Joined Blue Marlin as Global Creative Director in January 2006 after leaving his role as Creative Director at Coley Porter Bell. + Martin has 15 years' experience as a Creative Director, and an industry profile built around outstanding creative work with Unilever, Cadbury, Pernod Ricard, Kimberly-Clark, BAT, Nestlé, and GlaxoSmithKline. + He has numerous accolades under his belt, including a Clio Gold & Best of Show Award, a Design Week award, a DBA Design Effectiveness award, and a Pentaward. + Has also been nominated numerous times for a D&AD, and has been a member of many juries in recent years.

ANDRÉ HINDERSSON
Sweden, Creative Director and Co-founding Partner of Silver in Stockholm
+ His design work embraces brand and company identities, services, and packaging design for a wide range of clients ranging from iconic global brands such as Oriflame, and H&M to local heavy-metal record labels. + He lives in Stockholm but has had a second home in London since his student years at CSM. + A specialist on cosmetic packaging for years, André always aims to bring out the personality of the product, often adding a humorous twist. + Holds an MA in Communication Design from Central Saint Martins college (CSM) in London and a BA from Grafiska Institutet at Stockholm University. + He is also an accredited ISIA ski instructor.

BRIAN HOUCK
USA, Director, Creative Services, The Dial Corporation, A Henkel Company, USA
+ Bachelor of Fine Arts, Northern Arizona University. + Previous experience includes advertising for diverse companies in the Southwest and event design and staging for clients such as Norelco and Delta Airlines. + Has led the package design for Dial brands for 21 years including Dial Soap, Right Guard Antiperspirant, Purex detergents, Renuzit air fresheners, and Soft Scrub cleansers. + Winner of numerous industry awards in package design and printing.

YOJI NOBUTO
Japan, Art Director at Shiseido, Tokyo
+ Born in Tokyo in 1966. + Graduated from the School of Art at Tokyo University in 1992. + Started his career at Shiseido in 1992. + Worked at Shiseido, New York, and is at present working in Tokyo. + In charge of various design projects chiefly for cosmetics. + Has won several awards: Tokyo Art Directors' Club ADC Awards 2002/2004. + Gold Awards of Japan Package Design Awards 2003/2005, Japan Grand Awards of Package Design Awards 2005, Merit Awards of New York Art Directors' Club Awards, D&AD Awards, Excellent Awards of Japan Display Design Awards, among others.

ADRIAN PIERINI
Argentina, Founder and General Creative Director of Pierini Partners
+ Graduated, with honours, as a graphic designer in 1992. + Pierini Partners develops branding and packaging designs for companies in Argentina, Brazil, Mexico, China, Japan, Colombia, Paraguay, and the UK. + Started his professional career in some of the most prestigious design studios in Argentina, the USA, and Mexico. + Teaches courses on such subjects as "Design and Brand Image", "Packaging Design", and "Introduction to Strategic Design" in a private university in Argentina,

and gives a number of seminars on design in universities and institutions in Argentina, Bolivia, Chile, Colombia, Ecuador, Mexico, Peru, and Paraguay. + He has written various articles for specialised media and "Designers Go!" on applied methodology oriented to students and young professionals (Comm Tools Editorial, 2006).

OLOF TEN HOORN
The Netherlands, Head of Creative Team at Design Bridge, Amsterdam
+ Graduated from the Graphic Lyceum Amsterdam. + Started his career at Design Bridge in 1994. + Founded in 1986, Design Bridge is active in 50 countries worldwide through their three offices in London, Amsterdam, and Singapore. + Has won several awards: Winner of Norwegian Design Award, 2nd place Mobius Award, Nomination Dutch Design Award, Diamond Pentaward (best of show), Bronze Pentaward, 1st place Mobius Award.

JENNIFER TSAI
Taiwan, Managing and Creative Director of Proad Identity since 1987
+ Taiwan's Top 10 for excellence and China Outstanding Woman. + Jury of iF Communication Design Award 2008, red dot communication design award 2008. + Honoured for her work in branding design with 30 awards, including iF, red dot, Pentawards, and Good Design Awards. + Jennifer specialises in branding and corporate identities for many famous companies and brands. + In a fusion of Eastern and Western culture, she devoted herself to presenting the Eastern elements in Western design and to working on linking international alliances and associations, such as Global Design Source, Pan-European Brand Design Association, and Total Identity in Amsterdam.

LARS WALLENTIN
Switzerland, Designer of training courses
+ Born in Sweden and resident of Switzerland. + Worked for 40 years at Nestlé in its design department. + International reference in design management. + Teaches and organises conferences all over the world. + Involved in thousands of international packaging projects at Nestlé. + Author of numerous articles and publications on communication by design. + Launched in 2010 the website devoted to packaging design: www.packagingsense.com

ADRIAN WHITEFOORD
United Kingdom, Pemberton & Whitefoord (P&W)
+ Graduated with a 1st Class Honours Degree from Maidstone College of Art in 1983, then proceeded to complete a Postgraduate Degree at the Royal College of Art. + Agency experience includes: Conran Associates, The Partners and Lewis Moberly. + Formed Pemberton & Whitefoord (P&W) in 1987 with Simon Pemberton. + Clients include: Tesco, Nestlé, Colgate Palmolive, M&S, and Seicomart (Japan). + P&W were the only UK design consultancy commissioned to design own-brand packaging for Fresh & Easy (Tesco's first retail venture in the USA). + P&W have won over 60 international design and marketing awards.

YUAN ZONG LEI
China, Art Director at Jahwa Group, Shanghai
+ Born in Shanghai in 1961. + Syndic of the Shanghai packaging consortium. + Bachelor of Fine Arts, Shanghai Institute of Technology. + Started his career at Jahwa in 1992. + In charge of various design projects, essentially for packaging design, display design, and interior design. + Winner of numerous industry awards in packaging design.

INDEX

INDEX

ACKNOWLEDEMENTS

We would firstly like to thank all the people who took part in the Pentawards and in particular the winners of the last three years, who come from 39 countries and who made it possible to bring so much creative talent together in a single book. It is they who have made this publication possible.

Thanks to Benedikt Taschen for the trust he showed in us and to Julius Wiedemann, who revealed the potential of the Pentawards – without him this book would not exist.

We would also like to thank our jury of leading professionals from around the world and its chairman, Gérard Caron, whose advice aided us considerably in designing the Pentawards.

Finally, we would like to thank Daniel Siciliano Bretas and his team for the graphic-design and technical support provided in the day-to-day work from the start of the project. They not only were able to highlight the creativity and attractiveness of the presented designs, but also their efficacy.

Jean Jacques and Brigitte Evrard
Founders of the Pentawards
www.pentawards.org

DANKSAGUNGEN

REMERCIEMENTS

Zuallererst möchten wir all jenen Menschen danken, die an den Pentawards teilgenommen haben, vor allem den Gewinnern der letzten drei Jahre. Sie stammen aus 39 Ländern und haben es möglich gemacht, dass derart viel kreatives Talent in einem einzigen Buch versammelt werden konnte. Ihre Leistungen brachten dieses Buch überhaupt erst in die Welt.

Dank geht auch an Benedikt Taschen für das in uns gesetzte Vertrauen und an Julius Wiedemann, der das Potenzial der Pentawards aufgedeckt hat: Ohne ihn gäbe es dieses Buch gar nicht!

Ebenfalls bedanken wir uns bei unserer Jury aus maßgeblichen Profis aus der ganzen Welt und ihrem Vorsitzenden Gérard Caron, deren Rat und tatkräftige Unterstützung uns beträchtlich bei der Gestaltung der Pentawards begleitet hat.

Schließlich geht ein ganz herzlicher Dank an Daniel Siciliano Brêtas und sein Team für das Grafikdesign und die technische Unterstützung, die seit Beginn des Projekts in der täglichen Arbeit für dieses Werk geleistet wurde. Sie stellen damit nicht nur Kreativität und Attraktivität, sondern auch die Wirkkraft der hier präsentierten Designs heraus.

Jean Jacques & Brigitte Evrard
Begründer von Pentawards
www.pentawards.org

Avant tout, nous tenons à remercier tous ceux qui ont participé aux Pentawards, et surtout les gagnants des 3 dernières années, venant de 39 pays, qui nous ont permis de réunir tant de créativité dans un seul livre. Ce sont eux qui ont rendu ce livre possible.

Merci à Benedikt Taschen, pour sa confiance, et aussi à Julius Wiedemann, qui a su détecter le potentiel des Pentawards, sans lui ce livre n'existerait pas.

Merci également à notre jury composé de grands professionnels des 4 coins du monde, pour sa contribution inestimable, et à Gérard Caron, président du jury, dont les conseils nous ont considérablement aidés à construire les Pentawards.

Et enfin, merci à Daniel Siciliano Bretas et son équipe, qui nous ont apporté leur soutien graphique et technique au jour le jour, depuis le début du projet. Ils ont su mettre en valeur la créativité, le glamour, mais aussi l'efficacité des packagings présentés.

Jean Jacques et Brigitte Evrard
Fondateurs des Pentawards
www.pentawards.org

IMPRINT

© 2010 TASCHEN GmbH
Hohenzollernring 53, D-50672 Köln
www.taschen.com

To stay informed about upcoming TASCHEN titles, please request our magazine at www.taschen.com/magazine or write to TASCHEN, Hohenzollernring 53, D-50672 Cologne, Germany, contact@taschen.com, Fax: +49 221 254919. We will be happy to send you a free copy of our magazine which is filled with information about all of our books.

Editor
Julius Wiedemann
Editorial Coordination
Daniel Siciliano Bretas
Collaboration
Jutta Hendricks

Design
Sense/Net, Andy Disl and Birgit Eichwede, Cologne
Layout
Birgit Eichwede and Daniel Siciliano Bretas
Production
Ute Wachendorf

Cover Illustration
Sarah King (illustration and typography)
Back Cover
Truly Deeply for Gelati Sky (see page 196)

English Revision
Chris Allen
French Translation
Aurélie Daniel for Equipo de Edición
German Translation
Jürgen Dubau

Printed in Germany
ISBN 978-3-8365-1996-0